Prehistoric Architecture in the Eastern United States

Incised ceramic,
Moundville (Moore,
1905).

Prehistoric Architecture in the Eastern United States

William N. Morgan

The MIT Press
Cambridge, Massachusetts,
and London, England

This project is supported by a grant from the National Endowment for the Arts in Washington, D.C.

This book was set in VIP Spartan by DEKR Corporation and printed and bound by Halliday Lithograph in the United States of America.

Library of Congress Cataloging in Publication Data

Morgan, William N
  Prehistoric architecture in the Eastern United States.

  Bibliography: p.
  Includes index.
  1. Indians of North America—Architecture.
2. Earthworks (Archaeology)—United States.
3. United States—Antiquities. I. Title.
E98.A63M67   722'.91'0974   80-16998
ISBN 0-262-13160-9

OCLC 6421322

Engraved conch shell,
Spiro (Phillips and
Brown, vol. II, plate
36, 1975).

Contents

Preface

For thousands of years before Columbus came to the New World, people had been living in the Eastern United States establishing communities, developing their environments, and expressing themselves with art and architecture. This study is an initial examination of their architecture, a search for their accomplishments and a celebration of their spirit.

Although many studies have been presented on the architecture of Mesoamerica and South America before the arrival of Columbus in the New World, comparatively little attention has been paid to the architecture of the Eastern United States. This study is intended to present an overview of architecture in this area from about 2200 B.C. until the time of contact with Europeans sometime after A.D. 1500, which, to my knowledge, has never before been presented in a comprehensive publication for interested laymen, students, and architects. It is remarkable that three millenia of architectural experience in the Eastern United States have thus far gone largely unnoticed, particularly in light of our present-day concerns for environmental preservation, conservation of natural resources, and pollution control (including visual pollution). Most of the information in this study has been provided by archaeologists, anthropologists, historians, and other scholars to whom we are indebted for making this preliminary review possible.

The reconstructions presented here are based primarily on archaeological data where it is available, drawings and notes of early observers, aerial photographs, site visitations when possible, interviews with knowledgeable archaeologists, and examination of culturally related artworks. In some cases the data available convey a relatively clear picture of the work, but in other cases assumptions have been made subject to adjustment as additional information becomes available. Where assumptions have been made, they are noted insofar as possible. The reconstructions in this study are but one observer's interpretation, presented with the expectation that in the future we may improve and expand our understanding of the prehistoric architecture of the Eastern United States. This study is a beginning rather than a culmination, an inquiry rather than a definition.

This study examines primarily the relationships of elements in architectural environments rather than engineering technology or building construction. Emphasis often is placed on earth structures because they usually were primary elements in shaping the architectural environments of the prehistoric Eastern United States. This is not to suggest that structures of wood did not exist or were not important, but the comparative scale used here emphasizes large earth masses and excavations more readily than wood structures. Emphasizing earth structures also indicates a preference of the author, a conscious choice. My interest in the art of shaping earth began in the late 1950s when I was a student. A design problem for a museum in Oklahoma offered the possibility of shaping a butte, the site's dominant topographic feature, to create a museum. The proposal shocked my professors but the possibility was intriguing. I began to look more carefully at Frank Lloyd Wright's inquiries into earth architecture, for example, his proposed Detroit Auto Workers' Housing and second Jacobs House. In subsequent years as a Wheelwright Fellow of Harvard University, I visited Hatshepsut's mortuary temple at Deir-el-bahari, the Etruscan necropolises at Velletri and Cerveteri, the ruins at Persepolis, and the sanctuaries at Angkor Wat and Angkor

Engraved conch shell, Spiro (Phillips and Brown, vol. I, figure 64, 1975).

Thom. Articles and projects by Arthur Drexler, George Nelson, and Philip Johnson explored further the possibilities of earth architecture in recent decades. In my architectural practice, landscape and site planning moved toward a synthesis with architecture.

In 1968, while planning the Florida State Museum, I interviewed the archaeologist Ripley P. Bullen to ascertain his requirements in the new building. Spread out on a table in his cluttered office was a topographic survey of a truncated pyramid with an extended ramp. I quickly noted his office requirements and asked him to tell me about the pyramid and his work. He patiently explained more than I could absorb and gave me several pamphlets to read. Within three days I returned the pamphlets and asked for more information. He listed several sites for me to visit, the first being Crystal River. As the design of the new museum developed, it seemed to take on a character more akin to Florida's architecture before Columbus than after. One site visit led to another and my interest multiplied: Kolomoki led to Etowah and Ocmulgee, then followed Lake Jackson, Poverty Point, Marksville, Toltec, Winterville, Terra Ceia, Aztalan, Mount Royal, Shields, Town Creek, Chucalissa, Turtle, Mayport, McKeithen, Moundville, and others.

J. C. Dickinson, Jr., Director of the Florida State Museum, encouraged me to learn from Jerald T. Milanich, William H. Sears, and George Percy, all of whom assisted me and referred me to other scholars. Robert H. Spiro, President of Jacksonville University, and Dean Frances B. Kinne of the Faculty of Fine Arts and Music generously sponsored an assistance grant from the National Endowment for the Arts made possible by Bill N. Lacy and Roy G. Knight. Of exceptional importance in organizing and reviewing this study has been Stephen Williams of the Peabody Museum of Harvard University. At the suggestion of Arthur Drexler of the Museum of Modern Art in New York, aerial photographs of typical sites have been included to improve the study's credibility. Eduard F. Sekler of the Harvard Graduate School of Design encouraged and assisted me in this study from its inception and has been instrumental in its completion.

In the simplest of terms, this study suggests that we may be wise to stop destroying our architectural heritage, examine it further, and possibly learn from it with the view of rendering our future built environment more livable.

Methodology

The process of preparing this inquiry into prehistoric American architecture generally followed six phases: collection of information, analysis of data, selection of examples, interpretation of specific sites, presentation in a comparative format, and comparison of reconstructions to each other and to other sites outside of the Eastern United States. The process began in 1968 and intensified during 1977 and 1978. The sequence of phases was not concurrent for all sites: Some information was gathered a decade earlier than other information, mainly due to the absence of previous compilations in the field of prehistoric American architecture.

A great deal of information was gathered through personal interviews and subsequent communications with archaeologists, including Jeffrey P. Brain, Ripley P. Bullen, Hester A. Davis, Melvin L. Fowler, James B. Griffin, Charles R. McGimsey, III, Jerald T. Milanich, Robert S. Neitzel, George Percy, William H. Sears, Gerald Smith, Stephen Williams, and others. Comprehensive sources of information were books prepared by authorities in the fields of history, archaeology, social anthropology, or ethnology, including Squier and Davis, Cyrus Thomas, Clarence B. Moore, James B. Griffin, Franklin Folsom, James A. Brown, Philip Phillips, James A. Ford, Jesse D. Jennings, and Charles L. Hudson. My staff gathered additional information from the New York Public Library, Avery Library of Columbia University, Smithsonian Institution, and other sources. Telephone interviews and personal communications with archaeologists Jon L. Gibson and Melvin L. Fowler provided additional information on Poverty Point and Cahokia, respectively. Rochelle Marrinan's Ph.D. dissertation (1975) provided important chronological information on the Late Archaic Period on the Georgia Coast.

The analysis of information collected on each site began with an examination of site plans, or plane table maps, as archaeologists refer to them. Frequently, several maps or plans had to be assembled before the architectural character of a given site became apparent. Archaeological diagrams that omitted specific scales, north arrows, or dominant topographical features such as watercourses were suspended from consideration until missing information could be found.

Where this information was not found for an important site, a reasonable assumption was made, and this is stated in the text accompanying its interpretative reconstruction. In each case, verbal descriptions were examined for additional information relating to architectural characteristics, such as the height of earthworks. Where two or more contradictory site plans were available for the same site, an assumption of probable relative accuracies was made. In cases such as Mount Royal and Shields, where site plans were incomplete, missing elements are presented on the basis of early observers' verbal descriptions.

Finding two names for the same site occurred often: Selsertown now is known as Emerald, Towosahgy previously was called Beckwith's Fort, Knapp has become Toltec, Anna also is known as the Robson Group, Oldtown was known also as Old Town or Old Chillicothe, Perkins originally was called Bolivar, the Fuller site is also known as Chucalissa, South Charleston includes the Criel Mound sometimes called Creel, the Madira Bickel Mound is part of the Terra Ceia group, Squier and Davis's Prairie Jefferson site is apparently the Jerden site of the Lower Mississippi Survey, and the Troyville site lies beneath the present-day city of Jonesville.

Numerous inconsistencies occur in collected drawings and accounts. Squier and Davis's plates II and XX show north arrows differing ninety degrees from each other, and their description of plate XXXVIII, no. 4 (p. 113) refers to mound "E" as mound "A" and the winding path orientation as "west" instead of "east," which their drawing shows. Spaulding's map (Phillips, 1970, figure 84) shows a horizontal scale in meters rather than in feet, which would correspond to Phillips's text. Orientations frequently failed to indicate whether true north, magnetic north, or survey reference north is shown. Where subsequent verification of early accounts was lacking, sites rarely were retained for this study, and then only when they illustrated architectural characteristics not present at other sites. Generally speaking, greater credence was placed in more recent site plans, based on the assumption that more current survey techniques probably are more accurate. The several maps of the St. Louis site, for example, were based on the field notes recorded by Major Long's 1819 expedition using a hand-held compass and tape measure in dense undergrowth. Variations in drafting techniques presented an entirely separate series of problems requiring reasonable assumptions.

Stephen Williams, Jeffrey P. Brain, Philip Phillips, James B. Griffin, and Eduard F. Sekler assisted greatly by reviewing and correcting preliminary drafts, supplying missing information, and providing chronological data essential to the organization of the material presented here. While the assistance of these authorities has been invaluable, the author alone assumes full responsibility for the final outcome of this study.

Selection of eighty-two sites for presentation from the more than four hundred for which information was collected was influenced by several factors, the most important usually being the relative strength of data bases. In the interest of avoiding repetition and of presenting as comprehensive an overview as possible, attention was given to geographical and chronological diversity. Although individual masses occasionally are illustrated, mainly for their sculptural qualities, emphasis is placed on groups. The time period of 1000 B.C. to A.D. 1500 is emphasized, although the earlier shell rings of Fig Island and Sapelo also are included by way of establishing the background for subsequent developments.

Early in the selection process, a consistent scale on a 200-by-200-meter grid was adopted for all presentations. Several implications stemmed from this decision. Details such as palisades and marker posts became relatively small, and major sites such as Cahokia and Poverty Point were too large to be contained even within the expanded grid. In these cases, additional plan diagrams and perspective drawings are presented to illustrate the entire site plan. The decision to present north consistently toward the top of all plans resulted in selecting sites that clearly illustrated a typical conception without exceeding the format. For example, Oldtown is typical of many Ohio River Valley earthworks, but it was selected rather than other sites because its scale and orientation lend themselves more appropriately to the adopted format. The sole exception to the orientation of north toward the top of page is the reconstruction of Poverty Point, the reason for which is explained in its accompanying text.

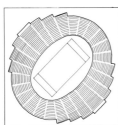
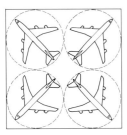

To assist the reader in comprehending the scale of a 200-by-200-meter grid, the three diagrams to the left illustrate a typical expressway cloverleaf, a football stadium seating about 70,000 spectators, and four Boeing 747 jet aircraft whose fuselage lengths are almost 100 meters each.

The precision of drawings presented in this study is based partly on my experience of building earthworks in the Southeastern United States (the crisp edges of the decade-old Florida State Museum is an example), on examination of aerial photographs, such as those of Marksville, Mississippi, and Newark, Ohio; on the linear clarity with which prehistoric artists executed their engravings and designs; and on the precision of dimensions and alignments noted by surveyors of prehistoric structures, such as for Newark and Spanish Fort.

Interpretations sometimes were hampered by the fact that different elements within the same site were constructed at different times. For example, there is evidence of several ramps on the central structure at Lake George, but it seems that all did not exist at the same time. It appears unlikely that all earthworks were shaped with the precision of Murdock Mound; for example, the earlier stages of Irene's major structure probably were much less sophisticated.

Concerning the architectural conventions adopted in this study, it must be emphasized that the rectangular open spaces define architectural relationships, which should not be confused with archaeological plazas. Although watercourses frequently are shown where they may have been, evidence for their existence except after heavy rainfalls or during floods is often lacking. Tree lines are used to emphasize architectural order rather than to suggest the existence of trees. The precisely square corners on orthogonal mounds have clear precedents in the presentation of Mesoamerican site plans (for examples, see Carnegie Institute publications), but this convention heretofore has not been applied to sites in the Eastern United States. Visitors to Uxmal, Palenque, Xochicalco, Copán, or other Mesoamerican sites probably would be unable to understand many of the still amorphous features of these sites without architectural reconstructions of their probable original shapes rather than their existing contours.

Presentation of each site followed four steps: interpretation, layout, review, and final drawing. I carefully reviewed drawings and descriptions in a search for proportions, ratios, steepness, data consistency, access, functions, evolution, chronology, surfacing techniques, colors, topographic influences, and related architectural considerations. From a series of notes and diagrams, an initial rough tracing paper site plan was developed over which a series of subsequent tracings were prepared in a search for probable design relationships, a process requiring, for most sites, between six hours and six days, frequently interrupted to seek additional information. Brief verbal descriptions were composed for each site emphasizing salient architectural characteristics.

Wherever possible, preliminary interpretations with accompanying text were submitted to knowledgeable scholars whose comments were incorporated into final presentations: Robert S. Neitzel (Marksville and Fatherland), William H. Sears (Big Mound City, Big Tonys, Fort Center, and Kolomoki), Jerald T. Milanich (Central and North Florida sites), Melvin L. Fowler (Cahokia), Stephen Williams and Jeffrey P. Brain (primarily Lower Mississippi Valley sites), James B. Griffin (primarily Squier and Davis sites in the Ohio Valley), Jon Muller (Kincaid), Christopher S. Peebles

(Moundville), James Brown (Spiro), Dan F. Morse (Parkin and Upper Nodena), Martha Rolingson (Toltec), Lewis H. Larson (Etowah), John S. Belmont (Greenhouse), William O. Autry (Mound Bottom), Bruce D. Smith (Shiloh), and Eduard F. Sekler (Comparable Sites).

Each interpretation was then submitted to architect William Ebert who methodically analyzed each detail. Through the use of photographic techniques, he adjusted plane table maps to a consistent scale, corrected imperfections, and developed accurate pencil-line drawings on tracing paper, including tree lines, rectangles of architectural relationships (not to be confused with archaeological plazas), watercourses, embankments, earthworks, and other site characteristics.

Final ink presentation drawings on mylar film were prepared by architect Thomas A. McCrary, who consistently brought his considerable talent to bear on each site. After preliminary examination of several rendering techniques, architect McCrary established the graphic standard for the entire study to which the visual design clarity of this book is largely due. The preparation of final drawings extended over a three-man-year period and involved three design-oriented practicing architects experienced in constructing earthworks in the Southeastern United States.

The final phase of this study involved the comparison of reconstructions in the hope of determining general characteristics that might be ascribed to prehistoric architecture in the Eastern United States. Based on the paucity of architecturally valid information and on the numerous assumptions implicit in this study, it would be wiser to withhold premature generalizations until more accurate data and analyses become available. At present, new information is being developed rapidly as a result of improved ceramic analyses, computer programs for data correlation, infrared aerial photography, improved archaeological research at new sites as well as at previously examined sites, and geological information relating to chronology, dendrochronology, radiocarbon dating, and other scientific techniques.

The information collected and analyses developed in this study have been catalogued with the view of assisting continued research in the field of prehistoric American architecture. This study may be likened to opening a window to obtain a view that we have not seen before. It now remains for us to examine more carefully the scope and details of this new perspective.

Introduction

Synthesis

Concerning meaning in the visual arts, Erwin Panofsky observed in his *Studies in Iconology* (1957, pp. 26–54) that meaning, as opposed to form, occurs on three levels: natural, conventional, and intrinsic. Natural meaning, the primary level, is a matter of practical experience or everyday familiarity with objects and events, which may be factual or expressional. For example, a rose is a rose and by any other name it smells as sweet. Conventional meaning, the second level, involves images, stories, and allegories whose themes and concepts must be understood before the meaning can be perceived. For instance, the symbol of a dove with an olive branch may mean peace to a western European but may mean something else or nothing to an Australian aborigine. Panofsky's third level, intrinsic meaning, involves essential tendencies of the human mind: values, intuitions, preferences, and ideas.

Embossed copper plate,
Peoria (Hudson, 1974).

Although we may identify a particular visual form, such as a conical mound in prehistoric American architecture, it per se conveys no natural meaning to us as a matter of our everyday experience. The second level of meaning escapes us because we do not know the conventions of prehistoric America and therefore cannot analyze them. At the third or intrinsic level of meaning, however, we may begin intuitively to perceive essential tendencies of prehistoric American architecture occurring in different places and at different times, a matter of synthesizing to identify the existence of meaning. At this point archaeology and architectural history come together as Phillips and Brown (1975, vol. I, p. 103) have suggested.

This study organizes architectural elements and compositions chronologically and geographically on the basis of apparently similar ideas from which we may infer the existence of an intrinsic meaning without actually knowing the nature of that meaning. The objective of this study is to present an overview of prehistoric American architecture by synthesizing what is known.

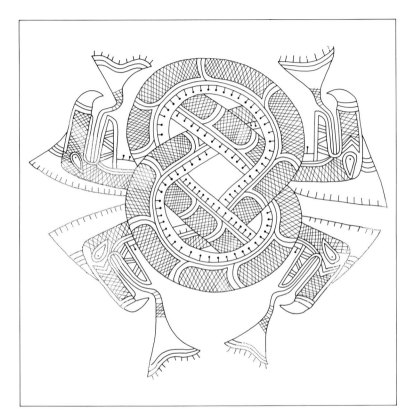

Engraved conch shell,
Spiro (Phillips and
Brown, vol. III, plate
69, 1975).

Evolution

Scholars believe that people entered the New World via a land bridge across the Bering Strait caused by a lowering of the ocean level due to glaciation. Small hunting groups numbering at most forty people apparently began to follow migrating herds of big game across the land bridge between 50,000 and 20,000 B.C. These bands migrated slowly across Alaska and Canada, following primarily a southerly route along the eastern slopes of the Rocky Mountains, where grasslands sustained large herds of mammoth, bison, and other big game. Over a period of many generations, a steady trickle moved southward, eventually crossing the Isthmus of Panama and spreading out across the North and South American continents.

In Eastern North America, migratory bands hunted deer and other animals and gathered food from the abundant forests and waterways. Population densities were comparatively low until about 7000 B.C., when the steadily increasing population began to employ improved techniques of hunting and gathering. Indigenous copper hammered and annealed into artifacts began to appear in the western Great Lakes. Shell mounds and tools began to appear in the Southeast. In the Eastern United States specialized burial practices began, including the interment of mortuary

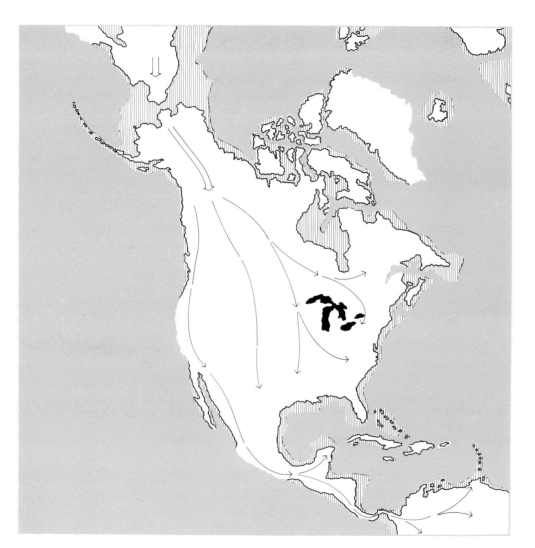

artifacts with burials. Along the Southeast Atlantic Coast from South Carolina to North Florida, migratory groups of shellfish eaters began to return periodically to the same places, depositing their discarded shells and debris in rings, thus producing the earliest architecture known in the Eastern United States. The Canon Point shell ring on St. Simons Island dating 2240 B.C. (± 90 years) is the earliest example yet discovered (Marrinan, 1975). At about this time the first pottery also appeared in the Southeastern United States.

Between 1300 and 200 B.C., settlements appeared in the Lower Mississippi Valley in the vicinity of Poverty Point. Here vast geometric earthworks and large mounds were constructed about 1000 B.C. Webb (1977) suggests that the ceremonial organization, site planning, and arts and crafts of the earthworks may be a result of Mesoamerican influences, but, this connection remains to be proved. The relationship of Poverty Point to later Ohio earthworks also is unclear. Period 1 of this study illustrates the architectural developments that occurred between 2200 and 1000 B.C.

Several distinctly new characteristics developed during the first millenium B.C. and reached a climax between 500 B.C. and A.D. 200, which is designated period 2 in this study. The use of ceramics became increasingly widespread, and agriculture, probably including maize, apparently began to supplement hunting and gathering in some areas of the Eastern United States. Elaborate ceremonialism developed, involving specialized mortuary practices, burial mounds, and associated earthworks. These mounds were usually circular or oval in plan and ranged in height from 1 to 21 meters in the case of the Grave Creek Mound in West Virginia. Elaborate grave artifacts were interred with the burials contained within them.

In Ohio, West Virginia, and Kentucky the Adena culture appeared. Adena burial mounds were typically steep earthern cones containing elaborate log tombs. Other Adena characteristics were circular enclosures and other earthworks associated with their burial structures and circular houses with paired wall posts.

Closely following the Adena culture was the Hopewell culture, which developed extensive trade networks over much of the study area. Large-scale Hopewell ceremonial centers appeared on river terraces in association with nearby extended villages or hamlets. Hopewell enclosures of square or octagonal plans often had earth mounds opposite breaks in their walls. Large burial mounds of specialized construction and elaborately furnished log tombs frequently dominated Hopewell ceremonial centers. By the time of its climax about the time of Christ, the Hopewell culture had attained a high level of artistic and technological achievement. Other regional developments of period 2 are illustrated in the Lower Mississippi Valley, Tennessee, and Florida.

Following a transition between A.D. 200 and 800, about which little is known, new architectural ideas appeared in the Eastern United States. Period 3 of this study began about A.D. 800, reached a climax around A.D. 1300, and generally declined after A.D. 1500, although architectural activity in some areas, such as Natchez in the Lower Mississippi Valley, continued into the early eighteenth century. Because more is known about period 3 than about the earlier periods, it has been divided conveniently into five geographical areas: the Upper Mississippi and Ohio Valley Area; the Lower Mississippi Valley Area; the Caddoan Area; the Tennessee, Appalachian, and Piedmont Area; and the Florida Area. A major factor in the success of period 3 apparently was the substantial improvement of agricultural production, particularly of maize.

Early in period 3 flat-topped pyramidal mounds appeared, serving as platforms for temples or residences. These structures often were grouped around plazas and ranged in number from one or two at smaller sites to as many as 120 at Cahokia in southwestern Illinois, the largest site known in the Eastern United States. Some platform mounds contained two or three terraces, although Monks Mound, the largest truncated structure known in our study area, contained four and rose to height of 30 meters above its plaza. The ceremonial centers and habitation areas of period 3 take on broad regional variations, which are described by individual sites presented in this study. Some contained palisaded enclosures and most contained sturdy wall-trench domestic structures with wattle-and-daub infill and overhanging thatched roofs. The origin of architectural ideas in period 3 is assumed, although not yet proven, to have been Mesoamerica, where truncated pyramids grouped around plazas appeared early and extensively. During each period in this study new ideas seem to have been combined with earlier ones, indicating an evolution with broad regional diversity rather than a sudden impact of foreign influences.

Reference: Jennings, 1974.

Communication

In order to understand the evolution of prehistoric American architecture, it would be helpful to understand as fully as possible the means by which ideas were communicated in the study area. The original Eastern North Americans had no written language, and their architects left no drawings or documents to record their intentions. In most cases, we do not know what they called themselves or what languages they spoke. To understand the people, we consider their known cultural and physical remains, the accounts of early European observers such as Le Moyne and Le Page du Pratz, and the records of interviews with their descendants, such as those of Mooney, Swanton, Adair, and Bartram.

According to Charles L. Hudson and Jeffrey P. Brain, the language families in the study area at the time of European contact were Algonkian, Muskogean, Iroquoian, Siouan, Tunican, and Caddoan. These languages appear to have been as different from each other as Latin is from German, Slavic, or Chinese. The problem of communicating verbally between one area and another would have been complicated further by linguistic dialects within each area as disparate as Italian is from French, Rumanian, Spanish, or Portuguese.

Engraved conch shell, Spiro (Phillips and Brown, vol. I, figure 44, 1975).

Embossed copper,
Etowah (Thomas, 1894).

In order to conduct extensive trade and exchange cultural ideas in the absence of written languages, the prehistoric Americans may have relied heavily on visual communication. In historic times, a Mobilian trade language permitted people of different backgrounds in the Southeast to speak with each other. Various visual symbols appear to have existed concurrently at Spiro, Moundville, and Etowah. The subsistence systems at these three sites apparently were related to agriculture. Common visual similarities seem to occur in their architecture: truncated pyramids with wooden structures on their summits, central open spaces or plazas surrounded by several mounds, evidence of religious ceremonialism related to burial practices, and locations near important rivers.

Environment

The map on the next page indicates the geographical locations of the sites reconstructed in this study, extending from the Great Lakes and lower Canada on the north to the Gulf of Mexico on the south and from the Atlantic Ocean on the east to the Great Plains on the west. The major topographical features of this area are the fertile basins of the Mississippi, Missouri, and Ohio rivers and their tributaries; the Appalachian Mountains; and the low-lying coastal plains of the Southeast through which numerous rivers flow from the uplands to the sea. The architectural development of the Eastern United States often appears to have been influenced by both geography and chronology: Ohio Hopewell sites differ from Mississippian settlements in the Yazoo Basin, and both differ from the earthworks of South Florida. Chronological separations between geographically proximate sites also occur: Jackson Place appeared within view of Poverty Point many centuries later, resulting in clearly contrasting architectural compositions.

The Natchez Trace, which interconnected the Lower Mississippi River with the Appalachian uplands, is a well-known example of the important overland roads developed in our study area. The Natchitoches Trace, an ancient route between Louisiana and St. Louis, is still visible today, particularly in aerial photographs.

Apparently waterways provided food, water, and amenities for aboriginal settlements and may have facilitated transportation, trade, and communications in some areas. At the fall lines of rivers, the points at which waterfalls or rapids prohibited continued navigation, portage was required. Here trade goods appear to have been

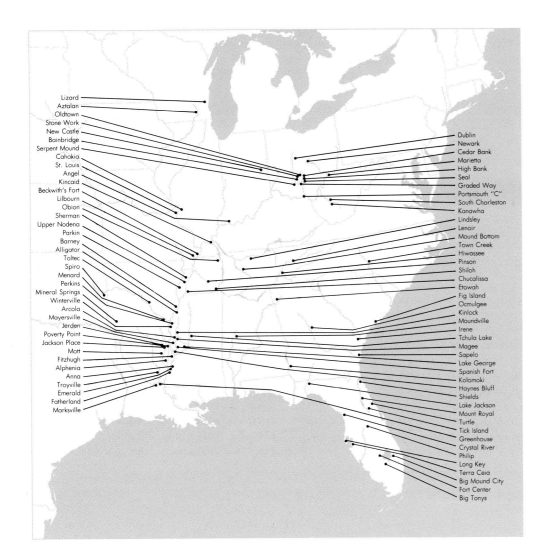

Lizard
Aztalan
Oldtown
Stone Work
New Castle
Bainbridge
Serpent Mound
Cahokia
St. Louis
Angel
Kincaid
Beckwith's Fort
Lilbourn
Obion
Sherman
Upper Nodena
Parkin
Barney
Alligator
Toltec
Spiro
Menard
Perkins
Mineral Springs
Winterville
Arcola
Mayersville
Jerden
Poverty Point
Jackson Place
Mott
Fitzhugh
Alphenia
Anna
Troyville
Emerald
Fatherland
Marksville

Dublin
Newark
Cedar Bank
Marietta
High Bank
Seal
Graded Way
Portsmouth "C"
South Charleston
Kanawha
Lindsley
Lenoir
Mound Bottom
Town Creek
Hiwassee
Pinson
Shiloh
Chucalissa
Etowah
Fig Island
Ocmulgee
Kinlock
Moundville
Irene
Tchula Lake
Magee
Sapelo
Lake George
Spanish Fort
Kolomoki
Haynes Bluff
Shields
Lake Jackson
Mount Royal
Turtle
Tick Island
Greenhouse
Crystal River
Philip
Long Key
Terra Ceia
Big Mound City
Fort Center
Big Tonys

exchanged between people from different ecological zones. Along these fall lines archaeologists sometimes find concentrations of cultural remains that expand our understanding of prehistoric America. Larger settlements sometimes were supported by two or more contiguous ecological zones: Poverty Point lay between upland and lowland settlements whose economies were interdependent, and Moundville was supported by hardwood forests upland to the north, fertile valleys and hills nearby, and lowland coastal plains to the south.

Environmental adaptation for agricultural production apparently established a pattern for unique architectural development in South Florida. In order to cultivate corn in low-lying terrain, irrigation canals were constructed to control water levels and provide fill for elevated agricultural plots. Early circular canals at Fort Center were expanded three times between 500 B.C. and A.D. 1. Later more efficient rectangular plots apparently were developed at Fort Center, Big Mound City, and Big Tonys, producing striking architectural compositions. Village middens augmented by excavated fill formed elevated platforms that protected residences from flooding and reduced the nuisance of insects. Similarly, the magnificent canals, lakes, and elevated platforms of Angkor

Thom and Angkor Wat in Cambodia employed techniques developed earlier for controlling water levels in rice paddies with earthern dikes and sluice gates.

Environmental adaptation and architectural evolution in Eastern North America apparently continued for 2,500 years, uninterrupted by massive foreign or major internal displacements. Here no parallel has been found with the Asiatic hordes that for centuries invaded Europe in successive waves of displacement. While Mesoamerica may have exchanged influences with Eastern North America, direct evidence of significant impact is lacking. By contrast, the Greek influences on Etruria and later on Rome were decisive, and China's influence on early Japan was extensive. The ideas that influenced the development of the Eastern United States appear to have been of domestic rather than foreign origin.

Many prehistoric sites first were visited briefly by small groups of hunters or gatherers. Sedentary communities sometimes were founded, abandoned, reoccupied, and expanded over a period of many generations. The fact that desirable natural sites sometimes were selected for settlements often assured their early occupancy and demolition by the European settlers who also sought desirable locations for their towns and farms.

Natural resources provided trade advantages for some sites. A quarry near Cahokia yielded stone suitable for the manufacture of durable hoe blades and other artifacts. Shell scrapers and conch vessels from the Southeast Atlantic Coast were valuable trade items inshore. Yaupon holly leaves, used widely in the preparation of the Black Drink, a ceremonial emetic, grew only in limited coastal areas. Copper suitable for annealing and hammering was found in limited areas such as the western Great Lakes and the southern Appalachian Mountains. Pearls common in some areas were rare in others. An extensive trade network apparently existed in the Eastern United States by the time that Poverty Point appeared about 1000 B.C.

European attitudes toward the aboriginal people of the Eastern United States varied substantially, according to Charles L. Hudson. Apparently, the Spanish viewed the people as potential religious converts and workers whose production could benefit Spain. To this end they established an extensive chain of missions across Florida for indoctrination, education, and organization. The French seem to have viewed Eastern North America as a profitable area for commercial concessions related to overseas trade. To this end they

encouraged the aboriginal inhabitants to increase supplies of goods valuable abroad. The English, however, viewed the people as obstructions to the efficient development of colonies in an environment ripe for exploitation. They and their successors systematically eliminated the people, first with economic enslavement, then with unreasonable seizure of land in payment of unfair debts, and finally with physical removal of those who survived the resulting famines, epidemics, and warfare.

Order

Architectural order is the disciplined relationship of elements in a composition. Because many prehistoric American sites have been destroyed or are in advanced stages of deterioration, and because we have no plans or other records to indicate the people's architectural intentions, we may seek to understand their conceptions of order by examining some of their well-preserved artifacts that illustrate design and inquiring into the apparent order of their social, economic, and political systems where they appear to have existed. Early French observers reported social order involving a matriarchial hierarchy, ceremonialism, and a ranked society at Fatherland in the Lower Mississippi Valley. It is difficult to ascertain how accurately they reported what they saw, how

Incised shell, Eddyville
(Phillips and Brown, vol.
I, figure 25, 1975).

Engraved conch shell,
Spiro (Phillips and
Brown, vol. II, preceding
plate 1, 1975).

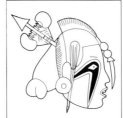

Incised pottery, Louisiana
(Hudson, 1974).

Engraved stone disc,
Issaquena (Holmes,
1906).

well they understood the Natchez people, or how widespread geographically and chronologically were the customs of these people. Burial practices of the Adena and Hopewell people seem to indicate that some interments were more important than others by the quantity and refinement of grave artifacts. The high level of artistic achievement of Hopewell and Mississippian artifacts indicates trade specialization, suggesting a relatively high degree of social organization. The skill in planning the large-scale earthworks of Poverty Point and the organization of labor required to accomplish the task are further indications of social order. However, this is not to say that the same degree of social order was present at all sites at the same time: Many sites near more orderly sites yield little or no evidence of artistic or architectural order.

The illustrations throughout the introduction of this book generally are more clearly ordered than others in which consistent design patterns are obscure or entirely absent. A fundamental and recurrent design element is the circle in which all elements are set an equal distance from the center, which sometimes appears as a dot. Concentric circles, such as the Dotted Concentric Circle

on page xxiv, extend this concept. Architectural examples of basic circles occurred at Fig Island, Sapelo, and the Adena sites. Concentric circles surrounded a central mass at Portsmouth Group "C." Steeply conical Adena burial mounds are a three-dimensional variation of the circle, of which Miamisburg is an example. Eleven platforms define the circular site at Tchula Lake.

A second recurrent arrangement of design elements is components symmetrically disposed about a single axis, such as in the Bilobed Arrow on page xxiv. The axial order of the Mount Royal site illustrates this concept in architecture. The multiple terraces of Sherman and Barney mounds are symmetrically disposed about a single axis. Two axes of equal order intersecting at a right angle are illustrated by the Mount Royal breastplate on page xxvi. Similarly, square platforms are set with biaxial symmetry on square bases in many period 3 temple mounds.

The introduction of a third axis forming approximately 60-degree angles at their intersection is illustrated by the Chunkee Player on the far left.

The Trilobate on page xxiv shows three axes emanating from one point of convergence. Variations of 60- and 120-degree axes do not appear to have been basic arrangements in prehistoric architecture.

The intersection of four axes forming 45-degree angles at their intersections appears in the Spider Web motif on page xxiv. This design conception and its variations occur frequently in prehistoric American design and architecture, of which the Hopewell enclosures at Newark, Marietta, High Bank, and Oldtown are examples. Pinwheels and spirals, such as those shown on the opposite page, lower center and right, occur more frequently in the design of artifacts than in architecture in this study.

By no means did concentricity or axiality dominate all designs in prehistoric art and architecture. The warrior's head shown on the left probably is a realistic portrayal of its subject. Asymmetrical order was achieved in the well-balanced Lake George and Big Tonys arrangements and in many other sites in this study. Little if any order is apparent at Crystal River and Tick Island.

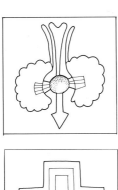

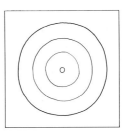

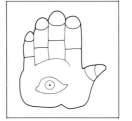
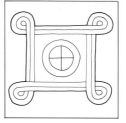

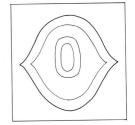

Motifs

Throughout this introduction are examples of prehistoric American design motifs that occurred at different times and places with varying frequency. What the motifs symbolized and whether they had the same meaning to different groups is unknown. Concentric circles, radials, biaxial symmetry, and other design characteristics appeared in architecture and planning as well as in motifs. Many other motifs are presented thoroughly in Phillips and Brown's *Pre-Columbian Shell Engravings,* volume I (1975), which is the source of the illustrations shown here, except as noted.

Top row: Bilobed Arrow, a variation of a frequently found motif (Williams, 1968); Concentric Radial T-Bar, a motif found at Spiro with variations found at Moundville and Etowah; Cross in Petaloid Circle, a motif found at Spiro; Dotted Concentric Circles, a motif appearing in many variations at Spiro; and Forked Eye Surround, a motif found widely with many variations.

Center row: Greek Cross, a nested version of a motif found at Spiro with many variations; Hand, a widely found motif frequently showing the front and back of the hand in the same view (Williams, 1968); Looped Square, a design found frequently at Spiro; Moundville Circle, found once at Spiro, but frequently found at Moundville; and Ogee, a motif found very widely in the Southeast at such sites as Spiro, Menard, and Mount Royal.

Bottom Row: Rayed Concentric Barred Ovals, a variation of the frequently found barred oval motif; Skull, a frequently found motif (Williams, 1968); Spider Web, a realistic Spiro variant of a relatively rare motif found at Mount Sterling, Illinois; Swastika Cross in Circle, a relatively rare motif found infrequently at Spiro; and Trilobate, a Spiro example of a motif found widely in the Southeast.

Reference: Phillips and Brown, 1975.

Design

The formal qualities of design considered in this study concern primarily sculpted masses and their relationships to each other. Secondary considerations include scale, construction materials and techniques, surfacing, color, orientation, access, and related characteristics. Particular forms and their relationships to each other seem to establish patterns that are found at specific places and times. Archaeological information is the major data source. The task of tentatively identifying and differentiating patterns is difficult and sometimes inconclusive because many sites are in advanced stages of deterioration or have disappeared; some were abandoned by their builders before completion or were constructed at different times under different influences; others have never been surveyed properly or have been restored only partially or incorrectly.

The design conception of given patterns embodies a specific ideal to which several sites may appear related, although no single site embodies all the elements of the ideal. The basis of determining forms and their patterns is subjective and therefore open to alternative interpretations. A primary consideration of each pattern has been its degree of organization: whether it appears unified or seems randomly scattered. Patterns lacking apparent design unity are presented less frequently, but even those that are included, such as Tick Island and Terra Ceia, seem to suggest conscious design considerations such as relative massing and proximities of elements or interconnecting elements. Patterns exhibiting more orderly components and relationships are represented by the geometric enclosures of the Ohio

Incised ceramic bottle
design, Arkansas (Phillips
and Brown, vol. III,
opposite plate 80, 1975).

Repoussé copper plate,
Mount Royal (Moore,
1894).

Hopewellians and truncated pyramids grouped around period 3 plazas. Factors considered in grouping design patterns included geometric characteristics, frequency of occurrence, chronological and geographical relationships, and similarities of architectural features, such as moats, causeways, ramps, plazas, enclosures, orientations, and structures.

Site

A central concern of architecture is the relationship of architectural elements to each other and to their natural environment over an extended period. Some environmental characteristics that prehistoric American architects may have considered when locating and planning their settlements apparently included the proximity of a nearby watercourse for drinking water, hygiene, fishing, and possibly transportation; views of dominant topographic features, such as a distant island or nearby valley; sufficient elevation to avoid flooding and to afford a refuge for outlying hamlets; sufficient distance from other settlements to assure appropriate areas for hunting, gathering, or agriculture; proximity to varied ecological zones to provide food supplies under changing natural conditions; and accessibility for trade or communications. An example of placing elements with respect to a dominant topographic feature is

Mount Royal on the east bank of the St. Johns River near Lake George in Florida. According to William Bartram, the site was composed of a pond connected by a long sunken avenue to a conical mound. The axis of these elements aligned with a small but well-defined island at the north end of the lake, creating a remarkable sense of place still evident today.

Moated D-shaped enclosures have been found at Marksville, Toltec, and other sites. These sites were on river banks with excavations and embankments around their inshore perimeters. The architectural elements of both sites were placed in axial arrangements closely related to the alignment of the nearby rivers. Shaping an existing hill to resemble a platform mound is a method of creating an impressive earthwork with relative ease of which Emerald is an example.

Site orientation often is related to dominant topographical features and sometimes to the points of the compass. Occasionally one or more of the elements within a composition may be oriented with respect to the cardinal points, but more frequently in this study site axes seem to be related to natural terrain.

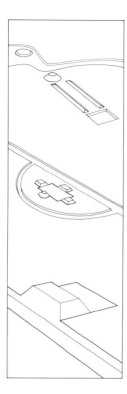

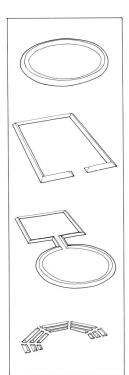

Enclosure

The earliest conception that America's first architects seemed to have was that of defining a special place, setting aside an opening in the wilderness and imparting a particular character to it. The shell rings of Fig Island, Sapelo, and other sites along the South Atlantic Coast appear to have been formed by placing discarded shells in circular patterns over an extended period of time. The interior surfaces of these enclosures apparently were kept free of habitations or debris, suggesting that they may have been used for ceremonial purposes. The shell ring sites may have been constructed by relatively small migratory groups of shellfish gatherers. By placing discarded shells in a ring rather than scattering them at random or depositing them in amorphous heaps, a relatively impressive structure could be created with relatively little effort. Shell structures resist natural erosion better than unprotected sand mounds along the South Atlantic Coast.

During the first millenium B.C. in the Mississippi and Ohio river valleys, earth enclosures of substantial size and complexity were developed. Rectilinear, curvilinear, and polygonal enclosures were constructed by excavating adjacent surfaces, sometimes creating moats, which may have served to visually augment the height of the wall. Adena and Hopewell enclosures frequently interlocked or were linked by parallel berms, creating processional ways, such as those at Newark. Burial ceremonies became increasingly important during this time, suggesting that the enclosures may have been related to the religious beliefs and practices of their builders. About 1000 B.C. at Poverty Point, vast earthworks were set in six concentric alignments resembling half of an octagon. Four aisles provided access to the central open space that faced eastward toward Bayou Maçon. These geometric earthworks and the nearby structures associated with them suggest a relatively high degree of planning skill and substantial organization of labor for construction.

Plaza

Architectural elements frequently were grouped around central open spaces in prehistoric America. These spaces sometimes contained ceremonial plazas or game courts from which all of the surrounding masses could be seen. This conception was the opposite of the Pyramids at Giza, the Athenian Acropolis, or Angkor Wat, where viewers moved around the central masses.

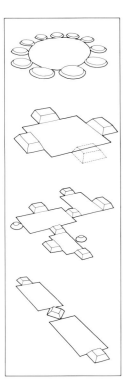

Circular plazas appeared during period 1 in shell ring sites, such as Sapelo and Fig Island, and during period 2 at sites such as Tchula Lake, where eleven low domiciliary mounds encircled the central open space. During the first millenium A.D. in the Mississippi River Valley, square or rectangular central spaces appeared, sometimes defined by masses on three sides with one side open and sometimes enclosed on all four sides. During period 3, multiple plazas were developed at larger settlements, such as Lake George and St. Louis. Fatherland's three masses were aligned on a single axis with two plazas rather than grouped around a central open space.

By no means did every site contain a single comprehensive geometric order such as a plaza. Crystal River is a baffling arrangement. Big Tonys and Big Mound City take on geometries of their own. Fort Center seems to obey time and terrain rather than geometry. The dominant masses of Falling Garden at St. Louis were placed along the edges of open spaces rather than in their midst. At Lake George the east plaza seems to have been constructed after the west plaza, so that the main pyramidal structure is centered in a single larger composition. At Cahokia, minor structures were placed in the large open space south of Monks Mound, forming two smaller spaces of more comprehensible scale. The main structure at Winterville was built near the center of the group of structures, separating one open space to the northeast from a second to the southwest.

Mass

The earliest masses found in the Eastern United States seem to have been refuse heaped into middens, frequently amorphous in shape and low in profile. In time middens augmented by earth began to take on specific shapes and functions, several examples of which are shown here. Burial mounds with a circular plan and domical profile appeared during the first millenium B.C., frequently in conjunction with linear earthworks and enclosures, such as those of the Adena-Hopewell people for whom burial and life after death apparently took on a special significance. In time, truncated conical mounds appeared. Relatively low house platforms were developed to serve as bases for wooden structures. Conical mounds without truncated tops occasionally are found, such as those on truncated platforms at Marksville.

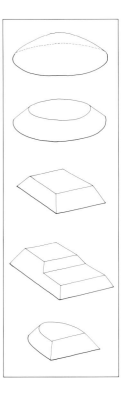

In period 3, square or rectangular truncated pyramids often served as platforms for temples or residences constructed of wood. Raising a religious structure above the surrounding terrain set it apart from the secular world and provided an appropriately impressive architectural character—a special high place. Residential platforms raised above grade gave protection against inundation during heavy rainfalls or minor flooding. Presumably higher platforms were reserved for more important civil and religious functionaries, perhaps to indicate their relative importance within community hierarchies. Multiple platforms creating terraces are sometimes found, particularly at larger settlements. The largest terraced structure yet found is Monks Mound, whose fourth level is more than 30 meters above Cahokia's main plaza. More frequently than not, terraces were arranged parallel to their adjoining plazas, providing multiple levels for temples or residences overlooking plazas.

According to Robert S. Neitzel, D-shaped structures occurred during earlier phases of construction at Greenhouse. The D-shaped structures reported by Squier and Davis (1848, plate XXXVIII, no. 4) at Jerden were apparently the result of erosion.

Shape

Variations of basic masses occur frequently in prehistoric America. Early earthworks in the shapes of birds, serpents, and animals have been found at Serpent Mound and Lizard, possibly reflecting the beliefs of their builders. Effigies are found more frequently among the Woodland and Hopewell people than elsewhere. Later, Mississippian builders concentrated on developing abstract geometric shapes such as truncated pyramids.

According to Melvin L. Fowler, ridge mounds found at Cahokia were elongated rectangles rising to ridges on which wooden poles were erected. These ridge poles were oriented with respect to the major site axes, apparently serving to define specific alignments or boundaries, but their exact functions are not yet clearly understood. Octagonal, square, and circular enclosures were found frequently in Ohio Hopewell earthworks, such as at Newark. Variations of basic geometric shapes were combined into large-scale compositions at Bainbridge, Dublin, High Bank, Marietta, Oldtown, Seal, and other Ohio Valley sites. According to early observers, Troyville's major structure was composed of a steep truncated cone set on two truncated pyramids and rose 24.4 meters from its 54.9-meter square base.

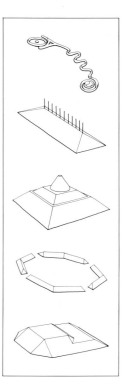

According to Harriet Smith, Murdock Mound was carefully faceted, by constructing a square platform on an octagonal base and cutting the base corners at forty-five degrees. Visually this would have shortened the length of the base while maintaining the full platform width, creating the illusion of steeper sides and greater vertical height. Faceting the corners of rectangular structures does not appear to have been widely practiced. Due to erosion, agricultural cultivation, dynamiting to remove tree stumps or artifacts, trampling of livestock, quarrying, and other forms of demolition, it is difficult to determine today the precise original shapes of many prehistoric American earthworks.

Comparison

The adjacent table compares some of the achievements of prehistoric American builders. Ordered by volume, selection was based on the strength of data for each earth structure. Monks Mound was the largest in volume and height, but the second highest, Troyville, was the smallest in volume. All were constructed primarily during period 3, except for Pinson, Grave Creek, and Portsmouth "C," which represent period 2. The structures compared are the major structures at

Site	Volume (cubic meters)	Maximum base dimension (meters)	Maximum height (meters)	Platform levels	Location	Configuration
Cahokia	615,144	241 × 316	30.5	4	Illinois	truncated pyramid
Etowah	121,813	85 × 110	20.3	3	Georgia	truncated pyramid
Moundville	112,000	52 × 116	16.8	1	Alabama	truncated pyramid
Lake George	76,840	84 × 84	18.4	1	Mississippi	truncated pyramid
Winterville	70,250	79 × 90	16.8	1	Mississippi	truncated pyramid
Emerald	69,070	133 × 235	10.2	1	Mississippi	truncated pyramid
Pinson	65,400	102 (diameter)	22.3	domical	Tennessee	burial cone
Kolomoki	62,510	61 × 99	17.2	2	Georgia	truncated pyramid
Grave Creek	52,975	97.5 (diameter)	21.3	domical	West Virginia	burial cone
Angel	51,788	107 × 203	13.4	3	Indiana	truncated pyramid
Mound Bottom	50,600	75 × 80	11	1	Tennessee	truncated pyramid
Portsmouth "C"	42,180	125 (diameter)	6.7	1	Kentucky	truncated cone
Obion	36,980	49 × 76	12	1	Tennessee	truncated pyramid
Toltec	30,910	46 × 85	14.6	1	Arkansas	truncated, elongated oval
Troyville	17,754	55 × 55	24.4	3	Louisiana	cone on two truncated pyramids

the sites listed. Volumes do not include associated earthworks or ramps except at Obion, where the ramp is a major feature of the principal structure. The volume shown for Emerald is one-third of the total pentagonal base, assuming that this represents the amount of earth moved to reshape the original natural hill.

Ascent

Movement through space, both vertically and horizontally, seems to have been an essential element of many prehistoric American sites. A typical sequence of movement through a period 3 settlement may have been to approach the site defined by a perimeter moat or enclosing wall, to enter through a portalway, to continue toward a central plaza signaled by several truncated pyramids, and to move between these masses into the central open space, which often was dominated by a major truncated pyramid and flanked by lesser structures. Because the summits of major mounds in period 3 settlements appear to have been occupied by important civil or religious edifices, it seems likely that ascent to these high places may have been limited to only certain privileged members of the society.

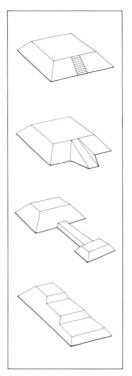

The simplest method of ascent to the platform of a truncated structure was by means of a stairway directly up the sloping side. Remains of ramps, sometimes utilizing clay or log steps, have been found projecting into open spaces at many sites. Evidence of several ramps ascending the same truncated pyramid has been found at several sites, but it appears that all these ramps may not have existed at the same time. It is more likely that they represent changing orientations at different stages of evolution, of which the east ramps of Monks Mound and the multiple ramps of Lake George's central structure are examples. William Bartram (1958) reported seeing spiral ramps during his eighteenth-century visits to the Southeast. Evidence of causeways connecting major and minor structures have been found at Winterville, Greenhouse, and possibly Troyville. Causeways lifted above low-lying terrain may have been utilized to give access to major structures and spaces at Big Mound City and Big Tonys. Multiple terraces assisted ascent to the summits of Monks Mound, Falling Garden, and other period 3 sites.

Excavation

Excavation into the earth was apparently the usual source of material from which above-grade masses were constructed. The closer the quarry

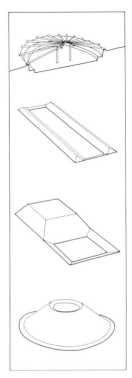

to the structure being erected, the easier the task. Earth lodges, such as the winter council house at Ocmulgee, consisted of a circular room with low earth walls near the center of which four vertical posts were erected to support the roof. Wood rafters spanned radially from the central support to the perimeter bearing wall. A layer of earth covered the timber roof.

A second example of space created below grade was the sunken avenue at Mount Royal, where excavated material was placed on two sides of the avenue, creating defining walls and directing attention to the mound at one end and to the pond and clearing at the opposite end. Borrow pits are common features in many period 3 sites, such as the ponds at Beckwith's Fort. Excavations often were found in close proximity to above-grade structures. This could have created an illusion of greater verticality, but the extent to which this possibility may have been exploited is not known. Excavations sometimes became ponds, serving as convenient sources of water and in some cases, such as Moundville, holding ponds for fish. Numerous fish hooks found at the bottoms of fish ponds suggest that fish trapped or caught in nearby streams may have been placed in the ponds to provide a dependable food source.

At several sites, excavations appear to have been combined with above-grade structures, combining positive and negative elements into a single composition. A rim around the top of a conical mound may have created a greater apparent height, provided visual privacy for the sunken summit, served as the base of a wooden roof structure, or formed the upper wall of a structure whose platform never was completed. An excavation around the base would have provided fill material for the main structure or served as a moat.

Earthmoving
The main method of moving earth in the prehistoric Eastern United States was by baskets carried by individual workers.

In order to obtain a reasonable estimate of the amount of time and effort that probably was required to construct Mayan structures in Mesoamerica, Charles J. Erasmus (1965) conducted an experiment in the summer of 1964 in Sonora, Mexico. He employed two workers who were descendants of the Mayas. Neither worker had previous experience in construction or earthmoving. One worker dug the earth with a digging stick, a method of excavation similar to that used in the study area, and loaded by hand a container with an average capacity of 20 kilograms per load. A second worker carried the loaded container 100 meters, deposited its contents in a conical mound, and returned for the next load. The experiment was conducted for five hours per day from 6:30 A.M. to 11:30 A.M., before the warmest time of the day. The men worked in full sun. At the end of one working week the men had produced a total average volume of 1.76 cubic meters of earth per day. The time required to carry the material exceeded the time required to dig it.

Earth in the Eastern United States is probably easier to dig than earth in Mesoamerica, and therefore the construction time in the study area may have been less than in Erasmus's experiment. Applying the same rate of earth digging and carrying to a typical earthwork in the study area, let us assume that Kolomoki's main structure was constructed in three equal phases of 20,840 cubic meters each. Taking William H. Sears's maximum population estimate to be

4,000, and dividing this by 5 persons per household, we estimate that 800 households may have provided 1 worker each for construction. Assuming 400 workers dug and 400 carried the material at an average rate of 1.76 cubic meters of earth produced per worker per day, we find that 29.52 days would be required to construct Kolomoki's 20,840 cubic meter mantle. Thus, Kolomoki's major structure could have been erected in less than a month by one-fifth of the population. We conclude that the construction of major earthworks in the study area was easily accomplished by relatively low populations utilizing simple construction methods.

We know that the sites in our study area typically were built by accretion over a long period of time in a series of phases rather than all at once. Erasmus's experiment suggests that construction was only a part-time source of employment. Construction work apparently was voluntary. Erasmus and other authorities believe that some of the reasons for prehistoric construction activity could have been "the desire for public approval and prestige, duty to the community, religious sentiment," or "pride in craftsmanship" (Kaplan, 1963).

Process

The process of constructing an earthwork in prehistoric America often seems to occur in a series of phases as later structures evolve. During their evolution, some structures changed not only their sizes but also their shapes, proportions, and orientations. Occasionally the primary functions of structures changed from domiciliary to burial, or vice versa, and sometimes their configurations changed from a D shape to a rectangular shape, such as at Greenhouse and possibly Jerden.

Sometimes the earliest phase of erection seems to have been a midden, often amorphous in shape and low in profile. The so-called canals at Key Marco suggested to early observers a series of complex, predetermined geometric ridges and sloughs, sometimes radiating and sometimes parallel. According to William H. Sears, it now appears likely that these ridges developed from rapidly accumulating middens formed by shells discarded from the shellfish eaters' residences. As the middens rose, earlier wood pole residences were rebuilt a short distance from their original locations. Over several generations, many midden ridges developed, forming a baffling myriad over the low-lying coastal island, apparently due more to pragmatic practice than to predetermined planning.

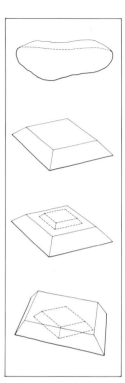

Surfacing materials often utilized in prehistoric earthworks frequently seem to have consisted of turf or clay, which may have been smoothed by hand. According to Jeffrey B. Brain, some earth structures at Lake George and Winterville seem to have been reinforced internally with compacted clay deposits to inhibit collapse of corners or sides. Clay facings offered the opportunity to change the structure's color: Murdock Mound appears to have been black, and Kolomoki's main structure bears traces of both red and off-white coloration in a series of layers. Shell cores and facings have been found at Crystal River, Turtle, Sapelo, and other southeastern coastal sites, but shell facings are not common elsewhere.

Settlement Patterns

Settlement patterns related to architecture help us to understand better the physical characteristics of prehistoric American sites, such as the density of residential areas; the orientation, sizes, and types of houses and the distances between them; the methods of inhibiting firespread between wood structures; the relationship of public to private zones; the effect of palisades on town planning; and whether palisades represent defensive systems or whether warfare played a role in prehistoric American architecture. Some authorities (Larson, 1972) believe that increasing population may have caused competition for limited arable land in period 3. Only about 2 percent of the land area now available for agricultural production in the Eastern United States is estimated to have been usable by the prehistoric Americans, who lacked modern fertilizers, flood control, irrigation systems, and other methods of improving cultivation.

It may be helpful to summarize the patterns that appeared in the Lower Mississippi Valley area, where more information is available, and set them in chronological sequence. Prior to the beginning of period 1 settlement patterns seem to have been limited to small groups in small camps in the uplands; no remains have been found in the flood plains (Williams, 1956). About 1000 B.C. large mounds and circular embankments appeared at Poverty Point, indicating either a large population for a short time or a smaller population over a very long period of time or both. At Jaketown, the cultural affiliate of Poverty Point, remains of an early circular house have been found. Its walls were constructed with small posts set singly into foundation holes in a slightly staggered pattern.

During period 2 in the Lower Mississippi Valley, distinctive pottery and small mounds appeared in the north and well-defined burial mounds were constructed in the south. Clear evidence of house types is lacking. Villages were relatively small and typically had adjacent burial mounds. Marksville had several burial mounds near its village area. At Spanish Fort, a typical period 2 site in the Yazoo Basin, a circular embankment enclosed a relatively large area, of which only one-fifth was used as a village site.

Early in period 3 pyramidal platforms were grouped around plazas in carefully planned villages. Populations definitely increased. In the south the truncated pyramids were not large at first, seldom exceeding four meters in height, but they were precisely related to their plazas. In the north information on early pyramidal mounds is lacking. Typical houses at Greenhouse were relatively large and circular. These were built both with and without wall trench foundations for supporting posts. Beckwith's Fort and Lilbourn were typical fortified towns with platforms mounds. Here large populations were concentrated in limited areas.

Broad variations of settlements occurred during period 3 in the Lower Mississippi Valley. In the south many large ceremonial centers appeared, such as Anna and Emerald. Emphasis seem to have shifted from precise arrangements to sheer size of truncated pyramids. Typical houses were square or rectangular in plan with wall trench construction, although some shift to wall post foundations occurred later. Lake George is an example of increasing cultural diversification with regional variations. Here a moated rectangular enclosure surrounded a large group of truncated pyramids grouped around two plazas with outlying rectangular wall trench houses. At Upper Nodena a circular structure, apparently related to special ceremonies, was placed on a platform mound. The fifty-odd houses at the site were rectangular or square in plan and utilized wall post construction.

Toward the end of period 3 a general cultural decline and population decimation took place throughout the Eastern United States. By the time of European contact, cultural activity had ceased in large areas of the Mississippi Valley. Natchez, one of the few sites that was active in early historic times, contained rectangular wall trench houses grouped in a fortified village.

In the past three centuries vast physiographic changes have occurred in the study area, rendering more difficult our "attempt to reconstruct cultures that no longer exist in an environment that exists in a profoundly modified state" (Phillips, Ford, and Griffin, 1951, p. 36).

Planning
Evidence of planning has been found at Cahokia, Moundville, Beckwith's Fort, Parkin, Kincaid, Lake Jackson, and many other period 3 sites. At the risk of oversimplification, it may be helpful to synthesize this evidence into a preliminary composite of planning ideas in the prehistoric Eastern United States.

According to Jon Muller (1978), the smallest settlement unit seems to have been a small camp, possibly 0.1 hectare in area. This may have been occupied only temporarily or periodically and may have served some special purpose, such as a base for hunters or gatherers. Camps are found in the vicinities of larger planning units.

Next in size was a farmstead, about 0.3 hectares in area, consisting of one to three rectangular structures measuring 3 to 6 meters on a

side arranged in an L- or U-shaped plan. Sometimes ramadas or corn cribs also are found at farmsteads. As the basic self-sufficient unit of period 3 sites, the farmstead contained all basic activities for economic development.

The next largest unit was a hamlet, which was 0.9 to 1.0 hectares in area and contained eight to fifteen structures grouped in clusters of farmsteads rather than randomly scattered over the site.

The secondary center was a large hamlet or village with one or more mounds, usually a plaza, and farmsteads arranged in wards or zones. The primary center was a typical arrangement for most of the sites presented in this study. At Kincaid, for example, only 6 hectares, or 8 percent, of the 70 hectares of land available was occupied; the balance of the area within the palisades was available to support the self-sufficient hamlets clustered around the main plaza and mounds. The site elevation was high enough to serve as a flood refuge within the palisade for the inhabitants of outlying hamlets and farmsteads. Although Kincaid's inhabitants also were concerned with basic subsistence, the site was primarily a center for distribution and administration. It was centrally directed and controlled, probably through the exercise of hereditary authority without force. This is characteristic of a chiefdom rather than a state that depends on the exercise of force to maintain its existence.

Structure

The remains of wood posts inserted into earthen holes or trenches and stabilized by backfill are found frequently at prehistoric sites. Free-standing posts at Kolomoki and those often found in plazas or athletic fields suggest that posts were used to display trophies or serve as goal markers for ball games. Cahokia's free-standing posts erected on the perimeter of circles at specific intervals may have served as observatories or woodhenges.

Set in lines at close intervals, free-standing posts also formed walls or palisades. Remains of bastions projecting outward from palisaded walls have been found at Aztalan, Beckwith's Fort, Etowah, and other sites. At many palisaded sites, smaller wood members were woven between the vertical posts and solidly infilled with wattle and daub. Entries through palisades sometimes were formed by simply omitting a section

of the wall, by overlapping the perimeter wall at the point of entry, or by creating towers with baffled entries like those at Town Creek.

At many sites, domiciliary structures were constructed of wall trench foundations with wattle-and-daub infilled walls supporting overhanging thatched roofs. These houses were similar in appearance to the thatched roof houses found in the Yucatán peninsula today. In larger wood structures, interior bearing posts were erected to support the central roof area. A less frequently found type of wood structure consisted of foundations in which a linear excavation contained a horizontal backlog reinforcing the bases of several upright posts.

Open sheds of post-and-beam construction formed sun shades for summer shelters at many sites. Structures partly recessed into the earth and enclosed with timber roofs were found at Ocmulgee and other sites. Winter lodges or council houses relied on interior posts and beams to support their roof structures, which often were covered with earth. Daylight penetrated the roofs of earth lodges through central openings, a conception similar to that of the Pantheon in Rome. The extent to which the prehistoric architects were aware of the design potential of interior space is not yet understood.

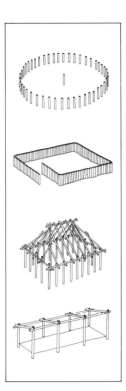

Engraved stone disc,
Moundville (Moore,
1905).

Reconstructions

The interpretive reconstructions of the eighty-two prehistoric American sites presented in this book are grouped chronologically into three parts, period 1 (circa 2200–1000 B.C.), period 2, (500 B.C.–A.D. 200) and period 3 (A.D. 800–1500).

Each part is preceded by a brief introduction, which attempts to identify that period's salient architectural characteristics. It appears that some of the ideas that evolved in period 1 may have recurred later in period 2, which reached its fruition between 200 B.C. and A.D. 200. Following a transition whose characteristics are unclear, new ideas manifested themselves between A.D. 800 and 1500, possibly reaching a climax about A.D. 1300. By the time of European contact, the architectural activities of period 3 were declining in most of the study area, although the earlier influences of period 2 seem to have survived into historic times in some areas, for example, among the Iroquois in the eastern Great Lakes region.

Each chronological period is presented generally according to the geographical proximity of sites. The description of each site includes the name of the site, immediately followed by the location of the nearest present-day city, which may be found on a current road map or in an atlas. Below most descriptions is a reference to an authority whose publication is listed fully in the bibliography. These publications contain additional information on the sites. In cases where several references are available, the primary source is listed, which is usually the origin of the site plan used as the basis of the interpretive reconstruction. The description of each site contains concise architectural information wherever available. The scale of all reconstructions is identical, and north is always oriented toward the top of the page, except in the case of Poverty Point, which is explained in the accompanying text.

An initial objective of this study was to develop a comparative analysis of each site in terms of proportions, steepness ratios, methods of access, functions, surfacing techniques and colors, and other architectural characteristics. Due to missing information on many sites, this analysis has not been possible. Other objectives of the study have been achieved and some findings developed that had not been anticipated initially. Often prehistoric American architects appear to have arranged their sites with careful regard to their visual environments, imbueing them with a special sense of

place, a conception seldom encountered in twentieth-century United States. Apparently, abstract orientation toward north or the cardinal points seldom preoccupied prehistoric architects. Often their settlements seem to have been organized with respect to natural terrain and related, in many cases, to a clearly perceptible order involving an architectural hierarchy. Their major building material appears to have been earth and they elevated earthworks to a high level of architectural achievement, another art lost to twentieth-century America. Unfortunately their earth structures have fallen easy prey to modern earthmovers, resulting in the rapid demolition of our architectural heritage.

Where a few examples of prehistoric American earthworks have survived, their durability is apparent, as evidenced by Monks Mound at Cahokia and the earthworks of Poverty Point. Internally reinforced earth structures have been found at Lake George and Winterville. By comparison, we recall that when vandals removed the protective copper roofing from one of Hadrian's Villa's domed structures built in the second century A.D., the exposed concrete dome weathered and collapsed within 200 years. Conversely Sapelo's monumental enclosure built more than 3,000 years ago is today still more than five meters

high, very nearly its original dimension. At Kiminaljuyú, early Mayan architects protected their clay structures with thin stone caps at the tops of walls to shed water away. Later Mayan monuments were entirely stone faced, a more effective method of erosion control. Often in the history of architecture we find the development of an architectural conception in advance of supporting technology, as in the case of Guarini's delicate binding arches for the stone cupola of San Lorenzo, which anticipated later steel or reinforced concrete construction technology. Prehistoric earthworks appear to have anticipated an effective erosion-control technology.

Metric System

Unit	U.S. Equivalent
Kilometer	0.62 miles
Meter	39.37 inches
Centimeter	0.39 inches
Square kilometer	0.3861 square miles
Hectare	2.47 acres
Cubic Meter (stere)	1.31 cubic yards
Liter (dry)	0.908 quarts
Liter (liquid)	1.057 quarts
Kilogram	2.2046 pounds

Prehistoric Architecture in
the Eastern United States

Period 1
Circa 2200– 1000 B.C.

Sapelo
Fig Island
Poverty Point

Fig Island
Poverty Point
Sapelo

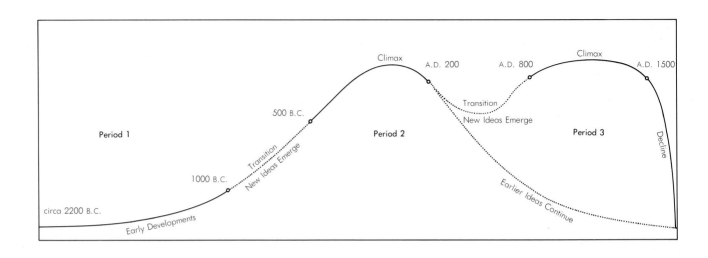

circa 2200 B.C.

Early Developments

Period 1

1000 B.C.

Transition

New Ideas Emerge

500 B.C.

Climax

A.D. 200

Period 2

Transition

New Ideas Emerge

A.D. 800

Earlier Ideas Continue

Climax

Period 3

A.D. 1500

Decline

Circa 2200–1000 B.C.

The diagram on the left suggests the presence of architectural activity in a large geographic area of the Eastern United States more than 3 millenia preceding Columbus's arrival in the New World. The diagram is general in nature based primarily on our greater understanding of more recent sites and the relative paucity of information on earlier sites. Although we know that architectural activity occurred in the study area as early as 2240 B.C. (±90 years), we are not yet able to discern a continuity in the architectural developments that appeared during period 1.

As early as 2240 B.C. (± 90 years), shell rings began to appear along the South Atlantic Coast, such as those of St. Simons Island, Sapelo, and Fig Island. These early architectural works illustrate several architectural ideas that reappeared at later times and at various sites in our study area: a central open space defined by a simple geometric mass constructed of debris and earth; a central space free of cultural debris, suggesting that it was a special place set apart from daily living; habitation areas separated from the central space; a defining structure augmented periodically by additional layers; and a location near major watercourses. The people who constructed the shell rings apparently were groups of migrating hunters and gatherers rather than farmers.

About 1000 B.C., large-scale geometric earthworks appeared at Poverty Point in the Lower Mississippi River Valley, arranged along a bluff overlooking the Bayou Maçon and its floodplain to the east. Here a special central place was set apart, but its defining geometric masses were much larger and more complex than the shell rings. Four streets or aisles radiated from the central place into the surrounding habitation areas and three large outlying earthern structures were aligned with the site's east-west and north-south axes in a close relationship with the natural terrain.

During the second millenium B.C. early pottery tempered by small, fibrous materials appeared in the Southeastern United States. The so-called Orange wares of the St. Johns River area in Northeast Florida and ceramics from the Savannah River area in Georgia are examples. By the time Poverty Point was built, extensive trade networks had appeared in the Eastern United States, extending from the Lower Mississippi Valley to the Great Lakes, the Appalachian Mountains, and coastal Florida. Settlements appear to have become more sedentary and more populous than the earlier sites of roving hunters and gatherers. When and where agriculture began in the Eastern United States is not known, although the Southeast seems a likely place in view of its fertile soil, favorable climate, and rainfall.

The problem of origin of architectural ideas remains to be resolved: Similarities to Mesoamerican architecture, such as the early Olmec earthworks at San Lorenzo in Central Mexico, have been suggested, but evidence of a direct connection is lacking. A possible relationship between the shell rings of the South Atlantic Coast and a similar structure of a slightly earlier time found at Puerto Hormiga on the Caribbean coast of Venezuela remains to be proved.

Sapelo

Sapelo Island, Georgia

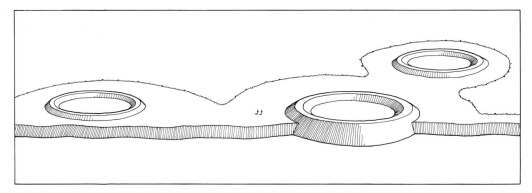

Constructed about 1700 B.C. near the north end of Sapelo Island, these shell rings are among the earliest known architectural structures in North America, substantially predating the earliest known architectural sites in Mesoamerica. According to McKinley (1873), Sapelo's central ring measured about 95 meters in outside diameter. Its encircling walls rose 3 meters from an 11-meter-wide base to a flat top about 4 meters wide. This main ring was constructed in at least three successive stages of mostly oyster shells with some conch, clam, and mussel shells, but very few bones or pottery intermixed. These shells made possible very steep sides that originally were inclined at almost a 45-degree angle. McKinley noted that along its easterly side the walls of the main circle rose almost 7 meters above the Mud River. Two other nearby shell rings were 76 meters in outside diameter with walls 1 meter high.

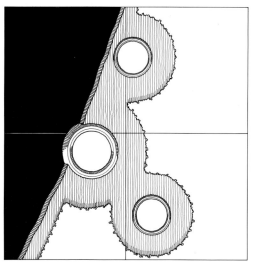

Surrounding the rings were hundreds of shell mounds one meter high and 3 to 7 meters in diameter that appear to be individual habitation sites built at a later time. The closest known burial mound, about 5 kilometers away, was also built at a later time. The purpose of the rings is assumed to have been ceremonial. Today erosion, cultivation, and quarrying have destroyed much of the site.

Reference: Williams, 1968.

Fig Island

Edisto Island, South Carolina

The Fig Island shell ring measured about 76 meters in outside diameter and contained a 2,000-square-meter open space within its 9- to 12-meter-wide encircling wall. Oyster shells constituted most of the ring's estimated 13,215-cubic-meter volume. Apparently the ring was constructed between 1900 and 1200 B.C. by the earliest pottery-making inhabitants of the southeastern Atlantic Coast. These pre-agricultural people subsisted largely on the resources of estuaries and tidal creeks. Twenty-three meters to the north was a shell crescent assumed to have been part of a second circular enclosure partially destroyed by quarrying or erosion. Habitations are believed to have been located at the outer edges of the ring.

The site is more than a meter higher than the surrounding tidal marsh of the North Edisto River estuary. Similar shell rings are found within 320 kilometers along the Atlantic Coast. The oldest yet recorded is on St. Simon's Island, and it yielded a radiocarbon date of 2240 B.C. (± 90 years), according to Marrinan (1975). The purposes of the rings may have been ceremonial, but this is not yet proved. According to some authorities, a similar ring found at Puerto Hormiga on Columbia's Atlantic Coast was constructed between 3000 and 2500 B.C., possibly suggesting early voyages between North and South America.

Reference: Hemmings, 1970.

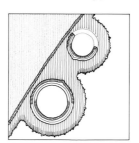

Poverty Point

Floyd, Louisiana

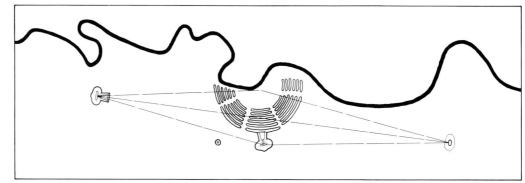

One of the earliest and largest prehistoric sites in this study is Poverty Point, which lies on a bluff overlooking Bayou Maçon to the east. Apparently constructed about 1000 B.C., the group consists of Motley Mound to the north, Lower Jackson Mound to the south, and two mounds and crescent-shaped earthworks near the center.

The central group of Poverty Point reconstructed on this and the next page is oriented with north to the left in order to present this unique group in its entirety. The central plaza or open space is about 595 meters in diameter and is flanked by six concentric rows of ridge mounds separated by four outward radiating aisles. In plan, the ridge mounds resemble half of an octagon. The truncated ridges are 3 to 3.7 meters high by about 25 meters wide and are set 46 meters apart. The ends to the east appear to have been terminated purposefully rather than eroded by the bayou. Near the center of the open plaza staggered postmolds have been found; their original purposes are not known as yet. Engaging

the westernmost ridge mound is an irregular 22-meter-high mound measuring 216 by 195 meters at its base. A platform 7 meters high, 73 meters wide, and 81 meters long lies between the summit and the engaging ridge mound. About 670 meters to the north of this irregular mound is a 6.6-meter-high conical mound 59.4 meters in base diameter containing cremated human interments.

Located 2.4 kilometers north of the plaza are the remains of Motley Mound, which was originally about 20 meters high and similar in configuration to the major central mound. Situated 2.4 kilometers south of the plaza are the eroded remains of Lower Jackson Mound, a relatively small and never-completed structure that originally may have been related to the main group.

Apparently the population of Poverty Point at one time may have been about 2,000 inhabitants. Evidence of nearby villages has been found both in the lower-lying terrain and in the uplands west of the bluff. Evidence found at Poverty Point suggests that a trade network existed 3,000 years ago, extending to Florida, the Appalachians, and the Great Lakes.

Reference: Webb, 1977.

Circa 2200-1000 B.C.

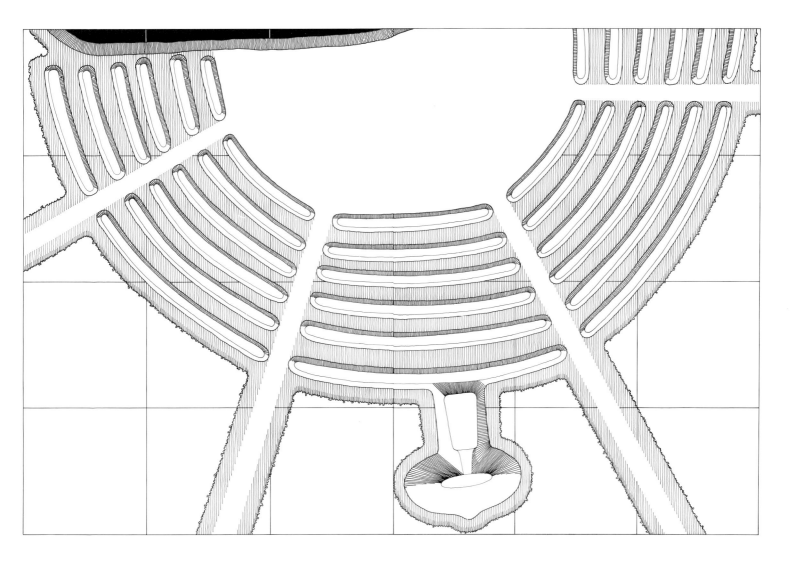

Period 2

500 B.C. – A.D. 200

Newark
Marietta
High Bank
Portsmouth "C"
Oldtown
Lizard
Serpent Mound
Cedar Bank
Stone Work
Graded Way
Seal
Dublin

Bainbridge
Kanawha
South Charleston
New Castle
Fort Center
Crystal River
Tick Island
Marksville
Tchula Lake
Spanish Fort
Pinson

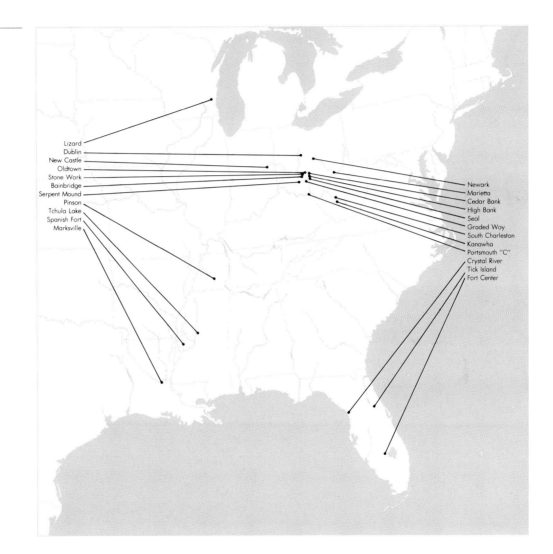

By 600 B.C., a new group of ideas had appeared in the Eastern United States, centered in the area of southern Ohio, western West Virginia, and northern Kentucky and extending with regional variations over much of the study area. New developments of period 2 included the more widespread use of ceramics and very possibly the introduction of agriculture, including maize, which would have allowed for the elaboration that led to the climax of Hopewell culture about the time of Christ. A third development was that of burial mounds and associated earthworks, which indicate a cultural preoccupation with mortuary practices and attendant ceremonialism.

An example of earlier variation during period 2 is the Adena culture, whose sites are characterized by steep conical burial mounds with elaborate log tombs, circular ceremonial enclosures and associated earthworks, circular houses with paired wall posts, and highly developed artifacts of stone and copper. Adena sites illustrated in this study are the eastern mound of the Marietta group, the circular earthworks of High Bank, Portsmouth Group "C," Serpent Mound, and Miamisburg (see aerial photographs). The Adena sites are particularly important because of their association with the Hopewell culture, which closely followed them in the Ohio area.

Hopewell sites appear to have been distinctly ceremonial centers with nearby habitation areas or extended villages and hamlets. They are located on river terraces and have complex large-scale plans with geometric earthworks ranging in height generally from 1 to 5 meters. Enclosure walls sometimes show a distinct disregard for terrain and appear to be clearly ceremonial rather than defensive, although their so-called hilltop fortification may have served this latter function. A characteristic of Hopewell sites is the placement of mounds opposite the breaks in square or octagonal earthworks, such as those of Newark, the central square at Marietta, Oldtown, High Bank, and Seal. Other Hopewell sites presented here are Cedar Bank, Stone Work, and New Castle. Bainbridge is probably a Hopewell site also.

Large burial mounds of complex structure dominated Hopewell sites. These are often circular or elliptical in plan and up to 10 meters in height. According to Stephen Williams (1963), their construction generally includes "a carefully prepared floor often with a layer of sand; posthole patterns; areas outlined with stone or gravel; a primary mound over burials and features; and a thin strata of sand, gravel, or colored earths between successive layers. Features on, or in, the floor include basins of 'altars', burial platforms, and log tombs—often subfloor—and pits. The basins are often filled with burial offerings, either whole or 'killed', and bones of individuals apparently cremated elsewhere. The platforms and log tombs are quite elaborate and were subsequently covered by small primary mounds."

Hopewell artifacts indicate a high level of art and technology with ample evidence of trade specialization. These include artifacts of stone, obsidian, flint, fresh water pearls, bone, antler, bear teeth, mica, marine conch shells, textiles, and copper sometimes overlaid with iron, silver, or gold. Less is known about Hopewell ceramics because they are seldom associated with ceremonial burials and relatively few village sites have been excavated. Hopewell artifacts indicate a broad trade dispersion over much of the study area: westward into Kansas, southward into Mississippi and Louisiana, southeasterly across Alabama and Georgia into Florida, and northeasterly into New York.

Florida sites active during period 2 are Crystal River, Tick Island, and the central area of Fort Center. The architectural characteristics of Florida sites are less distinct than those of the Ohio Hopewell but nevertheless indicate an emphasis on mortuary ceremonialism with its associated burial mounds and earthworks. Regional variations occurring in the Lower Mississippi Valley during period 2 are illustrated by Marksville, Tchula Lake, and Spanish Fort. The Pinson site in western Tennessee suggests a link between the Ohio River Valley sites and those of the Lower Mississippi.

The architectural features of some period 2 sites were built before 500 B.C. and some were added after A.D. 200. For example, Tick Island's southerly habitation area has yielded evidence of occupation as early as 4100 B.C., but its burial mounds probably date from slightly after period 2, according to Jerald T. Milanich. Fort Center's western circle dates from possibly 500 B.C., but its easterly features occurred after A.D. 800, according to William H. Sears. Marietta's truncated platform with ramps most likely was added during period 3, according to James B. Griffin.

The reasons for the decline of the highly ordered Hopewell culture after A.D. 200 are not clearly known. One reason may have been a shift in climate that would have reduced agricultural production in the Ohio Hopewell area. Other reasons may have been changes in cultural significance or changes in priorities.

The origins of new developments culminating in period 2 is likewise unclear. Asia has been suggested as a possible source, but because no evidence of burial ceremonialism occurs for thousands of miles across northern Canada and Alaska, this origin appears improbable. Mesoamerica may be a more likely source, but again direct evidence is lacking.

Elsewhere in the world between 500 B.C. and A.D. 200 the Athenians erected their classical structures on the Acropolis; the Temple of Edfu was erected in Egypt; the Great Wall of China was completed; and Roman architects built the Colosseum, Trajan's Forum, the Pantheon, and Hadrian's Villa.

Newark

Newark, Ohio

The octagonal and circular composition shown here was one of three groups of large earthworks on a fertile plain about 12 meters above the Raccoon Fork of the Licking River near Newark. The octagon is composed of eight nearly equal walls with corner entries. Located 18.3 meters inside of each entry was a 1.5-meter-high truncated pyramid with a 24.4-by-30.4-meter base. The octagon enclosed more than 18 hectares. Toward the southwest, two 91.4-meter-long berms set 18.3 meters apart flanked an avenue connecting the center of the octagon with the center of the circle. The geometrically precise circle enclosed more than 8 hectares within its 320 meter diameter walls. On the perimeter of the circle at the southwestern end of the site axis,

two walls turned outward for 30 meters as though to form an accessway, which, in turn, was blocked by a 52-meter-long mound several meters higher than the circular wall and set at a right angle to the site axis.

East of the octagon were three avenues flanked by 1.2-meter-high parallel walls. The two avenues toward the east and southeast led to two large geometric earthworks more than 3 kilometers away. Toward the south, the third avenue led 4 kilometers to the north bank of the Licking River.

The well-preserved and well-documented Newark earthworks help to confirm the scale and precision of other Hopewell sites, such as High Bank, Oldtown, and Seal. A comparable example of three earthwork groups set several kilometers apart and connected by avenues flanked by walls was found at Portsmouth. Newark's octagon contains the same area as the irregular square at Marietta.

Newark was occupied about A.D. 200 by Hopewell-related people whose monuments probably were related to the ceremonial burial of important persons in mounds within enclosures. Presumably lower ranked members of the society lived and were buried outside the enclosures. Today Newark's octagon and circle serve as a golf course, clearly visible in Dache Reeves's 1934 aerial photograph.

Reference: Squier and Davis, 1848, plate XXV, pp. 67–72.

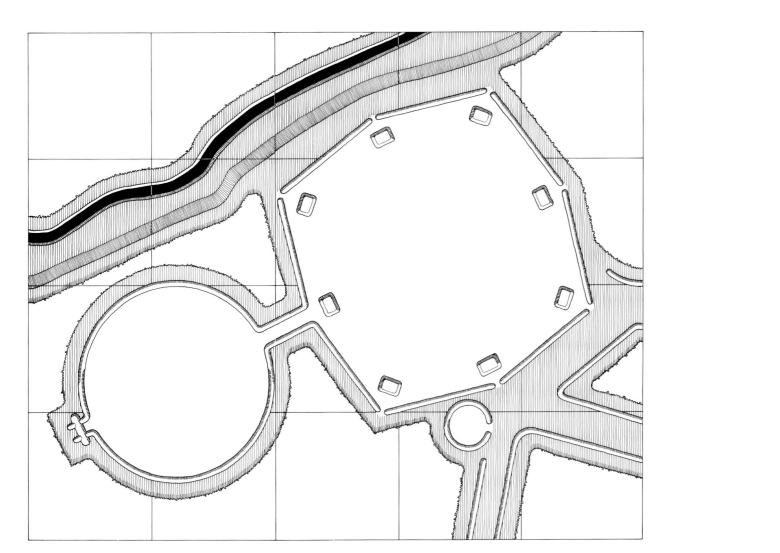

Marietta

Marietta, Ohio

The Marietta earthworks lay on a high sandy plateau 25 to 30 meters above the Muskingum River near its confluence with the Ohio River. The site occupied an 800-by-1,200-meter area and consisted of two large, irregular squares, a graded way descending to the banks of the Muskingum, an elliptical mound within a moated circular embankment, and related conical, pyramidal, and linear earthworks. The basis of this reconstruction is Charles Whittlesey's survey of 1837, published in Squier and Davis's plate XXVI with an accompanying description by Squier and Davis. Where the survey and description were inconsistent, Whittlesey's information took precedence.

Sixteen ridge mounds defined the larger square, which contained four rectangular truncated pyramids within its 18.2-hectare enclosure. The mounds were about 1.7 meters high and up to 9 meters wide at their bases. The 3-meter-high northwestern pyramid measured 40.2 by 57.3 meters at its base. The platform at the top was accessible by four graded ramps, each 7.6 meters wide and 18.3 meters long. The southeasterly pyramid rose 2.4 meters from a 36.6-by-45.7-meter base. From the platform, Whittlesey showed three ramps extending outward and a fourth recessed within the pyramid's southeast side, an unusual feature in prehistoric American architecture and possibly the result of recent alteration. A graded way, 207 meters long, led down to the Muskingum River to the southwest. This 45.7-meter-wide ramp was flanked by embankments that were 3 meters high on the upslope and 6 meters high on the downslope.

Ten ridge mounds and eight small conical mounds comprised the 11-hectare south square. To the southeast, a circular embankment with an inner moat enclosed a 9.1-meter-high truncated elliptical structure 65 by 70 meters in base dimensions. From its platform there was a comprehensive view of the earthworks, plateau, and rivers.

James B. Griffin (personal communication, 1978) suspects "the eastern mound at Marietta is late Adena, the central square is certainly Hopewell, and perhaps the western square. But the platform mounds with ramps I think are probably on the Mississippi period level [period 3]."

Reference: Squier and Davis, 1848, plate XXVI.

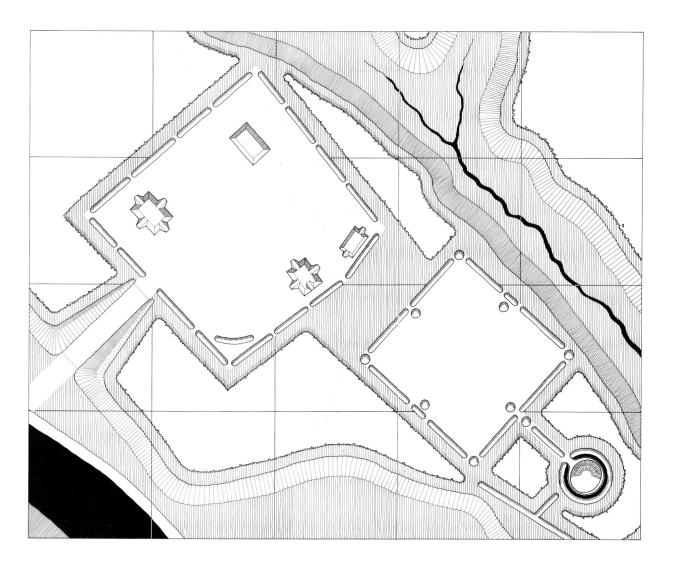

High Bank

Chillicothe, Ohio

The High Bank site consists of a circular and an octagonal enclosure and associated earthworks on the east bank of the Scioto River southeast of Chillicothe. The group derived its name from its position on the high bank of the river, which, at this point, was between 21 and 24 meters below the level terrace of the earthworks. According to Squier and Davis, the main site axis formed a right angle with the river and generally was parallel with the edge of a natural embankment to the southwest.

The general location plan and reconstruction shown here are based on E. G. Squier's plate II map of a 20-kilometer section of the Scioto Valley and Squier and Davis's plate XVI, which differ in minor details. Additional data conflicts occur in Squier and Davis's verbal description published in 1848, rendering it difficult to determine the precise architectural character of the site. In this reconstruction, the second largest circular embankment is shown completely intact, whereas it is shown partially eroded by the southwesterly bluff in Squier's surveys.

500 B.C.-A.D. 200

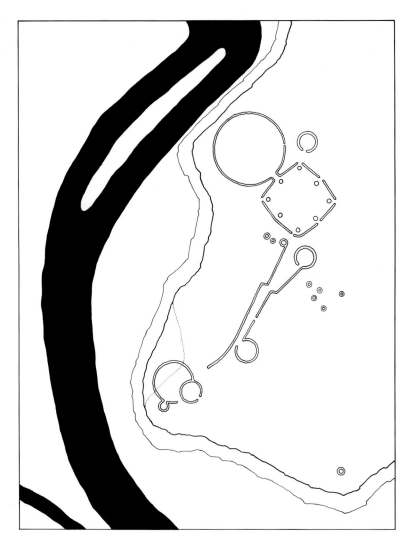

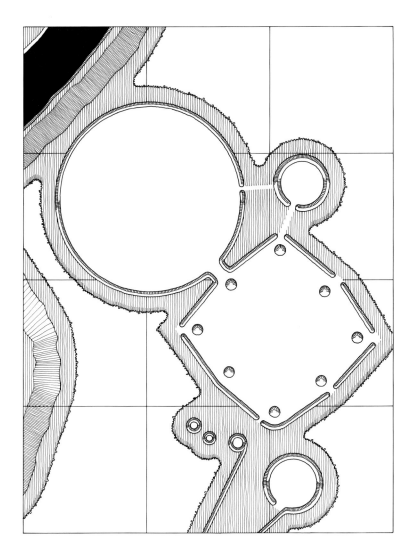

The irregular octagonal enclosure measured about 290 meters across in plan. Eight mounds were placed near the corners of the octagon, whose bold walls originally rose about 3.5 meters from 15-meter-wide bases. A walled opening toward the northwest connected the octagonal enclosure to a 320-meter-diameter circular enclosure with low walls. A 76-meter-diameter circular enclosure to the northeast opened toward the north corner of the octagon. Toward the south and west were several additional circular enclosures with an irregular arrangement of linear earthworks, which were still visible in 1848, though much eroded by cultivation. Six earth rings almost 15 meters in diameter with walls 60 centimeter high lay in a forest to the south. A large truncated mound exceeding 9 meters in height was the southernmost structure of High Bank.

James B. Griffin (personal communication, 1978) believes "the small earth circles and the large circles with one opening . . . are probably Adena and not Hopewell."

Reference: Squier and Davis, 1848, plates II and XVI.

Portsmouth "C"

Greenup, Kentucky

Group "C" of the Portsmouth Works was located on the south shore of the Ohio River about 10 kilometers east of its confluence with the Scioto River, the site of the present-day city of Portsmouth, Ohio. Four concentric earth embankments placed at irregular intervals enclosed a central open space and conical mound. The embankments varied from 0.6 to 1.5 meters in height and diminished from a 485-meter outer diameter to a 210-meter inner diameter. The truncated cone, 6.7 meters high, rose from a 125-meter-diameter base to a 20-meter-diameter platform, from which the surrounding earthworks were clearly visible. A graded way gave access to the summit from the southeast. Four 30-meter-wide avenues flanked by 1.2-meter-high ridge mounds provided access through the circular enclosures. The avenues were biaxially symmetrical about an axis 5 degrees east of north.

The westerly avenue followed the natural contours, sometimes steep, without intervening portals. The flanking earth embankments stood 1.2 meters high by 6 meters wide and were 13 kilometers long. Curving to the north for 2.5 kilometers, the avenue descended 15 meters to the banks of the Ohio River. From the north bank of the river, the avenue continued northwest an additional 4 kilometers to Group "B," the central Portsmouth Works. A similar avenue connected Group "B" with Group "A," 5.5 kilometers to the southwest, and recrossed the Ohio River to the Kentucky shore. A third avenue proceeded northwest from Group "B." In all, more than 32 kilometers of parallel earth embankments were reported to have bordered the three avenues of the Portsmouth Works.

James B. Griffin's guess (personal communication, 1978) was that Group "A" is Hopewell, Group "C" is probably late Adena, and Group "B" is a mixture of Adena circles and mounds.

Reference: Squier and Davis, 1848, plates XXVII and XXVIII.

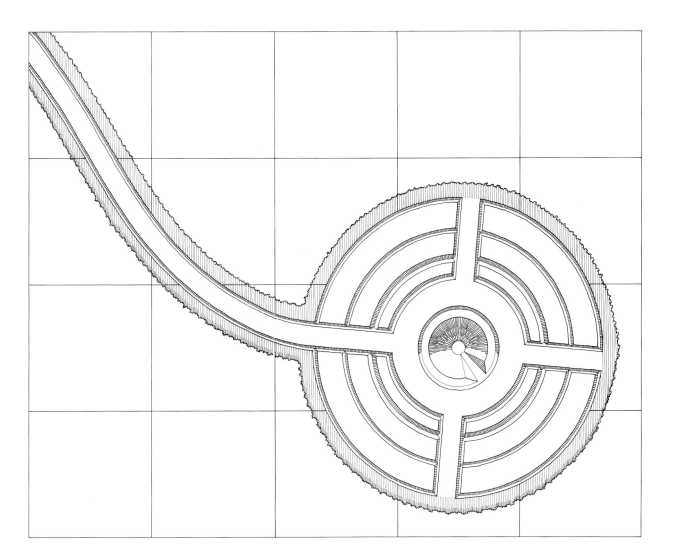

Oldtown

Frankfort, Ohio

The geometrically precise earthworks of Oldtown, also known as "Old Chillicothe," were situated on the north bank of the North Branch of Paint Creek, partly within the town limits of Frankfort, according to Squier and Davis. The group consisted of two circular earth embankments and a perfect square. The circular walls, about a meter high, were built of loam and gravel taken from topsoil, while the straight walls were made of clay taken from the subsoil, suggesting that they were added to the composition last. The square measured 329 meters on each side. Biaxially symmetrical entryways were at the centers and corners of the square. The point of tangency between the square and the larger circle was on a line passing through the exact centers of both figures and parallel to the creek's course. A similar alignment occurs between the centers of the smaller circle and the larger circle where they are tangent. The large circle was 524 meters in diameter and contained 21.6 hectares, the square enclosed 10.8 hectares, half the larger area; and the smaller circle was 235 meters in diameter, containing 4.3 hectares.

Within 32 kilometers of Oldtown are four similar earthworks, each composed of a 329-meter square, a 524-meter-diameter circle, or major portion thereof, and a 235-meter-diameter circle. The uniformity of dimensions and the accuracy of square corners suggest that the builders used a standard measurement length and understood a method of laying out exact squares, octagons, and other geometric shapes, a difficult task, at best, without accurate instruments. The arrangement of each of the four sites varies according to the natural terrain, particularly watercourses.

James B. Griffin (personal communication, 1978) comments that "Oldtown was certainly a Hopewell earthwork with many 'classic' features including the mounds opposite the breaks in the square earthworks. Probably the best preserved Hopewell earthwork."

Reference: Squier and Davis, 1848, plate XXI, no. 4.

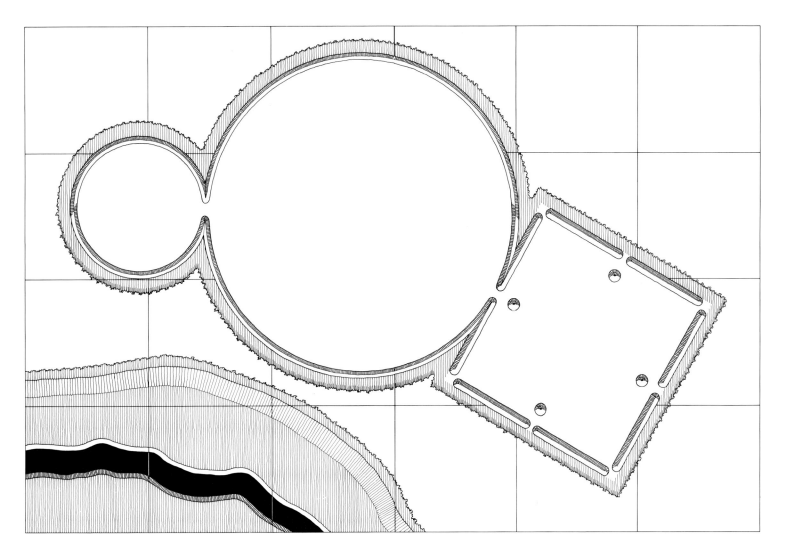

Lizard

West Bend, Wisconsin

About 5,000 effigy mounds have been found in southern Wisconsin. Thirty-one of them are in this group located 8 kilometers northeast of West Bend. At most one meter high, the mounds here represent panthers, birds, and a lizard as well as linear, conical, and oval geometric figures. Other sites contain eagle, water fowl, bear, buffalo, and turtle effigies. A panther effigy, 175 meters long, was found at Buffalo Lake, the longest recorded in Wisconsin. An unusual human effigy 65 meters long was located near Baraboo.

The effigy mounds are believed to have been constructed by Woodland people, possibly between A.D. 600 and 1000. Usually within the mounds are single or multiple burials, but because very few funerary objects have been found with these interments, it is difficult to establish exact chronology.

A variation of effigies is the intaglio, an excavation into the earth as deep as 30 centimeters in the shape of a panther or bear and never associated with burials. About ten intaglios have been reported, but the only surviving example is the panther effigy near Fort Atkinson. Ninety-eight percent of the North American effigies are in Wisconsin, but a few also are located in Illinois, Iowa, Ohio, and Minnesota.

Reference: Ritzenthaler, 1970.

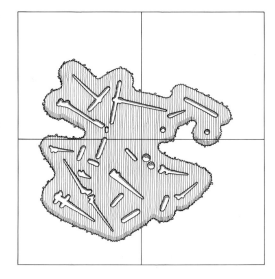

Serpent Mound

Peebles, Ohio

The largest serpent effigy yet found in the Eastern United States is located several kilometers north of Peebles, a town in south–central Ohio. The site is a plateau 45 meters above Brush Creek, which lies 30 meters to the west. A rocky natural precipice retains the eastern edge of the plateau, which slopes less abruptly down to Small Run toward the east and north. The northern tip of the plateau appears to have been artificially shaped to form a 3-meter-wide accessway around a 1.2-meter-high earth oval measuring 24 by 48 meters. The open space within the oval is slightly elevated above the surrounding plateau, and a circle of large stones was found in the center. The oval appears to be held in the distended jaws of the great serpent.

In 1846, the snake's body was more than 1.5 meters high and 9 meters wide, but erosion and cultivation have reduced these dimensions to about 1.2 by 6 meters. Winding southward more than 244 meters, the effigy terminates in a triple coil at the tail. Outstretched, the body would be

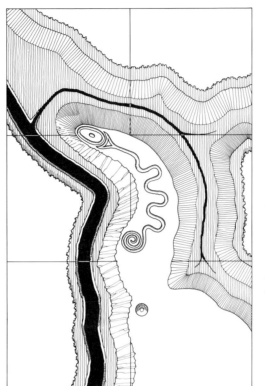

almost 400 meters long. The plateau's surface is slightly convex throughout the effigy's length. Small stones and lumps of clay first were placed on the plateau to outline the shape, then clay from the site was used to construct the earthwork.

The date of construction is not known, but evidence from a 3-meter-high burial mound 91 meters to the south suggests that the great serpent may have been built by Adena-related people who apparently occupied the area between 800 B.C. and A.D. 400. Presumably the Serpent effigy was related to the beliefs of its builders.

Serpent Mound was saved for posterity by the action of Professor Frederic Ward Putnam, Director of Harvard's Peabody Museum from 1876 to 1915. In a very early example of the preservation movement, he raised money to buy it and later turned it over to the state (Stephen Williams, personal communication, 1979). An aerial view is shown on page 157.

Reference: Squier and Davis, 1848, plate XXXV.

Cedar Bank

Chillicothe, Ohio

The Cedar Bank earthworks were located on the east bank of the Scioto River immediately north of Chillicothe. A bluff 21 meters above the river defined the site's westerly edge, and an earth embankment enclosed the 13-hectare site. The enclosure's 1.8-meter-high walls rose from 12-meter-wide bases. The north and south walls were 320 meters long, respectively, and the east wall measured 427 meters long. Two embrasures, 18 meters wide, bisected the north and south walls on the centerline of the main site axis, which was generally parallel with the bluff edge. The south wall extended to the bluff, but the north wall terminated 7.6 meters from it. The site thus would have been surrounded on three sides by embankments above the viewer's eye level, opening a broad vista of the Scioto Valley to the west. An excavation outside of the enclosure was 12 meters wide and 1.5 meters deep except toward the northeast where it joined a 2.4- to 3-meter-deep drainageway.

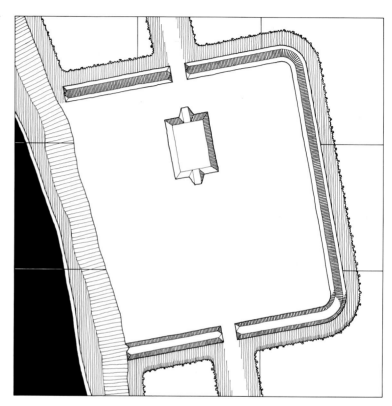

500 B.C.-A.D. 200

On the main site axis, 61 meters from the northern gateway, was a truncated pyramid, 1.2 meters high, with a 46-by-76-meter base. According to James B. Griffin, this structure probably was not of Hopewell origin. Ramps, each 9 meters wide, gave access to the summit from the north and south. To the east and south were several lesser geometric earthworks whose relationship to the principal enclosure is obscure. Sixteen kilometers to the south was the High Bank group.

This reconstruction is based on the account of Squier and Davis's plates II and XVIII and an accompanying description with three minor exceptions: The bluff washout near the southwest corner has been eliminated, the erosion gulley at the northern two-thirds of the east moat is not shown, and the Scioto River bank has been extended slightly northerly assuming recent silting. James B. Griffin (personal communication, 1978) doubts that the outer excavation, which Squier and Davis called a "ditch," actually held water except after a heavy rain. Both Thomas and Fowke have commented on inaccuracies in Squier and Davis's Cedar Bank rendering.

Reference: Squier and Davis, 1848, plates II and XVII.

Stone Work
Chillicothe, Ohio

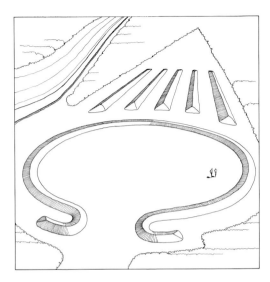

Possibly a conventionalized bear paw, Stone Work lies 24 kilometers from Chillicothe in the little valley of Black Run, which contains only a few stone structures. According to Squier and Davis, the Stone Work site consisted of an elliptical enclosure and five converging walls. The enclosing wall was about 5 meters wide at its base and 1 meter high. In plan, the enclosure measured 53 by 76 meters. On both sides of a 15-meter-wide entry, flanking walls curved outward 18 meters. Beginning 3 meters north of the enclosure, the five 30-meter-long converging walls diminished from 6 to 3 meters in width. Hopewellians probably built the Stone Work between A.D. 1 and 400.

Reference: Squier and Davis, 1848, plate III, no. 1 and plate XXX, no. 4.

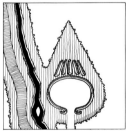

Graded Way

Piketon, Ohio

Of the several earth ramps constructed in Ohio, Squier and Davis considered the Graded Way, about 1.6 kilometers south of Piketon, the most remarkable. From the lower level at the north, the ramp ascended 5.2 meters in a horizontal distance of 329 meters, diminishing in width from 65.5 meters at its base to 61.9 meters at its upper end. Two flanking earth embankments averaged 9.6 meters in height and 21 meters in width. At the top of the ramp, a low embankment continued southward 786 meters and terminated in a group of mounds and geometric embankments partially shown in this reconstruction.

The earthworks contained sandy soil and fine gravel, but compact yellow clay at the site may have been employed originally to retain the exceptionally steep slopes, according to Cyrus Thomas's account (1894, pp. 491–492). A natural depression at the north end of the westerly embankment suggests an earlier stream bed, possibly the course of the Scioto River, which is today about 800 meters away.

500 B.C.-A.D. 200

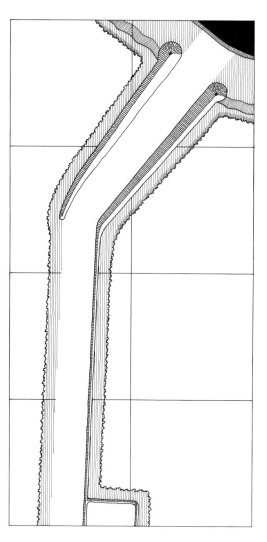

James B. Griffin (personal communication, 1978) points to evidence in Gerard Fowke's *Archaeological History of Ohio* (pp. 274–278) that indicates the Graded Way is "primarily a natural feature."

Reference: Squier and Davis, 1848, plate XXXI, no. 1.

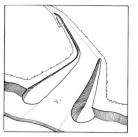

Seal

Piketon, Ohio

In Seal Township, Squier and Davis located the earthworks shown here together with several smaller but also geometrically precise works to the south along a natural embankment to the west of the site. The Scioto River apparently formed this embankment, but in 1847 the river was almost 1 kilometer further to the west. The circular earthwork contained 8 hectares within its 320-meter diameter and was connected to the 250-meter square enclosure by an avenue 30 meter wide, 145 meters long, flanked by parallel walls. A stream bed, 38 meters wide and 4.6 meters deep, cut through the avenue, which was slightly offset in its north-south alignment at its juncture with the stream. This suggests that the stream bed existed at the time of original construction. The avenue may have been graded artificially down to the stream level, but this feature was no longer in evidence.

Other similar large geometric earthworks included in this study are the circle and octagon at High Bank, the circular enclosure at Newark, which has the same dimensions as Seal's circle, a square with two contiguous circles at Oldtown, and the concentric circles with a curving avenue at Portsmouth Group "C." Seal's square and avenue were oriented within 3 degrees of the cardinal points, but the determining factor in orientation here, as elsewhere, appears to have been the natural terrain.

As is frequently the case with sites reported by Squier and Davis, we have no subsequent verification or more recent archaeological data to corroborate the original report. Although supporting data is lacking, James B. Griffin believes that Seal was built by Hopewell people about A.D. 1 to 300 (personal communication, 1978).

Reference: Squier and Davis, 1848, plate XXIV.

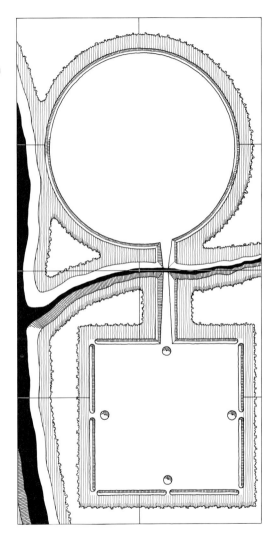

Dublin

Dublin, Ohio

Cyrus Thomas located this group of earthworks and moats 1.6 kilometers northeast of Dublin in Franklin County. He reported that the Scioto River lay about 400 meters to the west. This reconstruction illustrates the axial alignment of the site's two southwesterly mounds with respect to the river's presumed north-south course although Thomas made no specific reference to the river's orientation.

The westernmost mound, 1.5 meters high and 15.2 meters in diameter, lay about 152 meters west of a circular enclosure and moat. According to Thomas, the enclosure had an outer diameter of 49.4 meters and an embankment 5.5 meters wide by 61 centimeters high. The moat was 6.7 meters wide by 91 centimeters deep, and the embrasure, or level entry opening, was 6.7 meters wide. Within the moat, a 91-centimeter-high mound, 12.2 meters in base diameter, was located slightly off center.

The rectangular embankment measured along its centerlines, if extended to intersect at its corners, 87.5 meters on the north, 67.1 meters on the

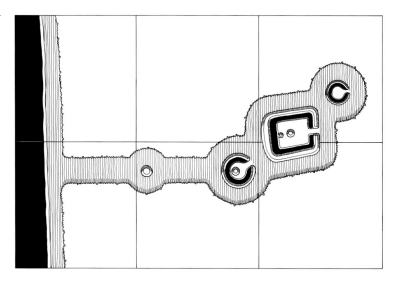

east, 79.9 meters on the south, and 64.6 meters on the west, but radial curves of 6.1 meters rounded its outer corners. The 61-centimeter-high embankment increased in width from 7.6 to 10.7 meters along its west side, which bowed outward slightly. The moat varied in width from 4.9 to 9.1 meters and in depth from 60 centimeters to 1.2 meters. Within the level enclosure were two mounds associated with burials, one 1.2 meters high and 10.7 meters in diameter and the other,

on the moat's edge, 30 centimeters high and 7.3 meters in diameter. The embrasure was 4.6 meters wide.

Located 40.5 meters northeast of the rectangular embankment was a 61-meter-high circular embankment with a 61-centimeter-deep interior moat. The enclosure's outermost diameter was 39.6 meters. The circular wall was about 3 meters wide; the moat was 4.6 meters wide. A 3.7-meter-wide embrasure faced toward the east.

Reference: Thomas, 1894, figure 310.

Bainbridge

Bainbridge, Ohio

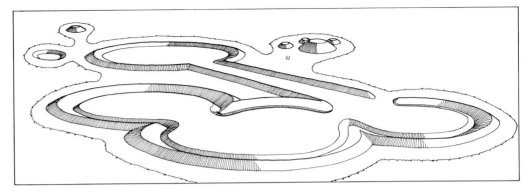

This group of circular earthworks, excavations, and mounds was recorded by Squier and Davis. Located 1.6 kilometers west of Bainbridge in the valley of Paint Creek, the diameter of the southernmost circular enclosure was 84 meters; the east and west enclosures were 69 meters in diameter. Parallel ridge mounds flanked a connecting avenue to the 61-meter-diameter north enclosure, which had no excavation. A circular excavation to the northwest was a borrow pit 3.4 meters deep. A 7.6-meter-high mound to the northeast was located near three smaller mounds. The site's westerly edge was bordered by lower-lying terrain.

Excavations within enclosing embankments suggest ceremonial rather than defense purposes. The relatively small scale and interlocking arrangement of the enclosures suggest that the site probably was not a village in active daily use.

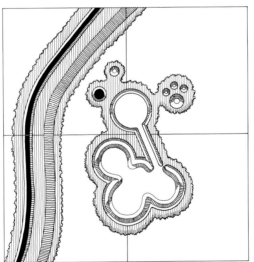

The reader may wish to compare this site with other small geometric earthwork compositions of the Kanawha River Valley in West Virginia, such as Kanawha and South Charleston.

James B. Griffin suggests that the Bainbridge site is probably of Hopewell origin (personal communication, 1978).

Reference: Squier and Davis, 1848, plate XXXII, no. 5.

Kanawha

Charleston, West Virginia

Along the Kanawha River 5 to 14 kilometers south of Charleston, Cyrus Thomas reported fifty earthworks. The four shown here are typical of what he found. Near the north banks of the river was a 46-by-128-meter rectangular enclosure with rounded corners. Where undisturbed by cultivation, the walls were 1.2 to 1.8 meters high. Along the enclosure's west wall Smith's Creek ran through a ravine 15 meters deep. A spring-fed moat lined the inner wall. Six stone-covered graves were found immediately outside the walls, three to the south and three to the north. To the west of the enclosure about 165 meters was a 1.5-meter-high conical burial mound 20 meters in diameter. The second burial mound shown here was 76 centimeters high and 9 meters in diameter.

On a 30-meter-high bluff south of the river, the Spring Hill earthworks formed an 8-hectare enclosure. The enclosing embankment extended several meters beyond the bluff's edge at three

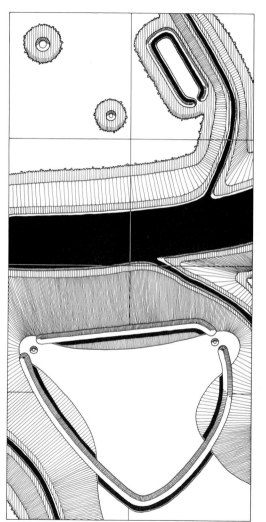

points. Moats lined the interior walls of the enclosure except along the plateau's southerly extension, where a moat once was reported to have been outside of the wall but no trace remained at the time of Thomas's observations. Extensive cultivation had reduced the embankment to a height of 60 centimeters and a width of 6 meters. The north wall measured 345 meters in length. In the 37.5-meter-wide northwest opening was a mound about 12 meters in diameter and originally about 2.6 meters high. A similar opening and mound occurred at the northeast corner. A spring on the north edge of the bluff within the enclosure provided fresh water for the site. The enclosure may have been a refuge in times of danger for the inhabitants of the extensive village once nearby.

One meter below the surface of the northwest mound was a 1-by-2.4-meter burial vault with a small conical chamber similar to that of the Criel Mound 3.2 kilometers to the northeast, referred to in the description of the South Charleston site. Other features observed in the Kanawha Valley were circular enclosures, graded ways, and rock-formed vaults.

Reference: Thomas, 1894, plate XXVII and figures 293 and 294.

South Charleston

South Charleston, West Virginia

The South Charleston Mound, earlier known as "Creil" or "Creel" Mound, is one of fifty earth structures on the banks of the Kanawha River immediately south of the present-day city of South Charleston. The principal structure of this group was a truncated cone, 51 meters in diameter at its base, 10 meters high, and 12 meters in diameter at its summit, according to Cyrus Thomas's account (1894, pp. 414–417). At the center of this mound near original grade was a wooden burial vault, 5 meters in diameter; walls, which were about 2.7 meters high, originally supported a conical wood roof. The vault contained eleven extended burials. Near its center was a second vault, a hollow dome "of very hard earth," 1.5 meters in diameter and 1.2 meters high, with a basin-shaped floor, 60 meters deep at its center.

Ninety-one meters northeast of the conical mound was a 64.6-meter-diameter circular enclosure, according to Thomas's 1887 plan. The 60- to 90-centimeter-high enclosure sloped gently outward but steeply inward to an inner moat. At the enclosure's center was a 9.1-meter-diameter conical mound, 90 centimeters high. Centered on the southeasterly portal was a 7.6-meter-diameter conical mound, 90 meters high, containing burial remains. From the enclosure's westerly edge a graded way, 74 meters long by 7.6 meters wide, descended to the river's bank. Tangent to the enclosure's easterly edge was a 44.8-meter-diameter excavation, 1.5 meters deep, according to an 1887 survey. The southwesternmost structure in this reconstruction was a 6.4-meter-diameter conical mound, 75 centimeters high, beyond which extended additional mounds on an axial alignment generally parallel to the river's course. A second circular enclosure with an inner moat lay 91 meters southwest of the principal mound, but its features had been badly obliterated by agricultural erosion at the time they were observed.

One of the few prehistoric structures of the Kanawha Valley to have escaped destruction, the South Charleston Mound stands today in a small city park beside highway U.S. 60 in downtown South Charleston.

Reference: McMichael and Mairs, 1969.

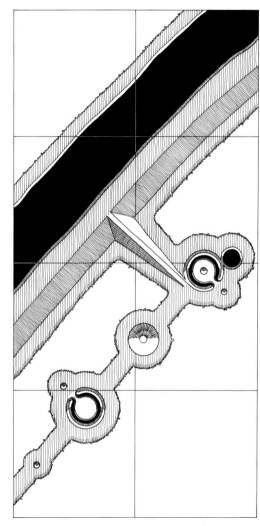

New Castle

New Castle, Indiana

New Castle was a Hopewell ceremonial center apparently in use between 60 B.C. and A.D. 230. The site is situated on a bluff 15 meters above the Little Blue River near its confluence with the Upper Blue River. The earthworks consisted of three mounds, two circular and one panduriform, and ten circular enclosures. New Castle seems to have been a ceremonial burial site because no village remains have been found in the vicinity.

The largest and westernmost of the ten circular enclosures was 76 meters in outside diameter with an entranceway or embrasure to the east. Within the encircling berm was an excavation, 1 to 2 meters deep, from which material was taken to construct the earthworks, presumably serving as an inner moat, as suggested in this reconstruction. Slightly west of the center was a 60-centimeter-high mound about 12 meters in diameter.

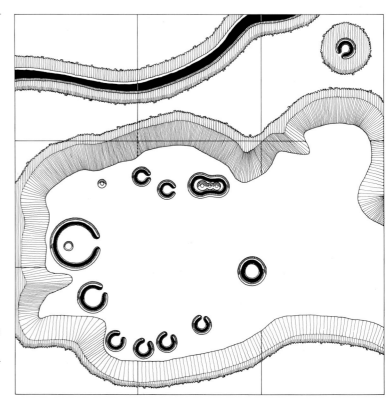

500 B.C.-A.D. 200

Eight smaller circular enclosures ranging in diameters from 49 to 27 meters constituted the main New Castle group. Each had an embrasure facing generally toward the panduriform mound. The tenth circular enclosure, 30 meters in diameter, lay about 300 meters to the northeast on a small hill.

The enclosing berm of the panduriform mound measured, overall, 66 by 41 meters, constricting to 20 meters near its center. The 2-meter-high berm and 2-meter-deep moat together averaged about 8 meters in width. The inner earthwork consisted of two mounds, each about 13.7 meters in diameter and 3 meters high, set 5 meters apart, linked by a third mound, which apparently was added later. On the west mound a cremation area was found, from which human remains were removed for secondary burial. More than a dozen burials are recorded, covered by layers of earth taken from the Little Blue River about A.D. 10. A ceremonial platform located on the east mound contained remains yielding the radiocarbon date of A.D. 40 ($\pm$ 140 years). The linking mound contained intrusive burials dated about A.D. 230.

Reference: Swartz, 1976.

Fort Center

Lakeport, Florida

Built between 500 B.C. and A.D. 1650 in two successive phases, Fort Center in one of the largest prehistoric sites in Florida. About 500 B.C. settlers began to build single-family, detached residences on mounds at widely dispersed intervals in the savanna area 5 kilometers west of Lake Okeechobee, near the banks of Fisheating Creek. As corn cultivation became increasingly important, they constructed a circular cornfield that they expanded twice to the 366-meter diameter shown here. A ditch, about 4.6 meters wide and 1.5 meters deep, surrounded the cornfield, apparently draining the soil to facilitate corn production. Several sand mounds, two levee middens, and excavation material formed two parallel ridges around the ditch, enclosing more than 10 hectares. Two causeways were located on the western side of the circular cornfield.

Between A.D. 1 and 500, a Hopewell-related ceremonial center was constructed east of the circular cornfield, consisting of a 7.6-meter-high ceremonial mound with a house, in which bodies were prepared for burial; an artificial pond 1.5 meters deep, near the center of which was a wood charnel platform; a 1.5-meter-high platform mound with five or six habitations; and an enclosing irregular sand embankment. Wood effigies and decorative carvings adorned the charnel platform, on which the partially articulated bundled burial remains of 300 individuals had been deposited about A.D. 500, when the platform burned and collapsed into the pond. A speculative reconstruction of the ceremonial center appears on page 35. The circular cornfield probably continued in use during this period.

After A.D. 500, ceremonialism declined at Fort Center. After A.D. 900, house mounds were built east of the ceremonial center, each located at the east end of a raised linear agricultural plot up to 457 meters in length and 43 meters in width. The house mounds were oval in plan and were formed like the agricultural terraces—by excavating material from the perimeter. These

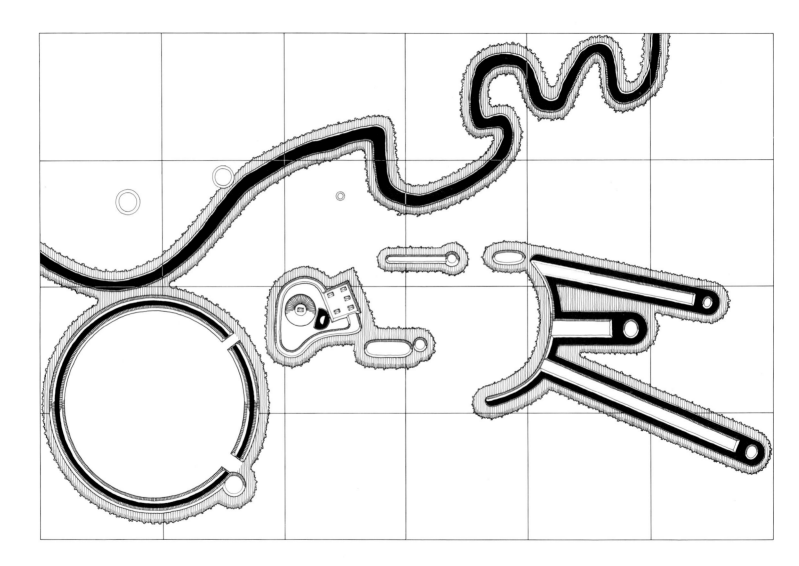

plots may represent a further advance in corn production. The houses and their plots probably continued in use up until the time of Spanish contact. Burials continued in the upper surfaces of the conical ceremonial mound during this last phase of occupation at Fort Center.

The evidence suggested by William H. Sears for corn production around the early period is the subject of continuing archaeological investigation. Like other Florida sites, Fort Center is quite different from Adena-Hopewell sites of the Ohio Valley or from later period 3 sites for that matter (James B. Griffin, personal communication, 1978).

Reference: Sears, 1971.

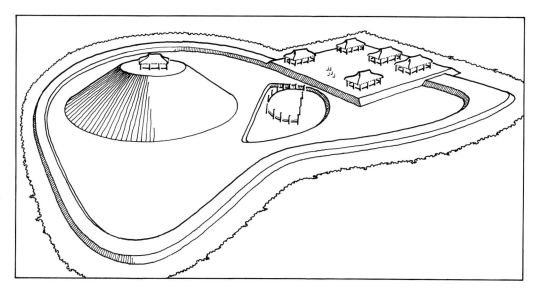

Crystal River

Crystal River, Florida

The village site and ceremonial earthworks on Crystal River lie about 7 kilometers east of the Gulf of Mexico near the present-day city of Crystal River. The site appears to have been occupied between 150 B.C. and A.D. 1350. The south temple mound rose steeply above the low-lying tropical riverbank. Constructed of alternating layers of shell and black earth, the truncated pyramid rose about 8.7 meters from a 30-by-55-meter base to a 15-by-33-meter platform. A 24-meter-long ramp led down toward the northeast, tapering in width from 6.4 meters at the summit to 4.3 meters at grade. Engaging the northwest side of the south temple mound, a low midden of shell and black earth exceeded 30 meters in width and 300 meters in length. This was described by Gordon R. Willey (1949A) as a habitation site. Toward the west end of the midden were two shell mounds, measuring about 3 meters in height. Traces of a ramp were found on the east side of the center shell mound.

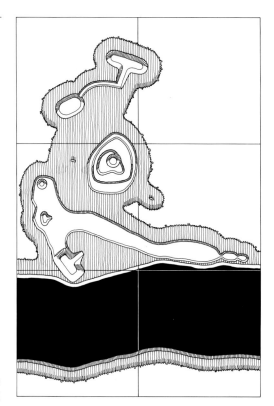

In the center of the site was a conical sand burial mound, 3.25 meters in height with a lower apron of layered shell and sand extending to the south and west. Enclosing the burial mound and apron was a 1.8-meter-high sand embankment, varying in width up to 23 meters. A second burial mound lay 30 meters to the northwest, an irregular oval about 30 by 45 meters in base dimensions. A shell causeway connected the northwest burial mound with the north temple mound, an imposing structure with a 9-by-55-meter platform, 3.7 meters above grade. In all, more than 450 burials have been found at Crystal River.

Two decorated stone slabs or stelae were found at Crystal River, suggesting possible contact with Mesoamerica, but a positive connection remains to be proved. Hardman theorizes that the earthworks and stelae may have been aligned with the solstitial and equinoctial positions of the sun, a giant calendar rather than a random arrangement of architectural elements.

This reconstruction is based on the site plans published by Clarence B. Moore after his visits in 1903 and 1907 and on more recent information published by Clark Hardman, Jr., in 1971.

Reference: Hardman, 1971.

Tick Island

Astor, Florida

Tick Island is bounded by Lake Woodruff and Spring Garden Creek, a tributary of the St. John's River in Volusia County. In rainy seasons the surrounding terrain becomes soft and swampy. The burial mound at the southern end of the site exceeded 5 meters in height and appeared to be 46 meters in diameter, according to Clarence B. Moore's account and partial site plan on which this reconstruction is based. The mound consisted of three successive layers of almost equal thicknesses: shell on the bottom, white sand in the middle, and brown sand on top. A causeway, 4.5 meter wide, rose 1.2 meters above adjacent grade. Its base averaged 7.6 meters in width and 119 meters in length when measured along its irregular centerline. The elevated way terminated to the northeast "at a large bean-shaped shell or refuse heap." Moore suggested that the Indians lived on the refuse heap and the adjacent shell fields. A second causeway led southwesterly from the elevated village midden, skirting the burial mound to which it apparently was not connected.

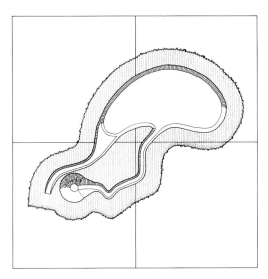

Similar arrangements of burial mounds connected by causeways to habitation areas were found at Terra Ceia. Unlike Terra Ceia, however, Tick Island contained no evidence of European contact, suggesting that it was abandoned before A.D. 1600. Numerous articulated, layered burials were encountered. Moore observed that the "great Tick Island mound as an ossuary exceeds any other on the St. Johns of which we have cognizance."

Reference: Moore, 1894.

Marksville

Marksville, Louisiana

A 1,000-meter-long earth embankment with an outer moat encloses the 16-hectare ceremonial site at Marksville. The site's easterly edge is a high bluff of the Old River, a bypassed channel of the Mississippi River. Today the Mississippi lies 48 kilometers to the east. In 1883 the embankment was observed to be 2.4 to 3.6 meters high. Three embrasures provided access through the enclosure to the south and west. A 91-meter-diameter circular embankment, 61 centimeters high and 6 meters wide, lay near the enclosure to the south.

Within the enclosure lay five mounds and a low eminence along the bluff's edge, occupied by trees and picnic facilities in 1977. The 4-meter-high northerly truncated pyramid measured 91 meters in maximum base dimension and had a conical mound on its platform. The southerly truncated pyramid rose 4.3 meters from a 72-by-88-meter base and also may have had a conical feature on its platform. Immediately east of

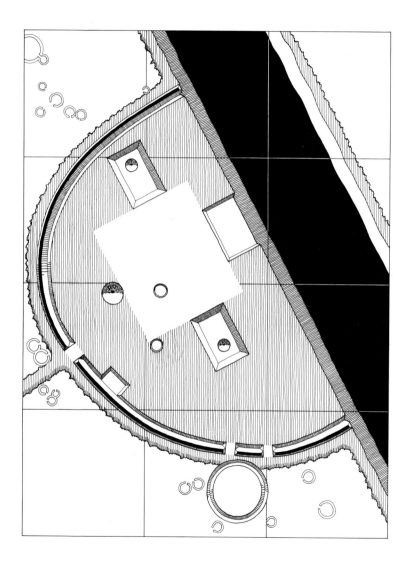

this structure was a semisubterranean structure, 7.6 by 7.8 meters, lined on two sides by posts, possibly a ceremonial or public building. The westernmost conical mound rose 6.1 meters from its 30.5-meter-diameter base and contained numerous burials. Constructed of two successive clay mantles, this mound contained a 7.6-meter square burial platform, 5 meters high, within which a tomb had been hollowed out. Vertical wood posts supported the tomb's log rafters, over which the second mantle was placed. Marksville's two remaining conicals rose about 1 meter from bases possibly 21 meters in diameter.

Earliest occupation and construction at Marksville occurred between A.D. 100 and 300. Like Marksville, Spanish Fort, Troyville, and possibly Toltec, suggest Hopewell influence in the Lower Mississippi Valley.

This reconstruction is based primarily on Alan Toth's 1974 account, the site plan (figure 2) published in *Southeastern Archaeological Conference Bulletin* 18 (1975), and the aerial photographs taken by Dache Reeves in the 1930s.

Reference: Toth, 1974.

Tchula Lake

Tchula, Mississippi

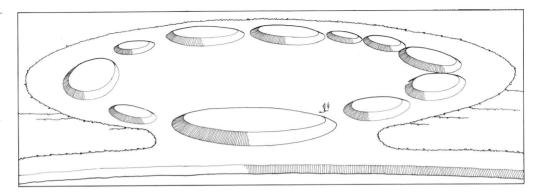

About 6 kilometers southeast of Tchula in west-central Mississippi is a group of eleven shell middens arranged in a circle on the west bank of Tchula Lake. Due to cultivation, the group today appears on first approach to be a single circular midden about 190 meters in outside dimension, but aerial photographs show that the site is composed of eleven low platforms, ranging from circles about 20 meters in diameter to ovals measuring at most 30-by-60 meters. The remains of the easternmost midden are about 1 meter in height, but a recently constructed road has destroyed much of this platform. Phillips assumed that all eleven middens were about 1 meter high. The 120-meter-diameter central area of the group was free of structures or cultural material, suggesting that it was purposely set apart for a special function. The surfaces of the middens are entirely white bleached shell, which gives a spectacular effect from a distance.

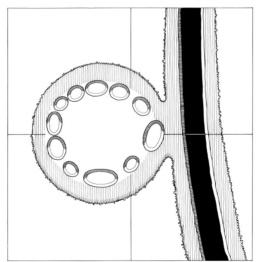

Sherds collected from the site in 1954 were consistently from the Deasonville phase of the Yazoo region, suggesting occupation and construction between A.D. 300 and 500. Other circular shell middens surrounding an open central space free of cultural material are Fig Island and Sapelo, but both of these sites are removed from Tchula Lake by more than 800 kilometers geographically and more than a millenium chronologically.

Reference: Phillips, 1970, pp. 270–272.

Spanish Fort

Holly Bluff, Mississippi

On the west bank of the Sunflower River, 9.6 kilometers south of Holly Bluff, lie the remains of a precise semicircular embankment with an outer moat (L.M.S. (Lower Mississippi Survey) 21-N-3). Although it is named Spanish Fort, this is an area the Spaniards never visited. This reconstruction is based on A. C. Spaulding's 1949 survey, which clearly shows the remarkable circularity of the enclosure; it is 570 meters in diameter measured from the center of the top of the embankment. The innermost octagon at Poverty Point is 590 meters in diameter, almost the same as Spanish Fort, and the semicircular embankment with an outer moat at Marksville encloses about 16 hectares, compared to the nearly 18 hectares at Spanish Fort. Similar structures have been found nearby at Little Spanish Fort (L.M.S. 22-N-14) and Leist (L.M.S. 22-N-1).

During his 1917 investigation, Calvin Brown observed that the embankment was 12.2 to 18.3 meters wide, approximately the same width as the moat. He noted a "semicircular refuse heap" in the southeasterly area of the enclosure and "medium sized mounds" flanking the enclosure at a distance of about 275 meters both up and down the river. According to Philip Phillips, the embankment is about 2.5 meters high and the moat is about 2.5 meters deep in areas which have not been cultivated or badly eroded. Phillips also found the midden to be 55 centimeters high and noted that the remaining four-fifths of the enclosure apparently was never occupied. Regarding the "medium sized mounds" that Brown reported, Phillips found possible remains of a mound flanking the enclosure to the east but none to the west and noted that the "symmetrical arrangement of these mounds would suggest some sort of relationship to the embankment, a characteristic Hopewellian feature."

Surface collections and stratigraphic tests suggest that Spanish Fort was occupied between A.D. 200 and 500. The site's precise, large-scale enclosure suggests a visual link to Hopewellian ceremonial centers in Ohio, such as Newark and Oldtown.

Reference: Phillips, 1970, pp. 305–315.

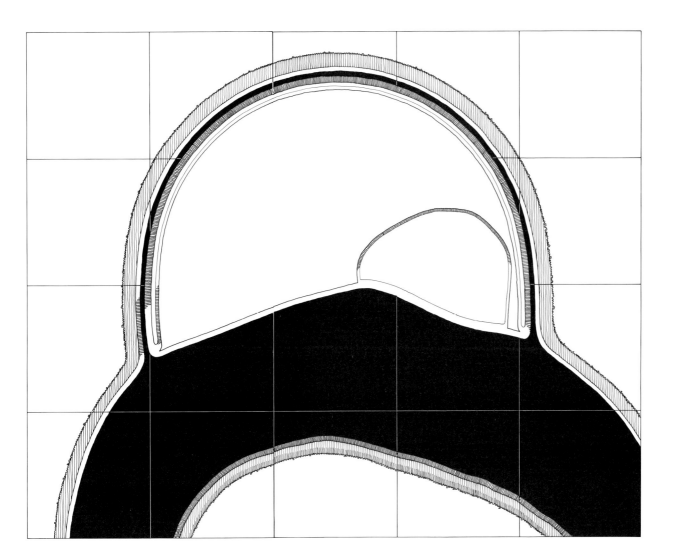

Pinson

Pinson, Tennessee

One of the largest groups of earthworks in the prehistoric Eastern United States lies 5 kilometers east of Pinson in southwestern Tennessee. The site extends for 4 kilometers along a high bank overlooking the flood plains of the south fork of the Forked Deer River and consists of thirty-four earth structures in three groups. This is shown in the site plan, except for four mounds lying west of the breastworks beyond the scope of the drawing. Due to the relative immensity of the Pinson site, only the central group is shown on the opposite page at the comparative scale of this study's 200-meter grid.

According to J. G. Cisco (1902), in 1840 Colonel Pickford Jones rode the entire distance of the palisades on horseback and observed its length to be at least 9.6 kilometers, not including the 1.3-kilometer palisade of the central group shown in the drawing to the right. Pinson's major structure rose 22.25 meters in 1916, according to William E. Myer (1922), whose survey is the basis of this reconstruction. Myer observed the

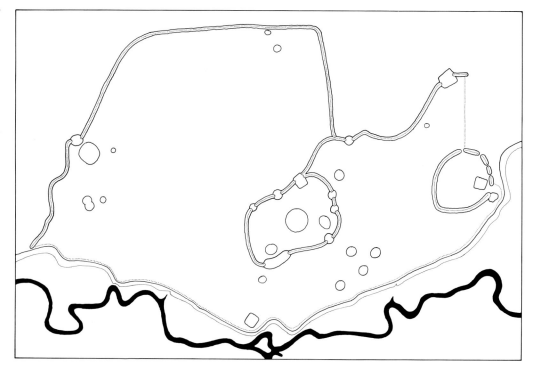

500 B.C.-A.D. 200

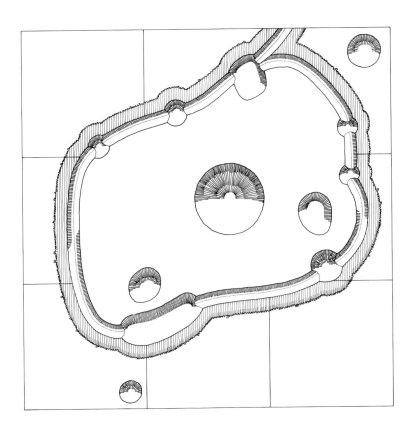

great structure to be 91.4 by 112.8 meters at its base and 11.6 by 18.3 meters at its summit. John B. Nuckolls (1958) and other scholars look upon this as probably a conical burial mound characteristic of period 2—the flat summit may be a period 3 addition or the result of recent alteration.

Archaeological investigations (Broster and Schneider, 1976) in 1974 revealed two oval structures in the central group yielding radiocarbon dates of A.D. 270 and 290 (± 70 years) with clear evidence of a relationship to both Marksville and Hopewellian cultures of the Ohio and Illinois valleys. In 1962, testing operations by Fischer and McNutt in the central group uncovered a rectangular trench wall house of about A.D. 850, indicating that Pinson also had been occupied in period 3.

Today only a remnant of the original enclosure survives in the eastern group, which is about 1.8 meters high. The remainder was destroyed by cultivation and erosion. Evidence for the original enclosure now is being sought.

Reference: Nuckolls, 1958.

Period 3

A.D. 800–1500

Upper Mississippi and
Ohio Area
Lower Mississippi Area
Caddoan Area
Tennessee,
Appalachian, and
Piedmont Area
Florida Area

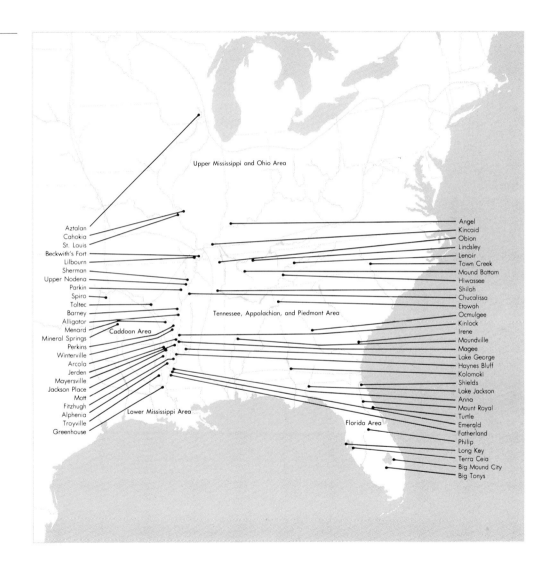

Upper Mississippi and Ohio Area

Aztalan
Cahokia
St. Louis
Beckwith's Fort
Lilbourn
Sherman
Upper Nodena
Parkin
Spiro
Toltec
Barney
Alligator
Menard
Mineral Springs
Perkins
Winterville
Arcola
Jerden
Mayersville
Jackson Place
Mott
Fitzhugh
Alphenia
Troyville
Greenhouse

Caddoan Area

Tennessee, Appalachian, and Piedmont Area

Lower Mississippi Area

Florida Area

Angel
Kincaid
Obion
Lindsley
Lenoir
Town Creek
Mound Bottom
Hiwassee
Shiloh
Chucalissa
Etowah
Ocmulgee
Kinlock
Irene
Moundville
Magee
Lake George
Haynes Bluff
Kolomoki
Shields
Lake Jackson
Anna
Mount Royal
Turtle
Emerald
Fatherland
Philip
Long Key
Terra Ceia
Big Mound City
Big Tonys

Between A.D. 200 and 800, architectural activity, ceremonialism, and trade networks declined in the Eastern United States. By about A.D. 750, truncated pyramids began to appear in the study area. These structures were built of earth in a series of layers and served as platforms for temples or residences of important religious or civil leaders. They usually were grouped around open spaces or plazas and ranged in number from 2 or 3 at smaller sites to 20 at St. Louis and Moundville, 25 at Lake George, and about 120 at Cahokia, the largest site in this study.

The origin of the temple mounds and plazas seems to have been Middle America, where their use was both very early and widespread. However, Mesoamerican structures normally were constructed of stone or rubble cores faced with elaborate exterior finishes rather than built of earth. The temple mound tradition appears to have arrived either by way of the Caddoan Area, possibly from the southwest, or by way of the Gulf Coast through Florida and Georgia or via the Lower Mississippi Valley.

Period 3 has been subdivided into the five geographical areas shown on the map on page 45. Beyond these five areas lie East Texas, the Ozark Plateau, the Great Plains, the upper and lower Great Lakes, and the North Atlantic areas of Eastern North America, where architectural developments do not appear to have attained as high a level of achievement as in the central area of the study.

During period 3, the Mississippian culture arose, characterized by distinctive ceramic items such as jars, bottles, and effigy vessels. A second Mississippian trait was the rectangular wall trench house of wattle-and-daub construction with a thatched roof. A third trait is ceremonialism, often including the use of temple mounds, although this is not the case in all areas of period 3. Characteristic Mississippian ceremonial objects included marine shell dippers, shell gorgets, repoussé copper breastplates, and distinctive masks.

The origin of the Mississippian culture is very complex. Possibilities include Southeast Missouri — Northeast Arkansas as well as the Tennessee-Cumberland drainage basin. The culture appears to have been widespread and pervasive, quite probably due to the considerable development of agriculture, with corn the major staple. According to Stephen Williams (1963), it "represents a socio-economic system that might have developed under the right conditions to a society on the Classic stage comparable to the Maya, Aztec, and the Inca." Prior to A.D. 1000 the Mississippian influence spread into Kansas, Wisconsin, Indiana, Georgia, Florida, and the Carolinas. However, the upper eastern seaboard area appears to have retained its general conservatism and resisted Mississippian intrusion. Apparently the Appalachian Mountains remained a formidable barrier to the northeasterly spread of Mississippian ideas.

Examples of period 3 sites in the Upper Mississippi and Ohio Area are Cahokia, St. Louis, Angel, Kincaid, and Aztalan. These large and highly developed sites include multiterraced truncated pyramids, of which 30-meter-high Monks Mound in Cahokia is the largest known, multiple plazas, and palisaded enclosures for ceremonial and sometimes defensive purposes, as was the case of Aztalan.

Twenty-eight reconstructions illustrate the Lower Mississippi Area. These sites are presented according to their geographical locations moving southward down the Mississippi River. Typical palisaded ceremonial centers with associated habitations are found at Beckwith's Fort and Lilbourn in southeastern Missouri, at Parkin and

Upper Nodena in northeastern Arkansas, and at Chucalissa in Tennessee. Barney and Sherman are truncated curvilinear structures in Arkansas with two and three levels, respectively, Toltec and Winterville are large D-shaped sites containing seventeen and eighteen mounds, respectively, defining multiple plazas. Alligator, Perkins, Menard, Kinlock, Magee, Jackson Place, Arcola, Haynes Bluff, Mayersville, Fatherland, Greenhouse, and Alphenia illustrate smaller Mississippian site variations. Lake George, Fitzhugh, and Troyville are larger sites of notable orthogonal discipline. Jerden and Mott have D-shaped arrangements with orientations toward watercourses to the south or east. Emerald and nearby Anna are both set on plateaus overlooking the Mississippi River to the west.

Spiro and Mineral Springs illustrate the enigmatic Caddoan Area, about which archaeologists generally know less than they do about other period 3 areas. Here there are many fewer constructions than further east.

The Tennessee, Appalachian, and Piedmont Area contains Moundville and Etowah, two of the most important period 3 sites in this study. Other sites exhibiting regional variations range from Town Creek in North Carolina, to Lenoir, Hiwassee, Mound Bottom, Shiloh, Obion, and Lindsley in Tennessee, and Kolomoki, Ocmulgee, and Irene in Georgia.

In the Florida Area, Lake Jackson shows more Mississippian influences than sites further south. Shields and Mount Royal, both on the eastern shore of the St. Johns River, had truncated platforms connected by graded avenues to ceremonial ponds. Turtle, Terra Ceia, and Long Key illustrate regional variations of mid-Florida. Big Tonys and Big Mound City illustrate unique elevated platforms with associated canals in large-scale curvilinear designs not found in other areas of period 3.

In all areas of the New World, including not only Eastern North America but also the Southwest, Mexico, and the Andes, an artistic peak seems to have been reached about A.D. 1300. After this time a general decline began, the reasons for which are unclear. By A.D. 1500 major architectural activity had ceased in most of the study area. Elsewhere in the world between A.D. 800 and 1500, Romanesque architecture evolved in Western Europe, Gothic cathedrals rose in France, and the Renaissance began in Italy. In Central Mexico, Monte Albán was completed; Uxmal and Chichén Itzá were constructed in the Yucatán Peninsula; and Angkor Wat rose in Southeast Asia.

Upper Mississippi and Ohio Area

Cahokia
St. Louis
Angel
Kincaid
Aztalan

A.D. 800-1500

Cahokia

Collinsville, Illinois

Cahokia was the largest and most complex site in North America prior to historic contact. The site is located 16 kilometers east-northeast of St. Louis in an exceptionally fertile area of the Mississippi River Valley known as the American Bottom. The Missouri and Illinois rivers join the Mississippi River a short distance north of Cahokia, placing the site in a favorable position for communications, transportation, and trade. To the north lie the central lowlands; to the southeast, the interior plateaus; to the south, the Lower Mississippi Valley; and to the southwest, the Ozark ecological zone. The combination of productive agricultural land, the confluence of major rivers, and access to diverse ecological zones was essential to Cahokia's development.

Central Cahokia may be inscribed in a diamond-shaped figure, measuring 4.58 kilometers east-west by 3.67 kilometers north-south and encompassing 13.4 square kilometers or 1,336 hectares. Approximately half of this area originally was occupied by about 120 mounds; the remaining area was too low for habitation. The site's dominant waterway is Cahokia Creek, whose course generally corresponds to the five-degree-east-of-north orientation of the complex. Today the Mississippi River lies 6 kilometers to the west. About 4.5 kilometers to the east lies a north-south line of bluffs in clear view of the site.

In the center of the site was the palisaded main plaza containing Cahokia's major structure, multiterraced Monks Mound, and sixteen smaller earthworks. Outside of the palisades lay more than one hundred truncated pyramids, conical or oval mounds, multiterraced structures, and lineal or ridge mounds that may have been boundary markers. Of these, only forty have been spared from encroaching agricultural fields, residences, highways, and commercial developments.

Monks Mound is the largest earth structure north of the Pyramid of the Sun at Teotihuacán and the Pyramid at Cholula in Central Mexico. From a 316-by-241-meter base it originally rose in four successive terraces to a height of 30 meters and contained an estimated 615,144 cubic meters of earth placed by workers carrying baskets weighing about 18 kilograms each. Radiocarbon dating suggests construction probably between A.D. 900 and 1200. A ramp slightly east of the main

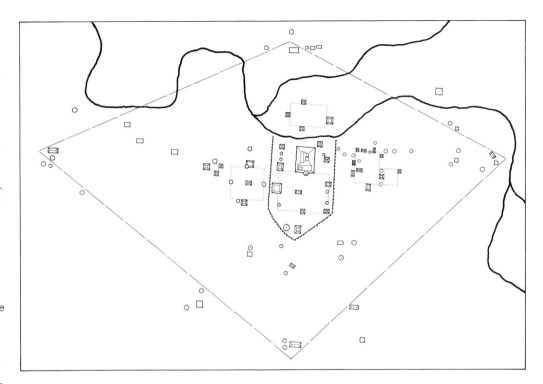

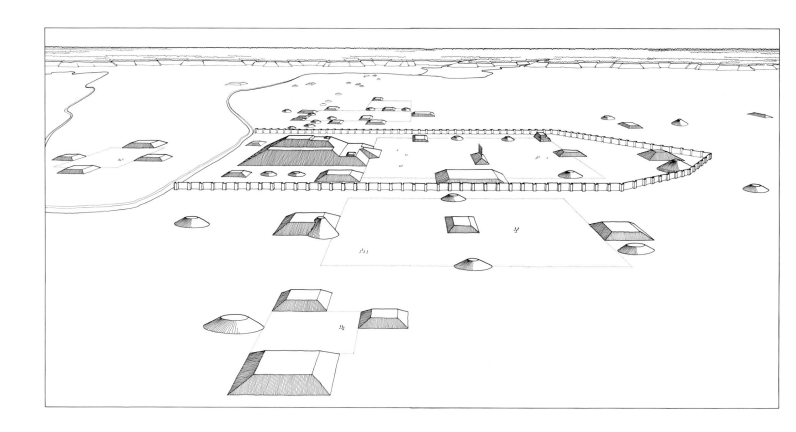

A.D. 800-1500

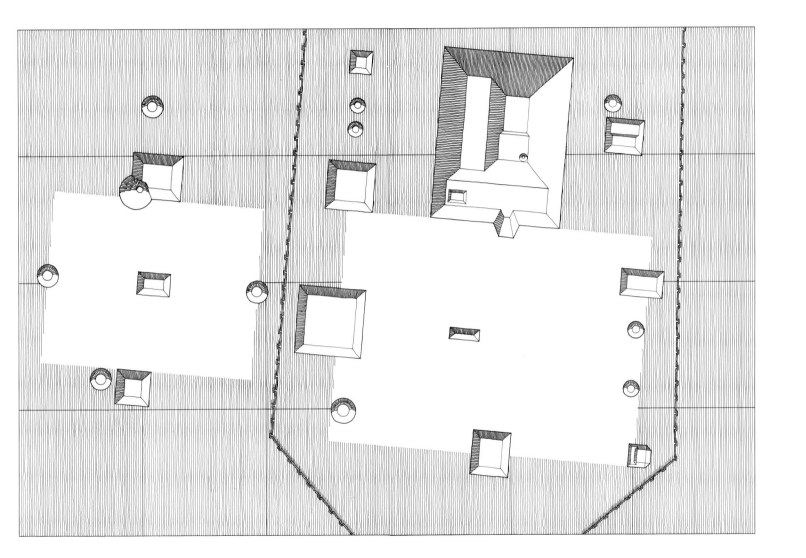

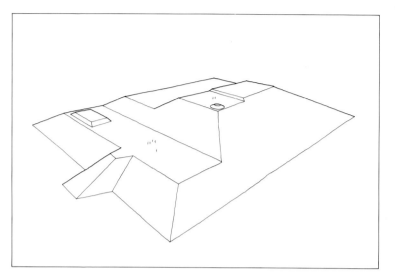

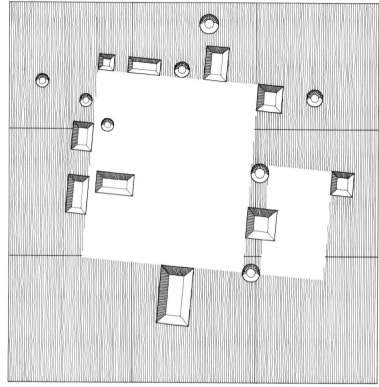

axis led to the first terrace, which was 11.7 meters above the plaza. Near the southwest corner of this terrace was a relatively low earth platform that appears to have been built at the same time that the fourth terrace of Monks Mound was being constructed.

The second terrace lies on the west side of Monks Mound about 20 meters above the level of the plaza. Although this terrace today is extensively eroded and its original configuration is not known, it is presented here in a manner consistent with the other reconstructions of this study.

The third terrace, 29 meters above the plaza level, measures about 40 by 48 meters and originally contained a 3-meter-high conical mound at its southeast corner.

The 30-meter-high fourth terrace is a 48-by-59-meter platform that originally was surrounded by a palisade and contained, along its northern edge, a wooden temple or residence 41 meters wide, 20 meters deep, and probably about 15 meters high. (Remains of domiciliary structures often are found on the platforms of Mississippian truncated pyramids.)

According to James A. Anderson (1973), the east palisade of the main plaza was built in four successive phases between A.D. 1150 and 1250. In final form, it consisted of 3-meter-square, outward-projecting log bastions set 21 meters apart over earlier circular bastions. The southwest palisade appeared to be more in the nature of a fence or screen, suggesting that it may have served visually to set off the plaza from other areas of Cahokia. This reconstruction assumes a uniform palisade around the main plaza as it may have appeared in the early thirteenth century. Subsequent to that time, two ramps apparently were added to the east face of Monks Mound. These protruding features are omitted in this reconstruction.

The plaza groupings suggested in this reconstruction are based on known earthworks apparently related by open spaces, although archaeological investigations have not yet been conducted to verify the existence or extent of plazas. The Ramey group is the largest earthwork group outside of the palisade at Cahokia. The original shapes of all of the mounds are not known. This reconstruction assumes rectangles of architectural relationship based on the site axis. A frequently found relationship at Cahokia is the pairing of a rectangular platform with a nearby circular

mound, suggesting that a charnel house may have been constructed near a burial mound. After initial preparation for interment in a charnel house, bundles of bones apparently were transferred to a secondary burial site for group interment. Frequently a mantle of earth then was placed over the burial mound, which continued to increase in size.

Four circles ranging in diameter from 73 to 146 meters have been found 914 meters west of Monks Mound. Warren L. Wittry (1973) terms circle number 2 a "woodhenge," a solar observatory, 125 meters in diameter, consisting of forty-eight wood posts set at equal spacing with four posts aligning with the cardinal points of the compass. There was a forty-ninth post 1.5 meters east of the circle's geometric center from which an observer could ascertain the equinoxes and solstices at sunrise in the year A.D. 1000. The posts were about 60 centimeters in diameter, possibly 9 meters long, and were set more than 2 meters into the ground.

According to Harriet M. Smith (1973), Murdock Mound, which is illustrated here, measured 35.2 meters square at its base and rose 10.1 meters in height. Its remains lie within the palisades, 400 meters south of Monks Mound. Built in several successive phases, Murdock's domiciliary structure was completed about A.D. 1370, long after major work apparently had ceased on Monks Mound. Some authorities theorize that after two centuries of labor on a central and dominant mound, the Cahokians may have abandoned Monks Mound in an incomplete state and may have begun to construct many smaller mounds such as Murdock Mound. If substantiated, this theory would suggest a turning point in Cahokia's social organization.

One of Murdock's distinguishing architectural features was corner faceting, which would have given greater vertical emphasis to the structure than would more frequently found square corners, which have lower sloping diagonal corner ridges. Murdock's sides apparently were coated with a fine mud, jet black in color even when dry, which may have further enhanced the original appearance of the finished structure.

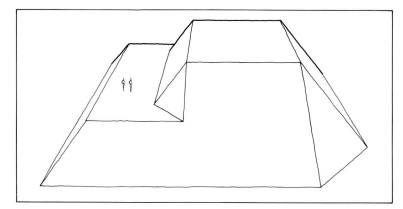

Cahokia appears to have been first occupied some time after A.D. 600. Maize agriculture provided food for an increasing population and rectangular houses were constructed with posts set in subterranean pits.

Between A.D. 900 and 1050, individual wall post construction appeared in houses, woodhenges were built, elaborate burial ceremonies developed, construction began on Monks Mound, small towns and farmsteads appeared in the vicinity of the main site, Cahokia's axis was established, and the site was organized.

Apparently between A.D. 1050 and 1250, Monks Mound reached essentially its final form, many public buildings and mound groups were constructed, the last woodhenges were completed, the palisade was erected, and Cahokia's population increased to possibly 15,000 persons with probably twice that number in nearby towns, villages, and hamlets. During this period of major activity, trade specialization and the arts and crafts flourished, sociopolitical systems became highly developed, and architecture and planning attained relatively high levels of sophistication.

After A.D. 1250, activity apparently began to decline at Cahokia, while Angel, Aztalan, Kincaid, St. Louis, and other period 3 sites seem to have begun to flourish.

One of the richest natural resources available to Cahokia was flint quarried in southern Illinois. This facilitated the development of an efficient flint hoe that could dig deeply and kill weeds that otherwise would hamper agricultural production. The need to know the best times for planting and harvesting may have led to the development of a calendar relying on woodhenges for solar calculations.

Like the other prehistoric American settlements, Cahokia exchanged trade over a large area of America, extending from the Gulf of Mexico to the Great Lakes and from the Appalachian Mountains to the Great Plains. Although Cahokia was large and complex, its influence on the development of prehistoric American architecture beyond its vicinity appears to have been no greater than other sites such as Etowah, Lake George, Marksville, Moundville, and Spiro.

The map of the Cahokia region to the right shows a 21-by-42-kilometer area of the Mississippi River Valley, southward from the confluence of the Mississippi and the Missouri rivers. Near the center is a diamond representing Cahokia. The four circles within 22 kilometers of Cahokia represent secondary communities, composed of several platform mounds, plazas, and associated habitations, located in relation to regional communications and transportation: Mitchell to the north, St. Louis opposite East St. Louis, and Pulcher to the south. The five squares within 18

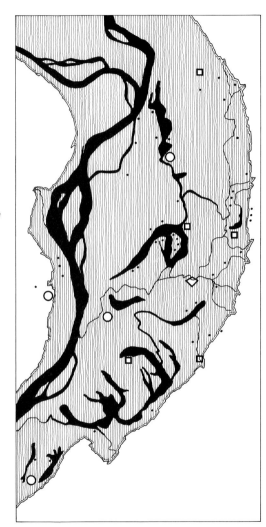

kilometers of Cahokia represent tertiary communities, each having one platform mound and associated habitations related to local agriculture and industry. The dots indicate sites without mounds, probably villages, hamlets, and farmsteads. See also the aerial photograph of Cahokia.

Melvin L. Fowler suggests that there may have been several reasons for Cahokia's decline, "one of these being the exhaustion of the resources in the immediate hinterland of the Cahokia site itself. There is some evidence for this in the changing of the kinds of woods that were used for building by the Cahokia peoples, switching from the longer growing hardwoods such as oak and hickories to softer more rapid growing species. Another factor in the decline of Cahokia may well have been the fact that the segments of the Cahokia interaction were growing economically in their own strength and that Cahokia as a center of redistribution of goods and services may no longer have been a viable solution to the problem of organizing large numbers of people" (Fowler, personal communication, 1978).

The basis for this reconstruction is primarily the information presented by Melvin L. Fowler (1973, 1974), Nelson A. Reed (1973), Warren L. Wittry (1973), Harriet M. Smith (1973), James A. Anderson (1973), and others in the Illinois Archaeology Survey Bulletin No. 7, revised edition, 1973. Prior to this Bulletin, the most comprehensive source of information on Cahokia was Warren K. Moorehead's work published between 1921 and 1928. Today archaeological investigations continue in the 192-hectare state park containing the remains of Cahokia.

Reference: Fowler, 1973 and 1974.

St. Louis

St. Louis, Missouri

Beneath present-day St. Louis lie the remains of more than twenty mounds on a 15-meter-high limestone bluff, the second terrace of the Mississippi River, which flows slightly west of south at this point. The main plaza was dominated by a 7-meter-high truncated pyramid, parallel to the plaza on its long axis. Opposite the main structure was a 3-meter-high platform mound. Along the plaza's easterly edge, following the bluff, was a row of four conical mounds ascending in height from 1.4 meters toward the south to 3 meters toward the north. Eight other platform and circular mounds completed the central group. In this reconstruction, rectangles representing the central group are in a 1 to 1 proportion; those representing the south and northwest groups are in a 2 to 5 proportion.

Falling Garden, a multiterraced mound consisting of three ascending platforms, commanded the south group. The lowest terrace was 1.5 meters above the plaza level, but there is no information concerning the heights of the second and

A.D. 800-1500

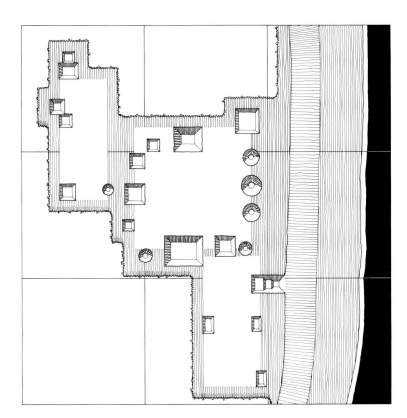

third terraces. Falling Garden is an exception to the usual arrangement for multiterraced mounds of the Mississippi period: It is not on the main plaza, it is not the major structure of the St. Louis group, and its longitudinal axis is at a right angle to its associated plaza rather than parallel to it. Falling Garden's highest terrace was at the bluff's edge with a commanding view of the river to the east.

The composition of the northwest group varies in the 1861 and 1904 reports of the Smithsonian Institution, although both are based on Major S. J. Long's 1819 survey. This reconstruction is based on Peale's account, containing data recorded in the field with only a hand compass and measuring tape when the site was densely overgrown. James B. Griffin believes that the St. Louis "group was surely in existence from about A.D. 900 to 1450 or so," and notes that it "was one of the larger compact Mississippian sites" (personal communication, 1978).

Reference: Peale, 1861.

Angel

Evansville, Indiana

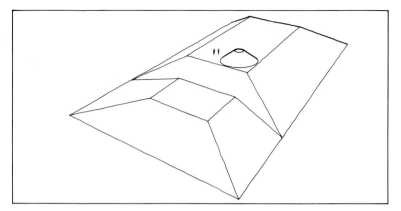

Angel is the northeasternmost Mississippian settlement in aboriginal America. The site lies on the
north bank of the Ohio River 11 kilometers east
of Evansville. Like Aztalan and Kincaid, Angel
was a fortified town that appeared, flourished,
and was abandoned between A.D. 1200 and
1450. This reconstruction is based on the account
of Glenn A. Black, who suggested that during
the time of prehistoric occupation, the river
flowed closer to the site's south edge than it does
today, and the narrow drainageway that defined
the island's perimeter to the west, north, and
east was more evident 500 years ago than it is
now. The site lies above the level of normal
spring floods.

A palisaded earth embankment, 1,920 meters
long and 6 meters high with outward projecting
bastions at approximately 36-meter intervals, enclosed the 40-hectare site inshore; it was interrupted by a 6-meter-wide entryway toward the
northeast (see opposite page). Within the embankment dwelt an estimated 1,000 inhabitants
in as many as 200 houses at a single time. They

A.D. 800-1500

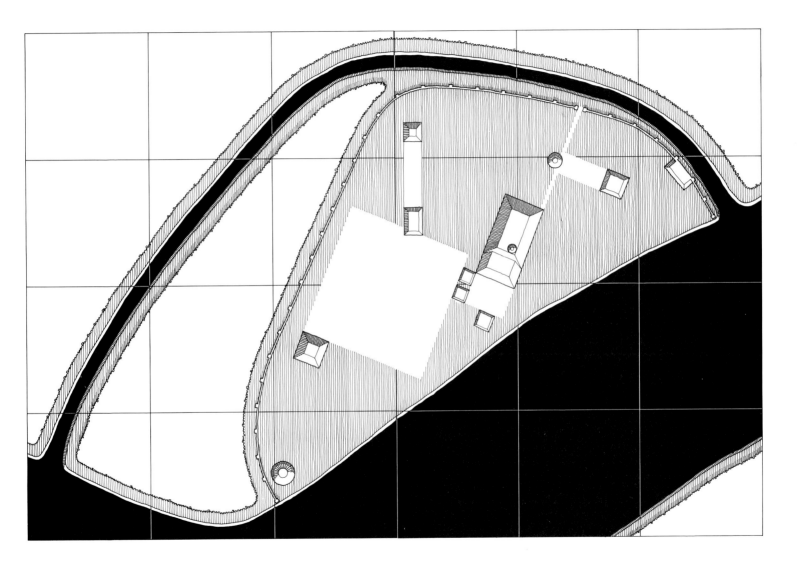

erected eleven earth structures, the largest of which was the three-level mound illustrated on page 58. It was oriented 22 degrees east of north, measured 203 by 107 meters at its base, and contained an estimated 51,788 cubic meters of earth. Gently sloping sides provided access to the 30-by-34-meter south terrace about 3 meters above adjacent grade. More steeply sloping walls surrounded the 37-by-76-meter main terrace, which was about 9 meters high. A platform more than 13 meters above grade surmounted the conical structure. A temple may have occupied the lower terrace, and the civil chief's residence may have been built on the main terrace. The truncated conical structure is assumed to have been built for ceremonial functions.

The second largest structure was a 4-meter-high truncated pyramid, 72 by 73 meters at its base and 20 by 23 meters at its summit, located 335 meters southwest of the three-level mound. A religious edifice may have been built on this mound. Between it and the largest mound was a plaza, notably free of archaeological debris associated with domiciliary functions.

North of the plaza were two truncated pyramids apparently oriented with respect to the cardinal points rather than to the site axis. The larger of these two structures is unusually well preserved, but cultivation had obliterated most of the smaller platform mound as well as other features of the site when it was purchased by the Indiana Historical Society in 1938.

Unlike many period 3 sites, Angel's composition is not oriented with respect to the dominant topographic feature, the Ohio River. A second peculiarity of the site is the lack of borrow pits near the earthworks. Black has speculated that earth may have been quarried from lower-lying areas around the site, particularly to the northwest.

Reference: Black, 1967.

Kincaid

Brookport, Illinois

Kincaid was a palisaded ceremonial center and habitation area located on the north bank of the Ohio River opposite the present-day city of Paducah, Kentucky. In all, nineteen truncated pyramids, platforms, conical mounds, and other features have been recorded within the approximately 70-hectare, 1.6-kilometer-long site. This reconstruction is based on the 1951 account of Fay-Cooper Cole and others and on information provided by Jon Muller (personal communication, 1979). Many of Kincaid's features remain to be thoroughly investigated and are shown therefore by dotted lines, pending further information.

The site is bounded on the south by Avery Lake, part of the drainage system of the Ohio River from which Kincaid derives its orientation, and to the north and west by several sloughs. Five major rivers converge within 50 kilometers of the site. During its occupation, Kincaid was fortified by a palisade with outward-projecting bastions

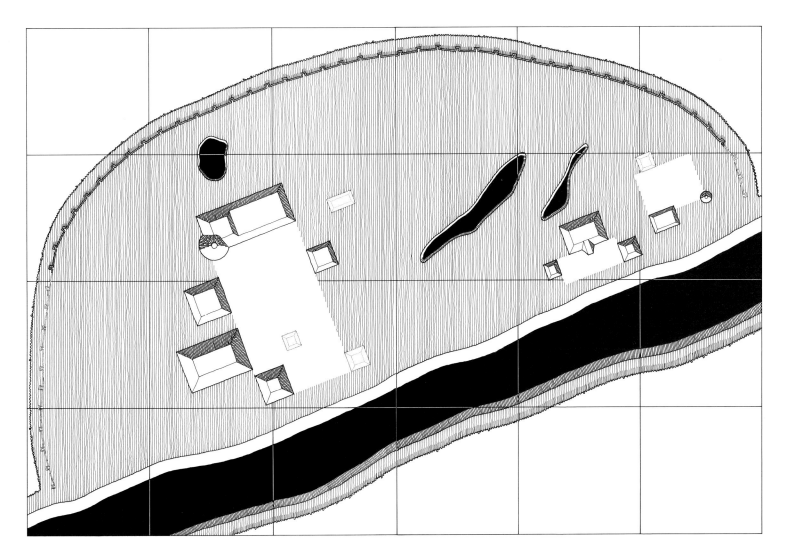

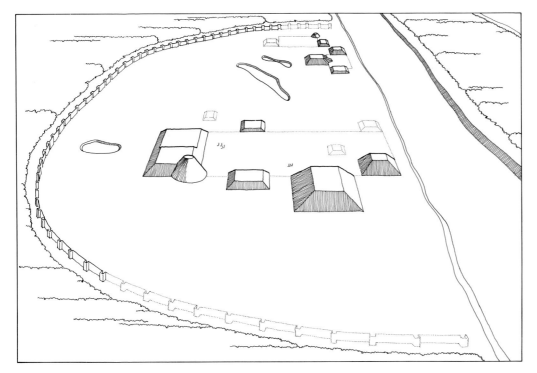

at possibly 30-meter intervals. Whether the bastions were square or round and how far the palisade extended is not yet known.

Dominating the plaza was a 6-meter-high truncated pyramid, 59 by 148 meters in base dimensions. An 11-meter-high conical mound at its westerly end was connected by a stairway to the lower second-level platform. A palisade or screen enclosed wooden structures on the platform. The well-preserved truncated pyramid on the plaza's westerly edge rose 12 meters from a 60-by-90-meter base. An extensively eroded square truncated pyramid, 9 meters high, occupied the plaza's southerly edge.

At most, about 100 houses were located in several hamlets within the palisade. These structures were approximately square in plan, and their sides were 3 to 6 meters long. Several round structures about 3 meters in diameter were located just south of the plaza.

Muller (1978) estimated that Kincaid's maximum population at a single time was about 500 persons. Major construction occurred about A.D. 1250, the same general period when building activity occurred at Angel.

Reference: Muller, 1978.

Aztalan

Lake Mills, Wisconsin

Aztalan is located on the west bank of the Crawfish River 3 kilometers from the present-day town of Lake Mills. It is the only mid-Mississippian period settlement discovered in Wisconsin and the northernmost Mississippian site in this study. A palisade 4 to 6 meters high surrounded the 8.5-hectare site, and two additional palisades were built within the enclosure, but all three may not have been standing at the same time. The palisades were constructed by erecting, at close intervals, posts of tamarack, pine, and oak to which wattle and daub was applied. Bastions or towers were built at about 25-meter intervals around the 1,340-meter perimeter of the palisade.

Aztalan's largest structure is a two-level truncated pyramid at the southwest corner with a residence or temple located on top. A smaller truncated pyramid in the northwest corner contained a crematorium. Aztalan's wood structures were rectangular in plan more frequently than circular, and presumably were built of wall pole construction with wattle-and-daub infill and thatched roofs.

The builders of Aztalan were farmers who supplemented their diets by hunting, fishing, and gathering mussels. According to James B. Griffin, occupation by Mississippian populations was about A.D. 1050 to 1350. Charred remains indicate that the palisade was destroyed by fire. Implements and ornaments of stone, bone, antler, shell, and copper have been found. Fine pottery was decorated with spirals, chevrons, and triangles incised in the wet clay before firing. Remains have been found of burials but not of cemeteries. In 1950 the site was acquired by the State of Wisconsin and is now being partially restored.

Reference: Ritzenthaler, 1970.

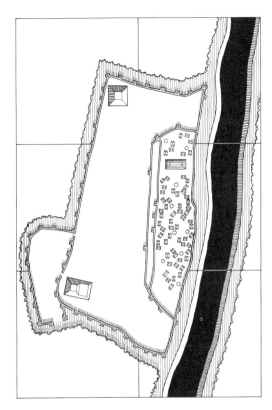

Lower Mississippi Area

Beckwith's Fort

East Prairie, Missouri

Beckwith's Fort, a 12-hectare palisaded ceremonial center and village is located on the Towosahgy State Archaeological Site 9 kilometers southeast of East Prairie. Pinhook Bayou, an old meander channel of the Mississippi River, lies 9 meters below the village level and defines the site's northeastern edge. Archaeological investigations now in progress on the site have found evidence of a palisade of upright logs on top of an earth embankment with an outer moat, but recent cultivation has obliterated most of this feature. Within the palisades were seven mounds arranged around a central plaza and seventy-three houses similar to those found at Lilbourn. The main structure measured approximately 55 by 76 meters at its base and was once 7.6 meters high, according to Cyrus Thomas (1894, figures 96 and 98). Evidence of wood structures has been found on top of several of the truncated pyramids. Due to cultivation and erosion,

A.D. 800-1500

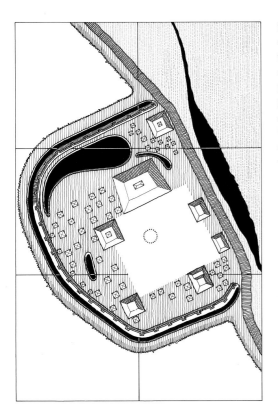

the original configuration of the mounds is not clearly known. The easternmost structure appears to have contained a 3-meter-wide lower terrace and a 6-meter-wide main platform. Within the plaza was a 21.3-meter-diameter circle of wood posts that may have been related to astronomical observations, but its precise nature is not yet known. In the northwestern area of the site was a large borrow pit. The site's axis corresponds with its dominant topographical feature, Pinhook Bayou.

In 1970, the remains of a bastion projecting 5.2 meters outward from the palisade were found, suggesting that bastions may have occurred at regular intervals around the site's perimeter. Similar arrangements have been found in the palisades at Aztalan, Cahokia, and other period 3 sites. Beckwith's Fort appears to have flourished between A.D. 1100 and 1400 and was a highly organized regional center for outlying villages and hamlets. Originally referred to as Beckwith's Fort by Cyrus Thomas, the site also is known as Towosahgy, an Osage word meaning "old town." The reader may wish to compare this site with Lilbourn.

Reference: Cottier, 1974.

Lilbourn

Lilbourn, Missouri

Lilbourn was a 28-hectare palisaded ceremonial center located 32 kilometers southwest of Beckwith's Fort on a 4.6-meter-high bluff overlooking West Lake, a tributary of the Mississippi River, which lies a short distance to the east. The earth embankment enclosing Lilbourn was about 1 meter high, according to Potter (1880). He described a truncated cone, 38 meters in diameter and 1.5 meters high, at the enclosure's northeast corner. Within the enclosure were eight mounds, an oval plaza, and remains of numerous habitations, as shown in this reconstruction, based primarily on Henrich's 1878 survey.

Lilbourn's major structure was a 6.4-meter-high truncated pyramid with an 82.3-meter-long trapezoidal base that varied in width from 42.7 to 64 meters. Its sides sloped upward at a ratio of approximately 2.5 to 1, and it contained remains of burials and a wooden structure. North of the main structure a truncated pyramid rose 3.4 meters, from a 36.6-by-45.7-meter base to

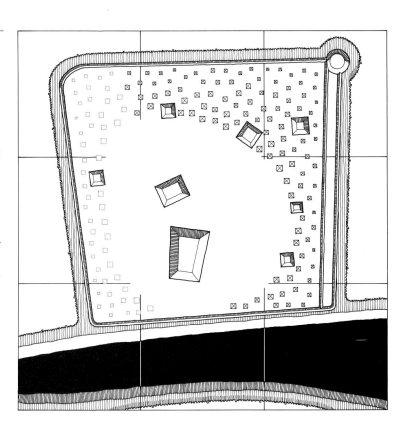

A.D. 800-1500

an 18.3-by-27.5-meter platform. Lilbourn's remaining earthworks varied from 2.7 to 2.1 meters in height and from 22.8 to 38.1 meters in base dimensions. In the plaza east of the main mound, remains have been found of three open-sided arbors or ramadas facing south, two rectangular pits whose sides had been fired brick red, a semicircular arrangement of large post molds suggesting a form of woodhenge (Wittry, 1969), and other structures for ceremonial or public functions.

The residential structures thus far investigated were aligned consistently with the south enclosure wall and appear to diminish in area from 33.5 square meters closer to the plaza to 17.6 square meters near the embankment, suggesting the possibility of a formal town plan based on a social hierarchy. Like Beckwith's Fort, Lilbourn was occupied from before A.D. 1100 until after 1350, its formal plan was adapted to local terrain, and its major structure was oriented for an unobstructed view of a large watercourse nearby to the south or east.

Reference: Chapman, 1976.

Parkin

Parkin, Arkansas

Parkin is the best documented of twenty-one similar palisaded sites along the banks of the St. Francis River. The 7-hectare site is raised more than 91 centimeters above the surrounding terrain by accumulations of village refuse and soil and is bounded by a wide moat or ditch on three sides and the river on the fourth. Toward the center of the rectangular site is an open area or plaza that is lower in elevation. Between the river and the plaza, the truncated ceremonial mound rises 7 meters with a 1.5-meter-high apron extending southward. Like other St. Francis-type villages, Parkin's orientation is as nearly north-south and east-west as the terrain permitted.

Occupation seems to have been concentrated between A.D. 1200 and 1650, with evidence of very late, historic activity at the site. Charles R. McGimsey, III (1968), suggests the single moat crossing shown in the reconstruction. Parkin's houses are believed to have been aligned in

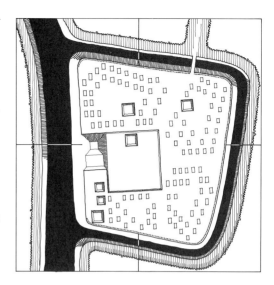

rows with the same orientations and possibly subdivided into wards, but their number and placement are not yet known. Undisturbed burials are found beneath house floors rather than concentrated in a cemetery. A wooden structure was erected on the apron of the ceremonial mound, which was built in several successive layers. The site lies within the present-day city of Parkin and is now an Arkansas State Park.

Reference: Davis, 1966.

Barney

Helena, Arkansas

Barney Mound consisted of two conjoined but unequal circular terraces surrounded by a moat. Cyrus Thomas reported the 4.6-meter-high terraces to be 103 and 61 meters in diameter. A conical mound on the larger terrace rose 6 meters above its 33-meter-diameter terrace base. The encompassing 3- to 3.6-meter-deep moat varied in width from 15 to 23 meters; Thomas did not mention a method of crossing the moat. Burned clay remains suggest possible domiciliary use. Thomas located Barney 1.6 kilometers from Rogers Mound in Phillips County, apparently near the Oldtown Works, which lie 20 kilometers southwest of Helena near the Mississippi River.

Reference: Thomas, 1894, figure 145.

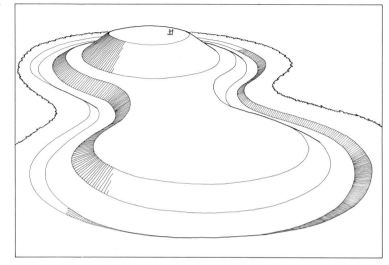

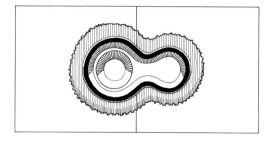

A.D. 800-1500

Sherman

Osceola, Arkansas

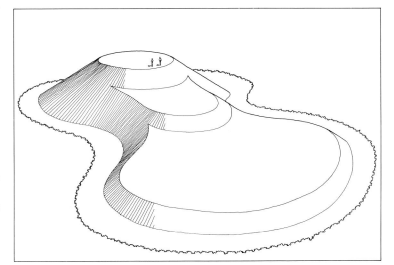
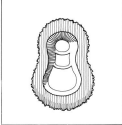

Sherman Mound is near Osceola, a northeast Arkansas town near the Mississippi River north of Memphis, Tennessee. It consists of three ascending terraces, 3.3, 4.4, and 6.3 meters high, in a curvilinear variation of shaped earth. According to an April 9, 1881, *Chicago Tribune* article, the lowest terrace was 39.3 by 48.2 meters; the intermediate terrace, 18.3 by 28.3 meters; and the upper terrace, 19.2 by 23.8 meters. The upper terrace showed evidence of burned clay, suggesting a domiciliary use. Cyrus Thomas's brief description includes an illustration (1894, figure 132) showing very steep sides, which is the basis of the drawing shown here.

Archaeological data on the Sherman Mound is lacking except for a few sherds collected on the site that suggest that Sherman was probably a period 3 site. The notable architectural quality of the Sherman Mound is its combination of multiple terraces and curves within a disciplined axial symmetry. The ascending tiers invite movement to the highest level, a sense of progression that is an arrangement often found in prehistoric American architecture. Other multiterraced or curvilinear mounds were found in prehistoric American architecture at Cahokia, St. Louis, Angel, Kincaid, Barney, Upper Nodena, Magee, and Lenoir.

Reference: Thomas, 1894, figure 132.

Upper Nodena

Wilson, Arkansas

The Upper Nodena site was a 6-hectare ceremonial center and village surrounded by a moat and palisade on elevated land west of an abandoned channel of the Mississippi River. Within the enclosure Dr. James K. Hampson observed, in 1900, twelve to fifteen mounds surrounding a major mound, 7 meters high, 34 by 37 meters at its base, with an apron or terrace extending along its northwest face. To the southwest across the plaza lay a 1-meter-high truncated pyramid on which remains of an 18-meter-diameter house were found, the only round house at this site. To the southeast, adjacent to a 28-meter-diameter, 90-centimeter-high truncated cone, lay a 31-by-46-meter chunkee field. Frequently found at period 3 sites, a chunkee field is a "specially prepared playing field for rolling a stone discoidal while attempting to throw an 8-foot shaft so that its distal end lands near where the stone stops rolling" (Culin, pp. 485–488).

In the northern corner of the enclosure was a 23-meter-diameter mound about 60 centimeters high, and in the west corner a lower mound 14 meters in diameter.

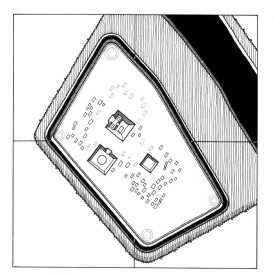

Within the clearly demarcated site were numerous rectangular buildings in an orderly plan, oriented according to the major mound axes; these buildings accommodated an estimated 1,100 to 1,650 occupants who practiced intensive agriculture. Although Upper Nodena was occupied between A.D. 700 and 900, major building probably occurred between A.D. 1400 and 1700. Other palisaded settlements near Upper Nodena were Parkin and Chucalissa.

Reference: Morse, 1973.

Winterville

Greenville, Mississippi

Winterville is a large Mississippian ceremonial center 6.4 kilometers north of the present-day city of Greenville. A notable feature of the site is its double plaza arrangement. The D-shaped perimeter suggested in this reconstruction is indicated by a forest edge rather than by an enclosing embankment or moat for which no evidence has been found. The site's northwestern edge is defined by the stream bed of an old Mississippi River channel that was probably an active bayou during Winterville's occupation.

Of the perhaps twenty-six mounds that originally existed, seventeen have been recorded. The largest structure is a 17-meter-high truncated pyramid. Its relatively steep sloping sides rise at an angle of about 33 degrees above the horizon. A 9-by-18-meter temple replica recently has been constructed on its 30.5-by-40.2-meter summit, from which a log step ramp leads down to the plaza. At the suggestion of Jeffrey P. Brain, this reconstruction shows a longer and more massive

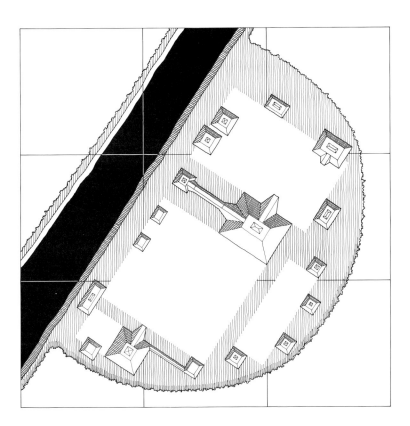

ramp than the recently restored version. An early survey indicated a second ramp leading down 90 degrees to the left of the first ramp and connecting a low causeway to a smaller truncated pyramid.

The second largest mound is 8.5 meters high, square in plan, with a ramp toward the northeast. The southerly plaza is flanked by 9 smaller mounds ranging in height from 1 to 3 meters. The two smaller rectangular open spaces shown here, one square and the other in the proportion of 1 to 3, suggest rectangles of architectural relationship rather than lesser plazas.

The third largest mound rises 5.5 meters above the ceremonial plaza northeast of the main temple mound. The proportions of the ceremonial plaza shown here are 4 to 7. The four flanking mounds range from 1.2 to 3.7 meters in height.

Apparently Winterville's major construction occurred between A.D. 1200 and 1350. Today barns and outbuildings obscure lower features, and roadways graze the site on several sides. The site has been preserved and is being partially restored.

Reference: Phillips, 1970, pp. 476–483.

Toltec

Little Rock, Arkansas

Toltec, also known as Knapp, is located 26 kilometers southeast of Little Rock on Mound Lake, an oxbow lake assumed to have been connected with the Arkansas River at one time. This reconstruction is based on a site plan and account by Cyrus Thomas (1894, plate X) and on more recently developed archaeological information. Although Thomas observed that most of Toltec's mounds were circular or oblong masses, their original shapes are not yet known. Considering the centuries of erosion and decades of cultivation that preceded Thomas's account, this reconstruction presents Toltec in a manner consistent with other period 3 sites in this area.

A 1.8-meter-high earth embankment enclosed the D-shaped site on three sides. Mound Lake lies about 3 meters below the plaza level and defines the site to the northwest. The 35-hectare enclosure measures about 853 meters along the lake and extends about 427 meters inshore. Thomas noted two portals in the southerly arc of the enclosure and two trenches, probably the result of nineteenth-century alteration, in the northerly arc. In 1883 a turretlike terminus was observed on the south side of the southerly trench.

The largest of Toltec's eighteen mounds is a 14.6-meter-high elongated cone that rises from a 45.7-by-85.3-meter base to a 15.2-by-27.4-meter platform overlooking the lake to the northwest and the plaza to the southeast. The second largest structure is an 11.6-meter-high truncated pyramid with a 53.4-by-61-meter base. The third largest structure rises 3.7 meters from its 27.4-by-30.5-meter base. Smaller circular mounds range in height from 60 centimeters to 3 meters and in diameter from 7.6 to 30.5 meters. Oblong mounds are 12.2 to 106.7 meters long. Two shallow excavations or ponds were also observed toward the center of the site.

Toltec may have had a small resident population with the majority of the community living in dispersed farming settlements. Information recently recovered at the site suggests that "occupation began a few hundred years prior to A.D. 700, and that most construction may have ended before A.D. 1000" (Rolingson, personal communication, 1979).

Reference: Rolingson, 1977.

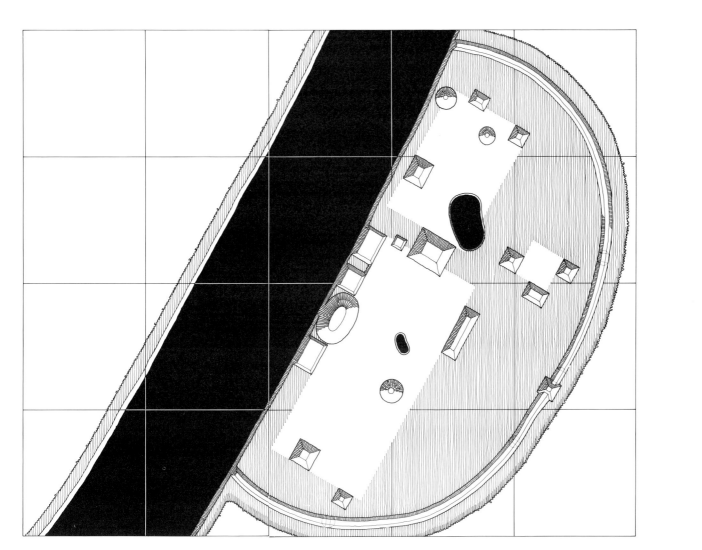

Alligator

Bobo, Mississippi

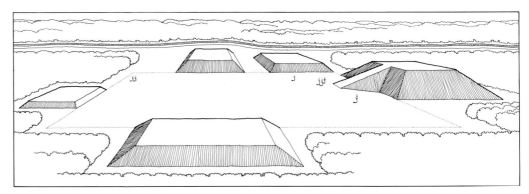

Alligator was a typical small Mississippian ceremonial center located in northwestern Bolivar County, Mississippi. The site's dominant topographical feature is an old meander stream of the Mississippi River that is presently occupied, in part, by Alligator Bayou; the river lies about 1.6 kilometers to the west.

The site consists of five truncated pyramids arranged around a central plaza that was generally parallel with a natural embankment overlooking lower terrain to the north. A ramp provided access to the 4.5-meter-high platform mound at the plaza's easterly end. Lower domiciliary platform mounds lay to the south and west, about 1.5 meters and 90 centimeters high, respectively.

This reconstruction is based partly on Phillips, Ford, and Griffin's description and plans and partly on the assumption that the old meander stream's south bank lay further to the north at the

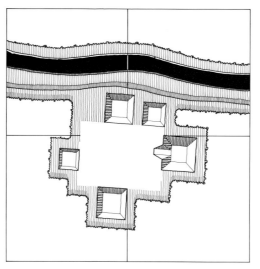

time the earthworks were constructed. Now extensively eroded by nature, cultivation, roads, fences, and buildings, Alligator appears to have been occupied first about A.D. 450 to 550. Following a period of apparent abandonment, the site probably was reoccupied sometime after A.D. 1000 by the people who built the mounds. Archaeological examination of the western domiciliary platform suggests that the village refuse of the earlier occupants was used to form the later mounds that were constructed of successive layers of earth in several building stages.

Reference: Phillips, Ford, and Griffin, 1951.

Perkins

Scott, Mississippi

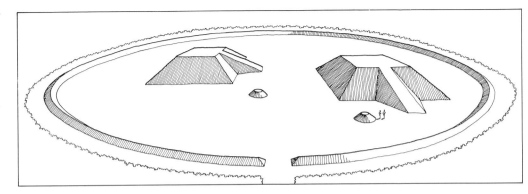

In Bolivar County, 2.4 kilometers east of the Mississippi River on Williams Bayou, Squier and Davis located a 223-meter-diameter circular embankment without a moat enclosing four mounds. A single opening through the 1.2-meter-high embankment provided access to the 3.9-hectare site from the east. The largest mound was a 6-meter-high truncated pyramid rising from a 46-meter square base to a 23-meter square platform with an access ramp to the east. The smaller pyramid was 41 meters square at the base and rose 4.6 meters to a 15-meter square platform with an access ramp to the north. Two conical mounds were each about 10 meters in diameter and 1.5 meters high.

This site has not been located in recent decades and, due to conflicting accounts of early observers, some doubt exists as to its orientation. The Squier and Davis version is shown here, based on their figure 22 (1848, p. 116). James B. Griffin (personal communication, 1978) has com-

mented that the "placement of these two platform mounds within the circle is most unusual. The platform mounds are certainly in the Mississippian Period." The shapes of these structures suggest that the truncated pyramids once may have had residences or temples on their platforms and the conical mounds may have contained burials.

Reference: Squier and Davis, 1848, figure 22.

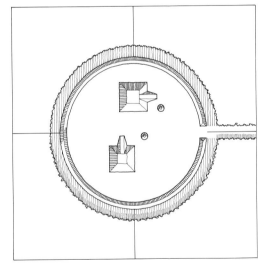

Menard

Arkansas Post, Arkansas

Eleven kilometers west of Arkansas Post lie the remains of a 15.2-meter-high conical mound with unusually steep sides, the principal element of the Menard site. From a 45.7-meter-diameter base, the mound slopes upward at an angle of 53 degrees above the horizon to a platform 22.9 meters in diameter. A central core of hard clay preserved the mound's form. Dr. Palmer's observations, published by Cyrus Thomas in 1894 (pp. 229–231), noted "two flanking wings," the larger, 6.1 meters high by 18.3 meters wide and 45.7 meters long, and the smaller, 2.1 meters high and 22.9 meters long. He also reported 8 hectares "of ancient dwellings," probably low platform mounds for habitations. The truncated pyramid and six smaller platforms shown in this reconstruction are based on the survey published by Phillips, Ford, and Griffin (1951, page 266, figure 37), which was drawn and generalized from a plane table map prepared for the National Park Service.

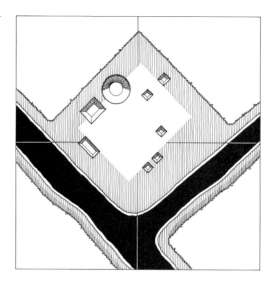

Since Thomas Nuttall first described the Menard site in 1821, it has become a key archaeological site of the Lower Arkansas River. Located at the extreme southern edge of Grand Prairie Ridge, Menard is well above flood level but convenient to the Arkansas River, which was once nearby to the southwest. Menard Bayou bounds the site to the southeast and extends northeasterly parallel to the heavily wooded ridge on which a continuous village apparently extended for several kilometers, including the recorded sites of Wallace, Poore, Massey, and Ellerton. Based on ceramic remains found on the site, the natural advantages of Menard's riparian situation appears to have been exploited for more than a thousand years preceding the Quapaw occupation encountered by the Europeans.

Traces of burnt clay on one of the platforms suggest the presence of a temple or residence. Erosion, cultivation, roads, and the migration of Menard Bayou and the Arkansas River have substantially altered the original character of the site. The dominant structure of Toltec, further up the Arkansas River to the northwest, also appears to have been curvilinear rather than rectilinear.

Reference: Phillips, Ford, and Griffin, 1951.

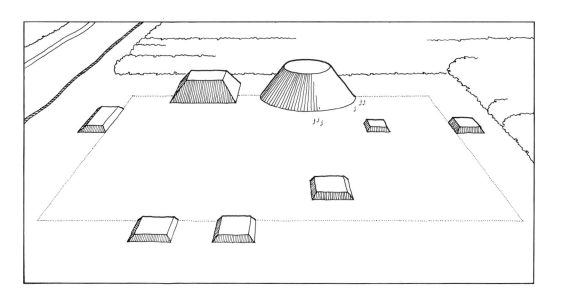

Kinlock

Tralake, Mississippi

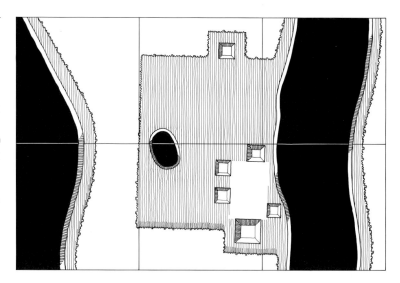

The Kinlock group lies near the present-day town of Tralake on a narrow neck of land formed on the east by the Sunflower River. It is bordered on the west by Dabney Brake, the eastern end of an oxbow lake that was formerly a Mississippi River channel but is now a swamp. Kinlock's dominant topographical feature is the river, now encroaching on the site from the east.

The site is a typical late period 3 arrangement, consisting of an extensive village area and five mounds compactly arranged around a plaza; a sixth mound is located 160 meters north of the plaza. Philip Phillips observed that the structures probably were originally rectilinear in plan with the possible exception of the 1.5-meter-high easternmost mound, which had been so badly eroded that its original form was no longer clearly discernible. The 5-meter-high southernmost mound is the largest of the group, and the

A.D. 800-1500

mound at the north end of the plaza is the second largest structure. The three remaining platform mounds are exactly aligned with a present-day road and have houses built on them, suggesting that one or more may not have been constructed prior to historic contact. Toward the center of the westerly village area is an excavation more than 150 meters from the Sunflower River. Phillips's figure 184 shows this feature as "Borrow Pit?", presumably suggesting that it may have been a quarry for mound building material, such as those of Beckwith's Fort and other period 3 sites in the Lower Mississippi Area.

Today Kinlock has been extensively eroded by cultivation, roads, fences, buildings, and the river. Extensive sherd collections gathered at the site suggest major periods of occupation between A.D. 300 and 500 and again between A.D. 1400 and 1600, during period 3 when major mound building presumably occurred. Minor indications point toward possible activity as early as A.D. 100 and between A.D. 700 and 1000.

Reference: Phillips, 1970, pp. 428–441.

Chucalissa

Memphis, Tennessee

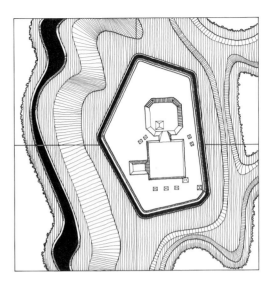

Located on a 30-meter-high bluff overlooking the Mississippi River flood plain 7 kilometers west of Memphis, Chucalissa was a palisaded village and ceremonial center. According to James B. Griffin, major activity at the site probably occurred from about A.D. 1100 to 1500. Chucalissa's maximum population appears to have been in the range of 1,000 to 1,500 inhabitants, most of whom lived outside of the palisade.

The enclosure consisted of an outer moat about 4.6 meters wide, an inner embankment, 4.6 meters wide and exceeding a meter in height, and a staggered row of posts, averaging 25 centimeters in diameter, 2.4 to 3 meters in height, and set about 60 centimeters into the crest of the embankment about 30 centimeters apart. The 61-meter square sunken plaza was about 60 centimeters below the surrounding grade. The civil chief's house was located toward the west end of the main truncated pyramid, a 46-meter square structure with 45-degree corners built in

several successive layers. Eight smaller wooden structures with wattle-and-daub walls and over-lapping bundled grass roofs have been reconstructed around the plaza.

This reconstruction, representing conditions in the late fifteenth century, is based on the 1977 on-site interpretation of Chucalissa's archaeological curator, Gerald Smith, and on Charles H. Nash's 1972 publication. Chucalissa is also known as the Fuller site (L.M.S. 12-P-2).

Reference: Reference: Nash, 1972.

Magee

Percy, Mississippi

The Magee site consists of six mounds and a village site 4 kilometers southeast of Percy in west central Mississippi. Deer Creek lies approximately 400 meters to the west, but this distance is slightly foreshortened in this reconstruction based on Philip Phillips's site plan. The site first was surveyed in 1941 and given the name "Deer Creek," but it is referred to here as "Magee" in order to avoid confusion with other Deer Creek sites, according to Phillips's recommendation.

Magee is a typical example of Lower Mississippi Area ceremonial centers of the second magnitude. It appears to have reached its final form toward the end of period 3, probably between A.D. 1400 and 1600. The largest mound of the group was estimated to be 12 meters high and 50 by 70 meters at its base. A clearly defined ramp led from the plaza up to its approximately 15-meter square summit. East of the summit was an apron or lower terrace about 2 meters above grade. As is the case with most multiterraced period 3 structures, Magee's terraces overlooked the plaza and the long axis of the major mound was parallel to the plaza rather than set at a right angle to it.

The second largest structure was a 4-meter-high and 35-meter square truncated pyramid located at the west end of the plaza. The third highest mound was the 3-meter-high rectangular mound defining the easterly edge of the plaza. Toward the southeast was a truncated pyramid measuring about 20 meters across and approximately 2 meters high. Both of the remaining mounds, one at the northeast corner of the plaza and one at the southwest corner, were about 60 centimeters high. The precise shape of the last three structures was difficult to determine due to extensive erosion at the time they were surveyed.

Although Magee is geographically closer to Arcola and other Deer Creek sites, a stronger cultural link with Lake George has been suggested, but conclusive archaeological evidence is lacking.

Reference: Phillips, 1970, pp. 464–467.

A.D. 800–1500

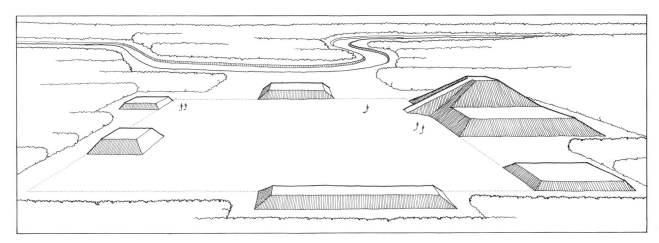

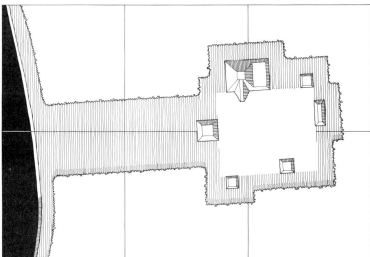

Jackson Place

Floyd, Louisiana

The Jackson Place site lay about 300 meters south of the closest ridge mound of Poverty Point within view of the present-day town of Floyd on the western edge of Bayou Maçon. All six truncated pyramids and their associated earthworks have been destroyed. The basis of this reconstruction is Clarence B. Moore's account published in 1913.

The six mounds were related to two rectangular open spaces, the larger in the proportion of 4 to 7 and the smaller in the proportion of 1 to 2. The truncated pyramid abutting both open spaces was Jackson Place's highest structure, rising 4.6 meters from a 37-meter square base to a 15-meter square platform. The northernmost mound rose 4.3 meters, and the two smaller mounds of the north group were 2.7 meters high. The southernmost mound rose 4.1 meters from a 54-by-63-meter base to a 29-by-41-meter platform. The westernmost mound was 2 meters high with two earthworks extending south and north. The unusual easterly curve of the northern ridge and

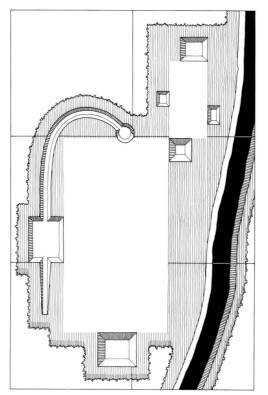

its round terminus were carefully recorded but not explained. Ponds caused by removal of material for mound construction and "humps and small rises" also were observed.

Cultivation, road construction, houses, and erosion by Bayou Maçon had altered some features of the site by the time of Moore's visit. The precise orientation of the earthworks and open spaces suggest that the bayou edge may have been more nearly north-south at the time of Jackson Place's original construction. The site seems to have been built mainly by period 3 people about A.D. 800 to 900, although the curving embankment and its terminus may date from period 2, possibly as early as A.D. 100.

Moore investigated the north group mounds only because houses stood on the other mounds. In the easternmost mound, then partly eroded by the bayou on the east and a road on the west, he found seven layered burials with associated funerary jewelry and pottery.

Reference: Moore, 1913.

Arcola

Arcola, Mississippi

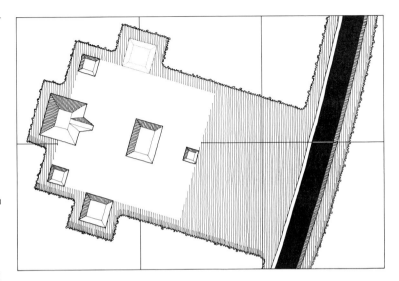

About 5 kilometers south of Arcola lies this well-preserved group of six truncated pyramids. A seventh structure was reported by Calvin Brown to the north but has not been found in recent decades. The reconstruction shown here suggests that the missing mound may lie below a railroad bed and highway that presently intersect where a truncated pyramid is indicated by dashed lines. The use of material quarried from mounds for civil engineering purposes is not an uncommon practice and may account for the missing structure at Arcola. The site's dominant topographical feature is Deer Creek, which lies about 200 meters east of the group. The bases of this reconstruction are the accounts of Phillips (1970) and of Phillips, Ford, and Griffin (1951).

Arcola was a later period 3 ceremonial center probably constructed between A.D. 1400 and 1500. The principal structure is the 13-meter-high westernmost pyramid that rises from a 60-by-70-meter base to a 22-by-27-meter platform. A ramp descends to the plaza toward the east.

The second largest structure is the southernmost, a 5-meter-high structure with a 40-by-45-meter base. This mound's easterly face has been damaged slightly by the railroad line now traversing the site. The seriously damaged central mound is about 4.6 meters high. The remaining low platform structures are 1.5 meters or less in height. These have been reshaped extensively by cultivation so that they now appear rounded rather than rectilinear. Clay daub found in the easternmost platform indicates an earlier domiciliary use and thus a rectangular shape.

The axis of Deer Creek at this site is approximately 16 degrees east of north, which closely corresponds to the alignments of Arcola's pyramids. An old unnamed bayou shown on Phillips's location plan passes immediately west of the group on a course parallel with Deer Creek's, but this feature does not appear to have been a major site determinant.

Reference: Phillips, 1970, pp. 461–464.

Lake George

Holly Bluff, Mississippi

The Lake George group lies on the south bank of Lake George about 2.5 kilometers southeast of Holly Bluff in east—central Mississippi. A moat and palisaded embankment define an area approximately 600 by 350 meters containing twenty-five surviving mounds and two principal plazas. Like many other large period 3 ceremonial sites, Lake George has been used as a plantation for many decades; its earth structures served as platforms above flood level for plantation residences, barns, and outbuildings. The trampling of livestock, extensive cultivation, and a road through the north sides of the plazas have contributed further to the erosion of the site. The main mound has been slightly damaged by the dynamiting of tree stumps to facilitate cultivation according to Jeffrey P. Brain (personal communication, 1978). This reconstruction is based on the accounts of Clarence B. Moore (1908), Jesse D. Jennings (1952 and 1974), and Philip Phillips (1970) and on personal communications with Jeffrey P. Brain and Stephen Williams during 1978 and 1979.

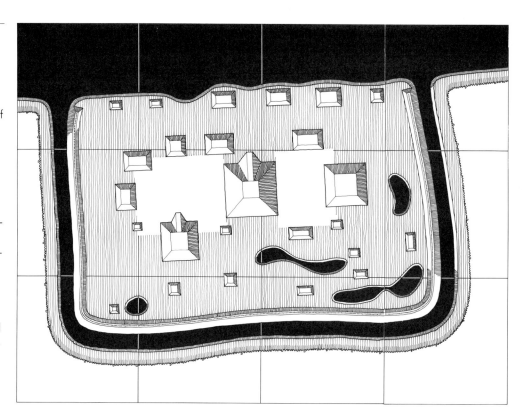

A.D. 800-1500

The site's orientation was about 3.5 degrees west of north. Jennings noted a ramp on the north face of the west plaza's south mound. Moore and Jennings mentioned ramps on the north and east sides of the main mound. The ramp arrangement shown in this reconstruction suggests probable conditions during the later period of development at Lake George, according to Stephen Williams, who conducted archaeological investigations of the site (personal communication, 1978). The shapes of the structures shown here are based on actual field tests of almost all of the mounds.

The main truncated pyramid once rose at least 18.4 meters from its 85-meter square base, dimensions similar to the major structure at Anna. The south mound of the west plaza was a truncated cone about 6.7 meters high, according to Moore, but Jennings reported that it was a truncated pyramid. Today the surrounding embankment is at one point 2.4 meters high. The entire enclosure now is apparent only in aerial photographs.

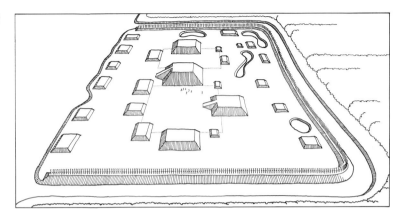

Lake George probably was occupied between A.D. 500 and 1450. Major activity apparently occurred between A.D. 550 and 1400. Until about A.D. 1100, construction was concentrated around the west plaza. Thereafter the emphasis in site construction and occupation shifted to the east plaza. The west plazas at both Winterville and Lake George were definitely of lesser importance after A.D. 1350. Both sites have similar site plans, except Lake George had an enclosing embankment with a palisade and outer moat during its later phase of occupation.

Reference: Phillips, 1970, pp. 278–289.

Haynes Bluff

Haynes Bluff Landing, Mississippi

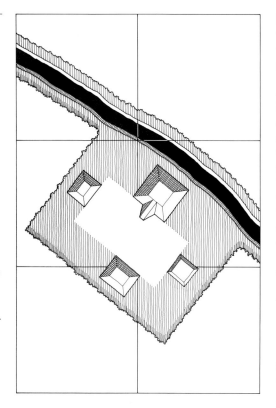

Haynes Bluff's site was one of the latest in the chronology of the prehistoric Eastern United States. All of the earthworks appear to have been constructed between A.D. 1400 and 1500, and the bulk of the main mound was erected after A.D. 1500. A very late period 3 site plan characteristic is the location of the major mound on the northeast side of the plaza. The earliest period 3 sites have the focal structure on the west side of the plaza, but their later placement tended to shift to the north side, modified by local topographical conditions. At Haynes Bluff the elements are grouped around a central open space, suggesting the relationship of a major temple mound to a plaza flanked by lower ancillary mounds. From the 9-meter-high main structure a ramp leads down to the southwest. The ramp's axis is equidistant from the bases of the 3-meter-high northwest mound and the 1.5-meter-high pyramidal mound that defines the plaza to the southeast. Clarence B. Moore (1908) referred to this pyramidal mound as "a knoll that

has served as a dwelling site." Midden material found in this mound substantiates this observation. A fourth structure to the southwest, also 3 meters high, completes the arrangement.

A stream along the northeasterly edge of the site has partially eroded the main mound, which otherwise remains in good condition today. The site axis of Haynes Bluff was approximately parallel with this stream. The site now lies on old Mississippi State Highway 3 between Yazoo City and Vicksburg, about 3 kilometers south of the confluence of Deer Creek and the Yazoo and 32 kilometers east of the Mississippi River. Only two of the mounds remain today. Cultivation, the trampling of livestock, road construction, and the recent construction of a paper mill have eroded the site. During the early eighteenth century, Haynes Bluff was the polyglot village of Tunica, Yazoo, Koroa, and Ofo, according to James A. Ford. The reader may wish to compare Haynes Bluff with other centralized plaza arrangements in the Lower Mississippi Area of period 3, such as Kinlock, Magee, Arcola, Mayersville, and Greenhouse.

Reference: Phillips, 1970, pp. 430–433.

Mayersville

Mayersville, Mississippi

Located on the east bank of the Mississippi River 1.6 kilometers south of Mayersville is an imposing group of six truncated pyramids flanking a main plaza with three smaller mounds to the southwest. Major occupation and mound construction at this site probably occurred during the period of A.D. 1200 to 1400.

The principal structure of Mayersville is 10 meters high with a ramp leading down to the plaza. The second largest mound, 7 meters high, defines the plaza edge near the levee. The central rectangular open space shown here measures 205 by 330 meters. A tenth mound may have been located near the north corner of the plaza, a possibility suggested by this reconstruction, but a banquette constructed along the bank edge in historic times has shown no evidence of such a feature. Additional mounds to the northeast may have been conical but probably were not associated with the main site.

Cultivation, the trampling of stock, and erosion have reduced much of the site, but some original rectangular outlines still are discernible. The northwest mound has been spared and is remarkably well preserved because of a small recent cemetery on its summit. A house now occupies the main mound. Altogether the Mayersville site is an impressive example of centralized plaza arrangements in the Lower Yazoo Basin.

Reference: Phillips, 1970, pp. 505–511.

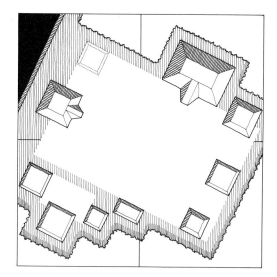

Fitzhugh

Mound, Louisiana

The Fitzhugh site originally consisted of seven truncated pyramids and an elevated way, 823 meters long, flanked by parallel excavations. The dominant feature of the natural terrain is Walnut Bayou to the north, 11 kilometers from the Mississippi River. The main axis of the mounds and elevated way are parallel to the bayou.

The largest mound at Fitzhugh lay 230 meters south of the bayou. From a 50-by-69-meter base, the temple mound rose 9 meters to a 23-by-38-meter level summit. A 3-meter-wide terrace, 3 meters high, extended along the entire north side, where a 6-meter-wide ramp extended 18 meters into the main plaza.

Across the main plaza lay a second mound, 4.6 meters high and proportionately smaller than the primary temple mound. The east end of the main plaza was defined by three square mounds connected by 1.2-meter-high links, 23 meters long to the north and 38 meters long to the south. The larger center mound was 29 meters square and rose 3 meters, while the smaller flanking mounds were 18 meters square and rose only 2.4 meters. The proportion of the main plaza suggested here is 4 to 7; the south plaza, 1 to 1.

The 823-meter-long elevated way was 23 meters wide and 1 meter higher than adjacent grade. Its flanking excavations were 1 meter deep, according to Hough's original survey. The south excavation was wider than the north, but both were about 610 meters long.

Originally covered with a heavy growth of black walnut trees, the site was first cleared in 1827 and since then has been extensively cultivated. This reconstruction is based on Squier and Davis's account and James Hough's survey. The aprons extending from the two highest mounds indicated by Squier and Davis are omitted on the basis of site observations by Stephen Williams (personal communication, 1978), who also noted that the main mound had been virtually destroyed. James B. Griffin suggests that Fitzhugh seems to have been occupied during the climax of mound building activities in the Lower Mississippi Valley, probably about A.D. 1300 to 1500 (personal communication, 1978).

Reference: Squier and Davis, 1848, plate XXXIX.

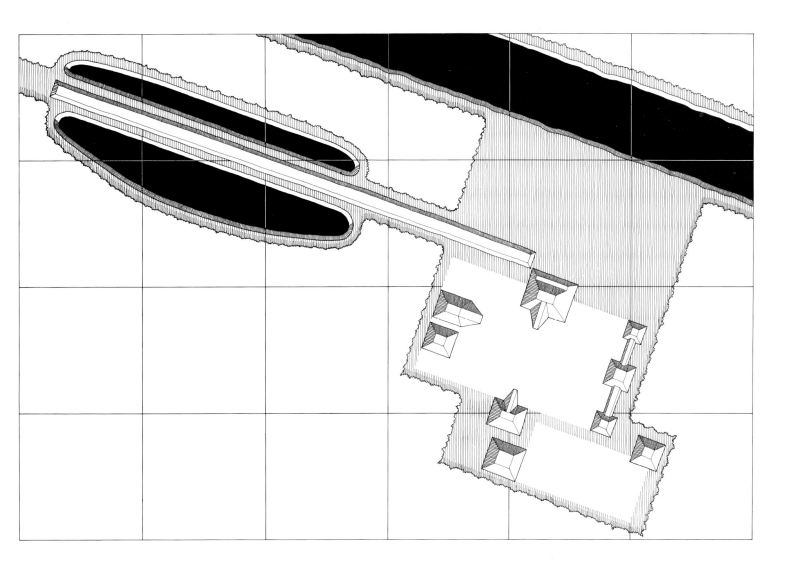

Jerden

Oak Ridge, Louisiana

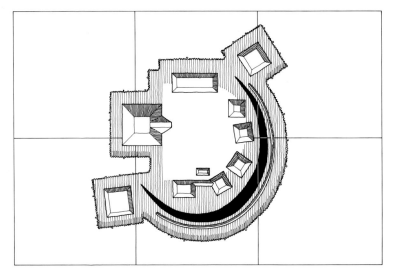

Four kilometers north-northeast of Oak Ridge is the Jerden group of seven truncated structures in a D-shaped arrangement with two outlying platform mounds, a moat with an outer embankment, and associated earthworks. This reconstruction is based partly on C. G. Forshey's 1845 description and survey published by Squier and Davis (1848, pp. 113–114) under the name of "Prairie Jefferson, Moorehouse Parish" and partly on unpublished information contained in the Peabody Museum's Lower Mississippi Survey files (L.M.S. 22-I-1).

Jerden's largest structure was a truncated pyramid that rose 15 meters from a 41-by-55-meter base to a 14-by-16-meter platform, according to Forshey, but by 1935 its height had diminished to 10.7 meters and its base had expanded to 67 meters square. Squier and Davis commented that this structure was built "of a series of strata or tables, one above the other, each surmounted by a burned surface," suggesting that wooden structures may have burned and collapsed and charred the surface of succeeding levels. The orientation and configuration of this structure and its

ramp are based on the 1935 report, which stated that Jerden's other six structures ranged from 1.8 to 4.2 meters in height.

Immediately north of the causeway interconnecting the two southeasternmost mounds was a small mound similar to the two small platforms associated with larger structures at the Mott site, which lies a short distance to the southeast. Defining the site to the south and east was a curving moat or borrow pit that diminished in size as it approached higher terrain toward the north-

west. Forshey (1845) noted that no watercourse lay within 8 kilometers of Jerden and speculated that the moat may have been constructed as a reservoir to retain rainwater. Outside of the moat was a curving embankment, 320 meters long, 3.7 meters wide, and 1 meter high near its center.

Thorough archaeological investigations remain to be conducted at the Jerden site, which bears notable similarities to the Mott site of period 3.

Reference: Squier and Davis, 1848, plate XXXVIII, no. 4.

Mott

Lamar, Louisiana

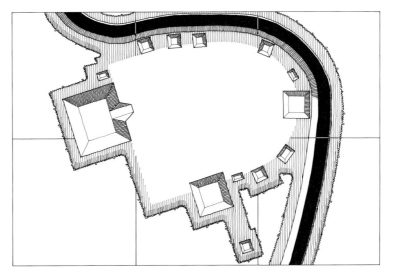

The Mott group of thirteen truncated structures is located 3.2 kilometers east of Lamar in a *D*-shaped arrangement similar to the Jerden site, which lies a short distance to the northwest. The Bayou Maçon once formed the north and east sides of the site and lay about 10 meters below the plaza level. This reconstruction is based primarily on Clarence B. Moore's 1913 description and Philip Phillips's survey for the Peabody Museum's Lower Mississippi Survey.

Although Moore reported that the Mott group consisted of only nine structures, subsequent investigations have revealed that there were thirteen, including one small remnant overlooking the bend of the bayou that may have served as a Civil War fortification. Mott's major structure was a truncated pyramid that rose 8.7 meters from an 87-by-96-meter base to a 46-by-61-meter platform, according to Moore, but Phillips's survey suggests this structure may have been more nearly square, probably with a ramp leading down to the plaza to the east. A 1.5-meter-high structure, measuring 11 by 17 meters in base dimensions, lay immediately north of the main pyramid, according to Phillips. Mott's second largest structure lay on the south side of the plaza and rose 5.2 meters from a 58-meter square base. Immediately to the east was a small platform mound in a relationship similar to the small platform on the north side of the main structure. At the east end of the plaza was a 3.8-meter-high structure whose base measured 41 meters square. During Moore's excavations, this structure yielded the remains of twenty-six burials. The remaining structures of the Mott group appear to have been rectangular domiciliary platforms, ranging from 1.2 to 2.5 meters in height and from 22.5 to 30 meters in base dimensions.

Today the site is privately owned and has been extensively cultivated, resulting in obliteration of many original features. The notable similarities in composition, scale, and orientation of the Mott and Jerden sites may be more than coincidence, according to Stephen Williams, but thorough investigations remain to be conducted at both sites.

Reference: Moore, 1913.

Anna

Natchez, Mississippi

On a high bluff, 19 kilometers north of Natchez, directly overlooking the Mississippi River to the west are the eroded remains of eight mounds that form the Anna group, also known as the Robson group. The largest truncated pyramid rises 15 meters above the plaza to which it is connected by a steep ramp. The seemingly random arrangement of elements conforms to the bluff edges. Apparently Anna was constructed and occupied between A.D. 1200 and 1500 and was built before Emerald. The reconstruction suggested here is a composite of speculative restorations by Jesse D. Jennings (1952 and 1974), which show eight earthworks in the group, and by Jeffrey P. Brain (1978), which show only six structures and the Mississippi River very close to the western edge of the site.

Reference: Jennings, 1952.

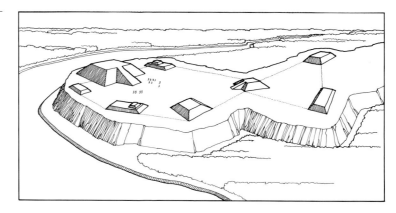

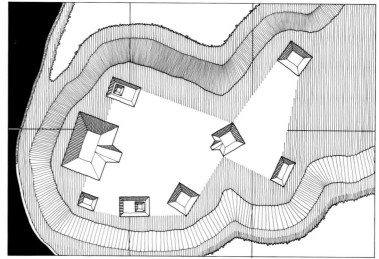

Emerald

Stanton, Mississippi

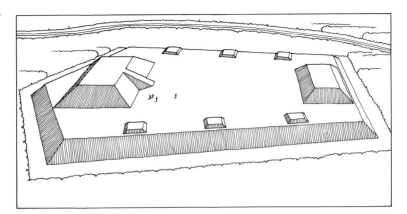

Located 2.4 kilometers west of Stanton is a 3.1-hectare earth platform and mound group known as the Emerald site, sometimes referred to as Selsertown. The site apparently was occupied between A.D. 1000 and 1700, with principal construction occurring after A.D. 1500. Jeffrey P. Brain (personal communication, 1978) suggests that the design of Emerald may have been influenced by Anna, its neighbor, which had been constructed earlier.

Emerald's base was a natural ridgetop that first had been a village site with rectangular wood structures. The sides of the platform were constructed of village debris and earth fill. Much eroded by cultivation, the original base appears to have measured, overall, 133 by 235 meters. The platform measured 105 by 195 meters and was 9 to 11 meters high. The larger truncated pyramid to the west was 48 by 58 meters at its base, 9.4 meters high, and 22 meters wide at its summit. To the east, the second largest mound rose at most 2.4 meters from a 24-meter-wide base. Squier and Davis (1848) reported "eight

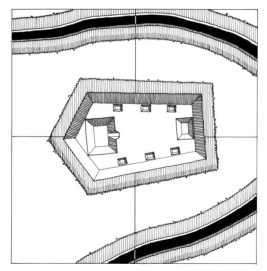

other mounds . . . regularly placed at various points," but Jeffrey P. Brain suggests that there may have been only four. Middleton (Thomas, 1894, pp. 263–267 and plate XIV) found two, both much eroded, one near the north edge of the plateau, measuring 12 meters in diameter and 60 centimeters in height, and one to the south, measuring 6.7 meters in diameter and 46 centimeters in height.

This reconstruction is based primarily on the accounts of John L. Cotter (1951) and Jesse D. Jennings (1974). Through deep ravines to the north and south of the site, two creeks flowed westerly toward the Mississippi River, which is 10 kilometers to the west. Graded avenues provided access from the east around a 12-meter-high natural ridge and from the lower creek level to the west. Today the west mound has been restored with a steep ramp leading down to the east. Burials and exotic artifacts have been found in the east mound. Extensive ceramic remains found near the mounds indicate domiciliary uses. The center of the plateau, however, contains neither ceramics nor mounds, suggesting that this area originally was a ceremonial plaza.

Reference: Cotter, 1951.

Greenhouse

Marksville, Louisiana

The Greenhouse site lies 5 kilometers north of the larger Marksville site. Both are near the banks of Old River, a bypassed channel of the Mississippi River, which has moved about 48 kilometers eastward since the time of original occupation. Site examination at Greenhouse by James A. Ford (1951) in the late 1930s, a personal interview with Robert S. Neitzel (1977), and information supplied by John S. Belmont (1979) are the bases of reconstruction presented here. According to Belmont, "Greenhouse is built on a natural tear-drop shaped island in the middle of an old river channel, predating the present Old River channel. The old channel was inactive at the time of occupation, except during floods." Ford (1951, plate 1) showed the island complete surrounded by water in the flood of 1939.

Principal components of the Greenhouse site are five domiciliary truncated pyramids and a low artificial platform with a cemetery, in use between A.D. 400 and 800. The plan shown here records the site as it was as late as A.D. 1200. The unifying element of the ensemble is a ceremonial plaza measuring 66 by 113 meters from the inner bases of the flanking mounds, a proportional ratio of 4 to 7. The major mounds to the northeast and southwest were the earliest to be constructed and were initially built in a D-shape with their flat sides defining the plaza edges. These major mounds were later reshaped so that their bases were about 33.5 meters square with platforms about 4.3 meters high. Today erosion has worn down the mounds about ten percent. The pyramidal sides appear to rise at angles in the range of 22 to 33 degrees above the horizon. Assuming a 27.5-degree average angle, major elevated platforms would measure 16.5 meters square. Apparently a wood pole and thatch structure was erected on each platform, probably to serve as the residence of a chief or priest or as a charnel house.

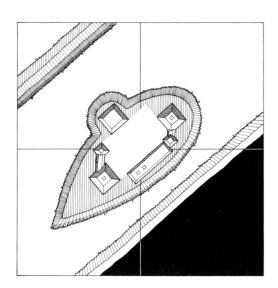

Later additions were a third truncated pyramid to the northwest, whose platform was 2.5 meters above the plaza level when construction ceased, and the low platform southeast of the plaza, which contained houses and a cemetery near its center. The northwesterly platform mound was centered precisely on the plaza and projected beyond the island into the old channel. A 1.3-meter-high causeway, on which a house was built, connected the northeast mound diagonally to the south with a smaller domiciliary platform. The final site element, a 2-meter-high truncated pyramid, measuring 17 meters square at its base, defined the west corner of the plaza and was connected by a low causeway to the larger structure immediately to the south. Evidence indicates that this was the last of the pyramids erected, and it was probably the residence of a new addition to the reigning hierarchy. This completed the complex symmetry of the site.

Greenhouse's main axis lies 49.5 degrees east of true north, parallel to the centerline of the island, which is the site's dominant topographical feature. Squier and Davis reported D-shaped platform mounds like those beneath Greenhouse's main structures at Jerden. Causeways also interconnected major and minor truncated pyramids at Winterville, Fatherland, and other period 3 sites.

Reference: Ford, 1951.

Fatherland

Natchez, Mississippi

Fatherland is an example of late linear site arrangements in the Lower Mississippi Valley, according to Robert S. Neitzel (personal communication, 1977). Here three truncated pyramids lie on a 366-meter-long axis oriented 28 degrees east of north. Constructed between A.D. 1200 and 1500, the site continued in use until 1730. Fatherland lies 4.8 kilometers southeast of the present-day city of Natchez on the east bank of the Mississippi River. Both historical and archaeological information describe the site.

In 1700, St. Catherine Creek was a shallow stream separating the ceremonial center from the village to the southeast. French explorer Dumont's sketch map of Fort Rosalie and its environs records eleven wooden cabins in the 1725 village, with each cabin roof ridge parallel to the main site axis. The map locates the village on the secondary site axis opposite the chief's mound.

During his 1700 visit, explorer Iberville recorded that after ascending the very steep bluff on the east bank of the Mississippi River "one finds . . . plains and prairies filled with little hills . . . and many roads from one hamlet to another or to cabins . . . a country of yellow earth [loess deposit] filled with a few little stones [calcified shells and bones] . . . [and nearby] begins the gray earth [prairie]." He further recorded eight cabins on the ceremonial plaza that may have housed guardians of the sacred precinct. The civil chief's house occupied the center mound, a square truncated pyramid rising 4.4 meters above the plaza level. The house and mound were oriented to the cardinal directions rather than to the site axis. The residence measured 15.2 meters square in plan, rose 6 meters in height, and was of wood frame construction, employing wall trench perimeter foundations with wattle-and-daub walls and a thatched roof. A square outer wall formed a windbreak around the residence. Entries were on the corners and so were the firepits, located so that the corner openings served as smoke outlets.

The temple mound, which lay 137 meters to the south, was a rectangular truncated pyramid on which a compound wood structure, 12.2 by 21.3 meters, was built. Up a ramp rising 3.2 meters above the plaza level, then into an arbor or portico 9.1 meters square and entirely open to the plaza, and through a small door was the interior of the temple, a 12.2-meter square structure constructed like the chief's house. Very little light entered the sanctuary, giving it an atmosphere of mystery. The temple housed the perpetual fire, sacred relics, and, in its floor, numerous burials of important persons and their entourages.

Fatherland's north mound rose about 1 meter higher than the center mound, but it was abandoned before historic times. It was probably square in plan and may have been the site of a temple or residence, but today it is extensively eroded.

Fatherland's mounds appear to have been built in four successive, distinctly plated layers of roughly equal thickness. A section through the temple mound reveals, in its earliest phase, mixed gray tan and black silt with lens concentrations. Phase 2 is composed of uniform gray tan silt, and

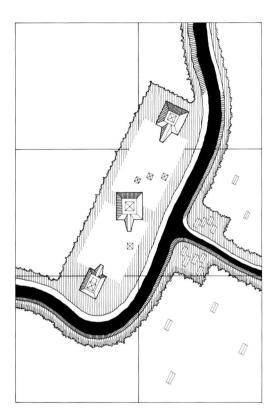

phase 3 contains tan silt. Bluish clay soil makes up phase 4. Remains of fire pits, burial pits, wood post foundation, and weathered surfaces, sometimes densely compacted by repeated foot traffic, assist archaeologists in determining successive building levels.

The plazas contained residences for dignitaries and served as amphitheatres for ceremonial events of particular significance to the Natchez people. According to French observers, the south plaza was the site of the ritual burial of the historic Tattooed Serpent, a revered warchief who died June 1, 1725. This elaborate ceremony was viewed by hundreds of mourners who watched the solemn funeral procession pass by and observed the final interment.

Today extensive erosion and cultivation along St. Catherine's Creek have destroyed some features of the site. The numerous hamlets and cabins for miles around the Grand Village of the Natchez have disappeared. A 2-meter-thick alluvial deposit once covered the plazas, but today Fatherland has been restored.

Reference: Neitzel, 1965.

Alphenia

Clayton, Louisiana

The four truncated pyramids shown here were located on the east bank and within view of the Tensas River a short distance west of Clayton, Louisiana. This reconstruction is based on Clarence B. Moore's plan and description and Peabody Museum's Lower Mississippi Survey data, which indicates the river bank about 200 meters to the west on a course slightly east of north.

The bases of the east and west pyramids both measured about 52 meters square, and the height of both structures was within 20 centimeters of 5.7 meters. Each pyramid also had a 21-meter square summit.

By the time of Moore's visit, the south mound rose less than one meter in height; it had been badly obliterated by cultivation since 1844. Apparently this mound had never been completed, but, obviously, it was placed on a four-sided plan that was biaxially symmetrical about an 80-meter square plaza oriented to the cardinal points.

The north pyramid rose 4.4 meters from a 40-meter square base to a 21-meter square summit. Partial exploration of this pyramid revealed multiple bundled burials, evidence of earlier wooden structures and firepits, and several successive layers of earth, suggesting construction by stages rather than all at one time.

Reference: Moore, 1913.

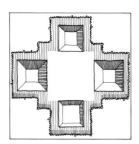

Troyville

Jonesville, Louisiana

Beneath the town of Jonesville lie the remains of Troyville. Because cultivation, erosion, reconfiguration as a fortification during the Civil War, the growth of Jonesville, and the removal of the major structure to provide fill for a nearby bridge approach in 1931 have altered the site, earlier accounts are the major sources of information on the probable original appearance of Troyville.

The approximately 21-hectare site is bounded by Little River on the north and Black River on the east. An embankment, at most 2.4 meters high and 7.6 meters wide, with an outer moat bounded the site to the south and west and was terminated by a platform mound at its juncture with Black River. George E. Beyer (1898 in Walker, 1936) recorded eight adjoining mounds within the enclosure and a ninth outside to the northwest; earlier accounts suggested as many as thirteen mounds. Four artificial ponds within the site were connected by navigable canals to Black

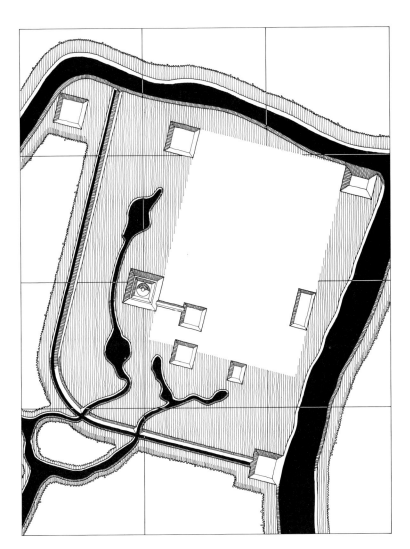

River, 4.8 kilometers south of the site, indicating that the center of the site had been accessible by canoe, as suggested by Thomas (1894, pp. 250–252). Thomas also reported that the two southeasternmost platforms within the enclosure were 4.6 meters high with a 22.9-by-27.4-meter base and 2.4 meters high with a 27.4-by-61-meter base.

Troyville's major structure rose 24.4 meters, second in height only to Monks Mound in the prehistoric Eastern United States. This structure apparently consisted of a conical mound set on two truncated pyramids, as illustrated on page xxx. From a 54.9-meter square base, the structure rose 9.2 meters at a 42-degree angle to its first terrace and continued more gently upward 4.6 meters to its second terrace. The conical mound then rose 10.7 meters at a 50-degree angle to its 2.4-meter-diameter third terrace. Winslow Walker suggests that stepped log ramps may have provided access to the first terrace from its four corners. A likely candidate for the Anilco of De Soto's narratives, Troyville's structures are characteristic of period 3, although occupation at the site probably began much earlier.

Reference: Walker, 1936.

Caddoan Area

Mineral Springs
Spiro

Mineral Springs

Mineral Springs, Arkansas

Mineral Springs was a highly complex ceremonial center composed of eleven mounds and two cemeteries. The dominant natural element of the site was a 3.7-meter-high sloping bank separating the higher terrace level from lower creek bottomlands to the east and south. A natural promontory to the southeast suggested the three site groups shown in this reconstruction: lower group, promontory group, and inshore group. The lower group consisted of a conical mound, 23 meters in diameter and 2.1 meters high, and two lower burial mounds of 16.8- and 21.3-meter diameters.

Toward the center of the southern promontory group was a rectilinear platform mound, 21 by 27 meters at its base and 1.8 meters high. At the westerly corner was a truncated cone, 24.4 meters in base diameter, rising 2.4 meters to a 7.6-meter-diameter summit on which a house was built. The small round mound at the easterly corner of the promontory group was 12.2 meters in diameter, under which the remains of an earlier house were found.

A.D. 800-1500

The largest mound at Mineral Springs lay near the center of the inshore group. This truncated pyramid measured 26 by 53 meters at its base and rose 2.4 meters to a 15-by-44-meter platform, on which was located a 12.2-meter-diameter conical mound, 1.8 meters high, used as the base for a temple or residence. The three remaining round mounds varied from 15 to 23 meters in diameter and supported houses. Radiocarbon samples from two of the houses indicate construction between A.D. 1250 and 1550.

Occupation of Mineral Springs appears to have begun in preceramic times and continued through period 3, in all more than a thousand years. Elaborate mortuary customs were practiced in later times, and the inhabitants apparently were organized into a stratified social system.

Little is known of the village area and subsistence methods employed in this important ceremonial complex. The architectural characteristics of Spiro and Mineral Springs appear to have been distinctly different from those of Lower Mississippi Area sites.

Reference: Bohannon, 1973.

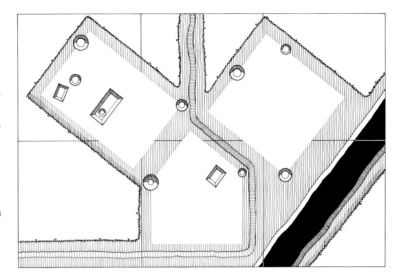

Spiro

Spiro, Oklahoma

Nine kilometers northeast of Spiro near an old channel of the Arkansas River is a 32-hectare ceremonial site containing a burial group of three mounds to the east and a ceremonial group of six mounds to the west. At the time of Spiro's prehistoric occupation the river was further to the north and a stream flowed along the site's southerly edge, conditions similar to those existing today.

The burial group's northernmost structure, Craig Mound, was a 10-meter-high cone, 34 meters in diameter at its base; it is now rebuilt. Originally constructed in nine successive phases over an extended time, Craig Mound was used variously for occupation, as a mortuary, and as a deposition for burials that were processed through the mortuary. The great mortuary at the mound's base contained incredibly rich burial materials, which may make it the King Tutankamen's tomb of the Eastern United States. Numerous burials with associated mortuary artifacts were found on each of its earlier levels. Three smaller contiguous burial mounds extended 57.3 meters to the southeast. Cedar posts encircling burial areas have been found in several locations. Two low conical burial mounds a short distance to the southeast have been obliterated by plowing.

Upland to the west, six mounds were arranged around a 200-by-275-meter oval-shaped open space, free of habitations or debris, suggesting possible ceremonial uses. The 53-by-61-meter easternmost truncated pyramid, once 4.6 meters high, was constructed in at least five phases. Its original wood structure was covered by the first truncated mound, whose gently sloping westerly side may have served as an access ramp. To the north was a 2.4-meter-high platform mound, 18 meters in base dimensions, constructed in two stages. Characteristic of Caddoan architecture, the remaining four mounds were buried houses, probably charnel houses, ranging from 9 to 21 meters in diameter and 0.6 to 1.5 meters in height.

According to Phillips and Brown (1975, vol. I), Spiro probably was first occupied between A.D. 700 and 950, when some of the Craig burials were made. Caddoan culture appeared about A.D. 1000, when most of the village around and between the two mound groups and accretional burial mounds were built. Between A.D. 1200 and 1350 Spiro was used as a mortuary/temple town rather than as a habitational site. The great mortuary dates from the early part of that period.

Reference: Brown, 1966.

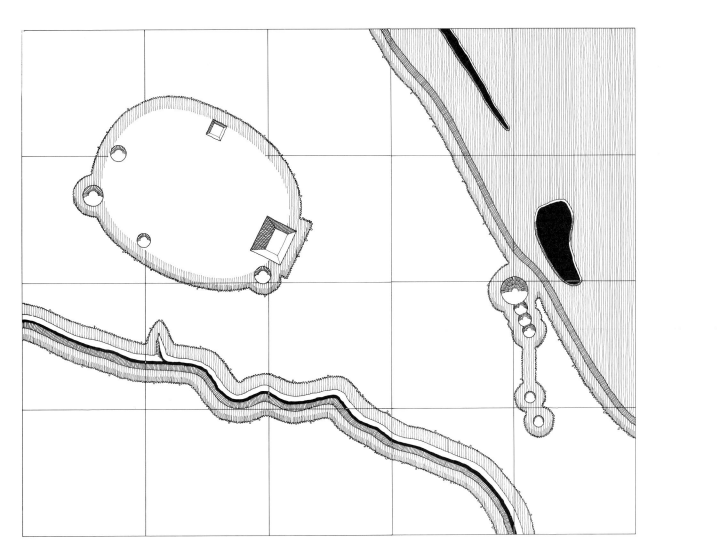

Tennessee, Appalachian, and Piedmont Area

Hiwassee

Dayton, Tennessee

The Hiwassee site was located 11 kilometers south of Dayton on a 325-hectare triangular island formed by the Tennessee and Hiwassee rivers prior to the construction of the Chicamauga Dam and Lake. The fertile island supported aboriginal agriculture. Oak and cedar forests abounded on the mainland. First occupied during period 2, the site contained at least three separate chronological and cultural divisions: Hamilton, Mississippian, and Historic. Cherokees last occupied Hiwassee Island in 1818.

Twenty-two conical mounds and two truncated pyramids were found on the site in 1885. On the northern tip of the island within a wooden stockade was an extensive village midden, two conical burial mounds, a low circular platform, a 23-by-160-meter excavated pond, a central plaza, and a 6.7-meter-high compound truncated pyramid 45 meters long. The steep-sided compound structure (far right), the fifth of seven stages, was created during period 3 to serve as the community's ceremonial focus.

A.D. 800-1500

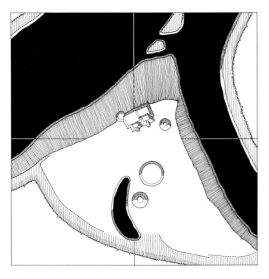

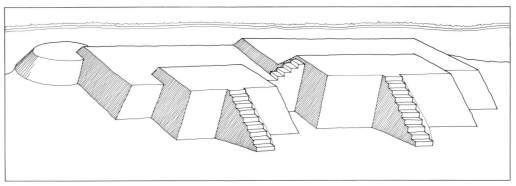

Quadrilateral and circular wood structures were
erected on successive levels with complex arrangements of platforms and stairs. The walls of
temples and residences were constructed by setting upright timber posts close together. These
were infilled with wattle and daub and protected
by overhanging thatched cane roofs.

Reference: Lewis and Kneberg, 1976.

Obion

Paris, Tennessee

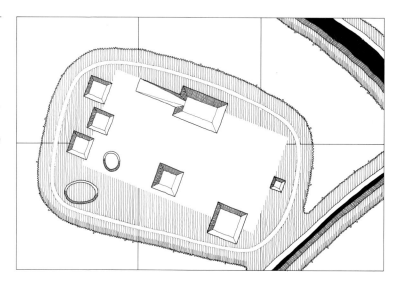

The Obion site is located 35 kilometers northwest of Paris on the south shore of the Obion River, which lies about 300 meters to the northeast. The site is situated on the second terrace of the river, which is 18 meters higher in elevation. A small tributary of the Obion River defines the site's southeast boundary. A 213-by-274-meter habitation area lies immediately northwest of the mound group but is not shown in this reconstruction.

Obion's major structure rose steeply about 12 meters from a 49-by-76-meter base to a 25-by-52-meter platform. An exceptionally long ramp projected westward 70 meters, almost the length of the mound itself, and diminished in width from about 21 meters at its base to 9 meters at the summit. South of the main structure, six platform mounds formed a rectangular open space. The maximum base dimension of these structures ranged from 18 to 49 meters. Two oval depressions were located in the southwesterly area of the site. On the north side of the main structure was evidence of a deep trench leading in the

direction of a fine spring 213 meters to the north on the lower river terrace. Remnants of a wall or ridge have been found along the southern edge of the group, suggesting that a palisade originally may have enclosed the site, as shown by dotted lines in this reconstruction and pending future confirmation of this feature.

Occupation and construction at the Obion site appears to have occurred between A.D. 900 and 1300. On an aparently natural mound, north-

west of the site near the riverbank, a comparatively large number of flint implements but very little pottery was found. The main Obion group contained relatively few flint implements but extensive pottery. This reconstruction is based on Madeline Kneberg's plan (1952, figure 106A), a site plan compiled by Elizabeth Baldwin from a C. H. Nash map in University of Tennessee files, a B. W. Merwin map in Peabody Museum files at Harvard University, and on information from Peabody Museum records.

Reference: Kneberg, 1952.

Lindsley

Lebanon, Tennessee

The Lindsley site is located near Lebanon, about 96 kilometers east of Nashville in the Cumberland Valley. Spring Creek, a tributary of the Cumberland River, probably flowed northward along the eastern boundary of the site several hundred years ago, as shown in this reconstruction, but today its channel has shifted about 140 meters further to the east. The site is barely above creek level to the east but rises approximately 7 meters toward the west. On a 9.3-meter-high bluff southwest of the main enclosure are six low mounds built of earth and stones that had been "heated and burned by long continued fires," according to Professor F. W. Putnam. Another low mound lay northwest of the enclosure near the creek.

A 200-by-275-meter oval earthen embankment with a 1-meter-deep outer moat enclosed the 4.25-hectare site. At the time of A. H. Buchanan's 1877 survey (Putnam, 1878), the embankment was about 30 centimeters high. At nearly equal intervals on the outside of the embankment

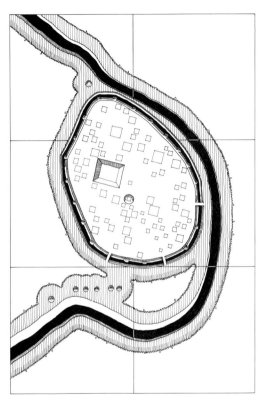

were bastions, 46 centimeters higher than the main wall. These projected outward to the moat's edge; the wall segments were inset 1 meter. Three causeways provided access through the enclosures to the south and east. Inside the enclosure the main structure rose steeply 4.6 meters from a 37-by-42-meter base to a 23-by-29-meter platform. It was built in successive layers of compacted clay, contained no burials, and probably had a house on its summit originally. Southeast of the main structure was a 90-centimeter-high burial mound, 14.3 meters in diameter; it contained sixty stone graves arranged in a hollow square three tiers high in two or three irregular rows. Within the enclosure were nearly 100 circular ridges up to 1 meter high and 3 to 15 meters in diameter, probably the remains of rectangular wood structures, according to Philip Phillips (1939, pp. 221–236).

Lindsley has yielded notable examples of ceramics, copperwork, stone and shell carving, and several types of woven fabric. Major activity at the site probably occurred between A.D. 1100 and 1400.

Reference: Putnam, 1878.

Mound Bottom

Kingston Springs, Tennessee

About 30 kilometers southwest of Nashville is the Mound Bottom Archaeological Complex. The northerly group shown in the area map is known as Mound Bottom; it is also shown in the comparative scale of this study's 200-meter grid. The southerly group, called the Pack Site, consists of the South Plaza group and two smaller groups enclosed by a palisade to the north and west and the Harpeth River to the south and east. A 1-kilometer-long embankment, 20 meters wide by 1 meter high, interconnected the Pack Site and Mound Bottom. The complex probably was constructed between A.D. 1200 and 1300.

In 1804 observers noted that Mound Bottom was enclosed by an impressive palisade with gateways (Haywood, 1973), but erosion and cultivation subsequently have obliterated this feature. A 50- to 75-centimeter-high earth embankment surrounds the plaza's east end. At the west end of

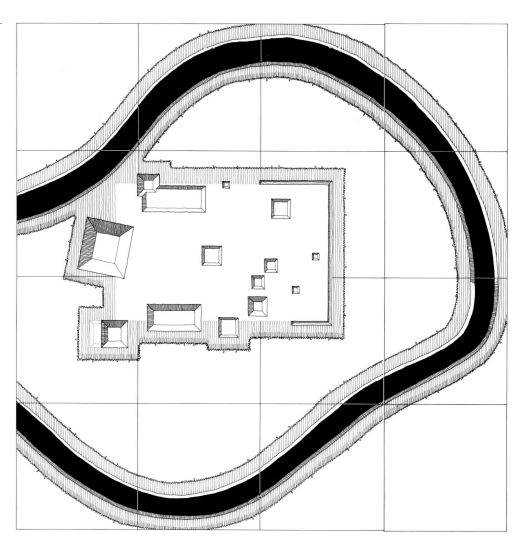

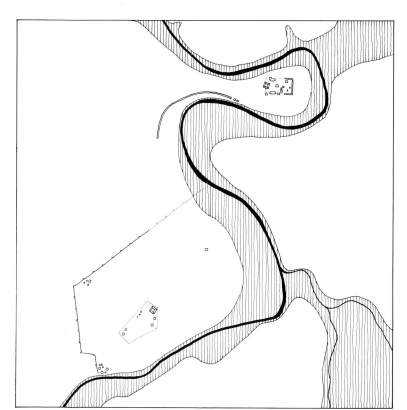

the plaza, Mound Bottom's largest truncated pyramid rises 11 meters from a 75-by-80-meter base. At the plaza's southwest corner a 35-by-40-meter structure rises 4 meters. Flanking the plaza to the north is a 1.75-meter-high rectangular platform mound with a 40-by-100-meter base. The 3-meter-high platform mound flanking the plaza to the south measures 40 meters by about 85 meters. In the center of the plaza is a 1-meter-high structure, which may have supported a post, possibly used for solar observations. Mound Bottom's remaining earth platforms range from 3.5 to less than 1 meter in height.

This reconstruction is based on an excellent 1974 map provided by the Tennessee Division of Archaeology and on Michael J. O'Brien's thorough description.

Reference: O'Brien, 1977.

Shiloh

Pittsburgh Landing, Tennessee

On the west bank of the Tennessee River about 15 kilometers southwest of Savannah, Tennessee, are more than sixty prehistoric earthen platforms, truncated pyramids, and other features comprising the Shiloh group. The axis of the site apparently was derived from the line of the high bluff overlooking the Tennessee River to the east. The Shiloh group is located on an irregular plateau rising more than 6 meters above lower-lying terrain to the north and south. A crescent-shaped palisade, interrupted at one point by recent erosion, originally enclosed the site to the west. In 1915 Clarence B. Moore recorded "seven beautiful, symmetrical, aboriginal mounds," Shiloh's largest structures, within the palisade.

Shiloh's southernmost structure is a 3.1-meter-high elliptical burial mound constructed during period 2. Here in 1899 Colonel Cornelius Cadle found the remains of a log tomb containing three burials with associated grave artifacts, including a 25-centimeter-high human effigy pipe exhibiting an exceptionally high level of craftsmanship.

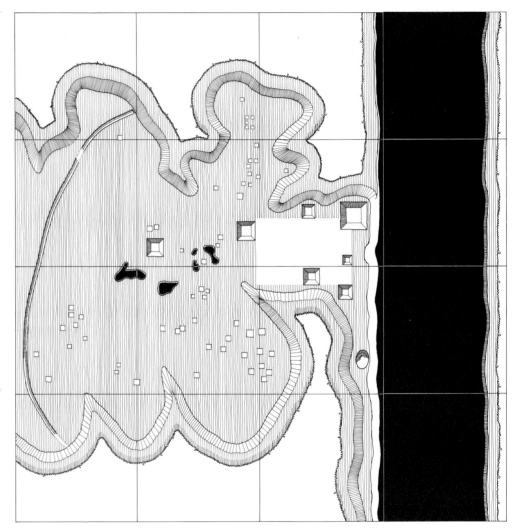

110   A.D. 800-1500

The seven truncated pyramids north of the burial mound probably were constructed between about A.D. 1000 and 1250 and are clearly characteristic of period 3. According to Moore (1915), Shiloh's highest truncated pyramid rose 4.4 meters above an approximately 38-meter square base at the northeastern corner of the plaza. The group's westernmost structure was 3.5 meters high. The remaining four platforms ranged from 3.0 to 1.5 meters in height. Shiloh's comparatively well-preserved structures have almost perfectly square bases and are more notable for their disciplined proportions than for their large sizes.

James B. Griffin has found indications of trade during period 3 between Shiloh and Cahokia, which is more than 400 kilometers to the north near the Mississippi River. Today the Shiloh group is part of a National Military Park commemorating a Civil War battle fought at Pittsburgh Landing in 1862. The site derives its name from the biblical Shiloh, the site of a temple on a mountain (Folsom, 1974).

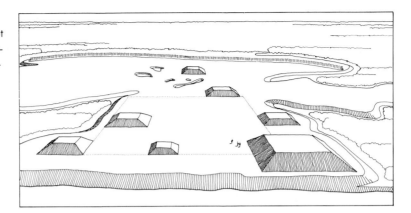

This reconstruction is based on the 1933–1934 plane table map drawn by S. J. Williamson, which is housed in the National Anthropological Archives, National Museum of Natural History, Smithsonian Institution, Manuscript Collection Number 4851 (Frank H. H. Roberts). It is also based on a map of Pittsburgh Landing prepared by an unknown Smithsonian Institution artist between about 1933 and 1935. The latter document shows the palisade and some, but not all, of Shiloh's house mounds, according to Bruce D. Smith (personal communications, 1979).

Reference: Moore, 1915.

Lenoir

Lenoir City, Tennessee

A conical burial mound with a large apron or lower terrace lay on an 83-hectare island on the southeast bank of the Little Tennessee River at its confluence with Town Creek and the Holton River. According to Cyrus Thomas, the conical top was 33 meters in diameter and 3.6 meters high. It was constructed of three successive layers of earth, each capped by a fired clay mantle, suggesting the burning of wooden structures. The mound contained sixty-seven burials, all but two extended, with ornamental pottery, beads, pipes, shells, red paint, and other mortuary objects. In the mound's core was a firepit shaft, tapering from 2.4 meters in diameter near the surface to 1.2 meters at original grade. In the lower clay mantles were the charred remains of numerous cedar posts, 15 to 45 centimeters in diameter, arranged in the form of three separate structures: a 6-meter-diameter circle, an irregular triangle, and an oval.

The 2.4-meter-high apron widened to 116 meters and then converged at a point 174 meters west of the conical mound following the bank of the Little Tennessee River. The lower terrace also contained burials and appeared to have been

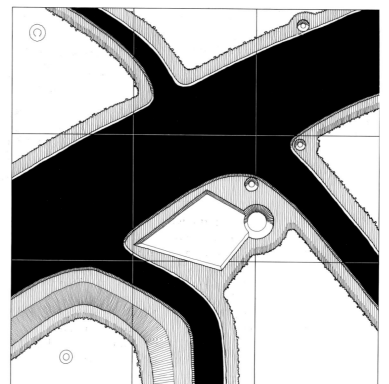

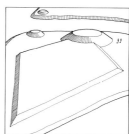

constructed after the completion of the main conical mound. Seventeen other smaller circular burial mounds were found within 1,200 meters of the main mound on both shores of the river.

Reference: Thomas, 1894, figures 276 and 278.

Town Creek

Mt. Gilead, North Carolina

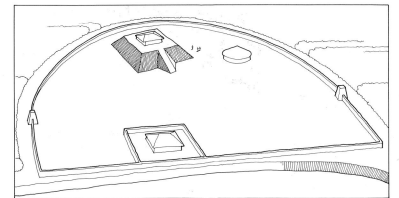

Nine kilometers east of Mt. Gilead is a 6-meter-high bluff overlooking Little River near its confluence with Town Creek. Here between A.D. 1450 and 1650 migrating people from the south surrounded a D-shaped ceremonial center with a 2.7-meter-high palisade of upright logs interwoven with cane, suggesting that the new people may have found their neighbors hostile.

The reconstruction shown here suggests the site's appearance about A.D. 1600. The palisade extended 111 meters along the bluff and 90 meters inshore. Entry towers provided access from the north and south. A third entry, partially subterranean, penetrated the bluff's edge to the east. Village habitations were located outside of the palisade.

The principal structure was a truncated pyramid, rising 5.2 meters from a 26-meter square platform. Beneath this structure was Town Creek's earliest ceremonial building, an earth lodge sunken partially below grade. In time this structure collapsed and a mantle of earth and rubble fill was placed over it, forming the truncated pyramid shown here. The temple or council house atop the pyramid had an entrance at its southeast corner. An opening at the roof's apex admitted light and emitted smoke from the fire within. An earth ramp led down to the east, projecting 10 meters into the plaza or ball court.

A round wood burial house with a conical roof was located between the platform mound and the north entry tower. A 13-by-21-meter wood privacy fence formed a secondary enclosure around the chief's house or minor temple at the bluff's edge.

Town Creek is a relatively small and unsophisticated site that is oriented with respect to its dominant topographical feature, Little River. According to Stephen Williams (personal communication, 1979), Town Creek is characteristic of the easternmost spread of Mississippian influence in the Eastern United States. Today the site has been restored and is open to the public.

Reference: Coe, 1976.

Moundville

Moundville, Alabama

Moundville was a period 3 ceremonial center and habitation area second only to Cahokia in size. Located 27 kilometers south of Tuscaloosa on the southeast bank of the Big Warrior River, the 120-hectare site contains twenty truncated platform mounds with related features. A thick palisade with outwardly projecting bastions originally surrounded Moundville and formed an arc around the southern portion of the site, as shown in the reconstruction.

All of Moundville's structures were platform mounds rather than burial mounds. The 16.8-meter-high main temple mound measured 52 by 116 meters at its base and contained more than 112,000 cubic meters of earth. The 6.4-meter-high platform in the center of the plaza measured 82 by 107 meters maximum at its base. Moundville's remaining structures were mostly 4 to 5 meters high.

A.D. 800-1500

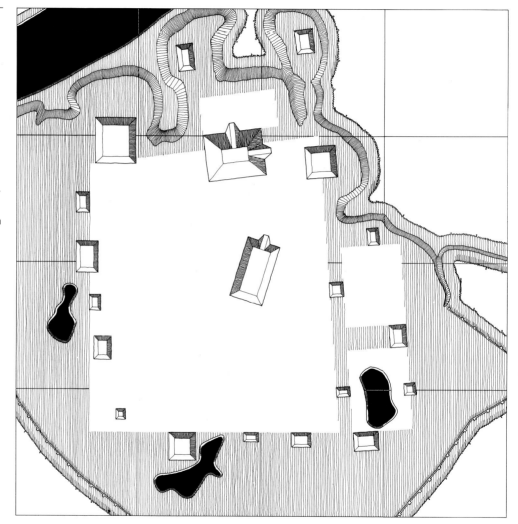

Three ponds were located near the central open space. Archaeologists have found numerous fish hooks on the bottom of the ponds, suggesting they were used to store fish.

Moundville appears to have been organized as a ranked society. The site contained elite residences in its northeast zone and public buildings at the northeast and northwest corners of the plaza. Charnel houses and a "sweat house" were constructed on the plaza's perimeter. Residential areas were located east, south, and west of the plaza.

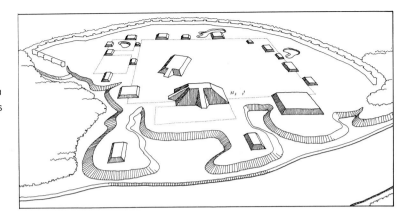

Moundville's population, who subsisted on agriculture, may have been about 3,000 persons at one time. Occupied and constructed between A.D. 1200 and 1500, as the population increased, villages developed within 20 kilometers of Moundville. These villages were grouped in a hierarchial arrangement of secondary centers with platform mounds and tertiary settlements without platform mounds. All of the settlements were elevated well above the river to avoid flooding. Like the comparable ceremonial centers of Etowah and Spiro, Moundville flourished after A.D. 1300, about the time that Cahokia was beginning its decline. Extensive excavations at Moundville have yielded more than 3,000 burials, seventy-five structures, and more than a million artifacts.

Because Moundville is located on the northernmost edge of the gulf coastal plain, immediately south of the Cumberland plateau fall line, Moundville's inhabitants had access to widely varied ecological zones that assured their subsistence and presented opportunities for extensive trade.

This reconstruction is based primarily on the 1905 and 1907 accounts of Clarence B. Moore and on an excellent 1969 map and additional information provided by Christopher S. Peebles in 1979.

Reference: Peebles and Kus, 1977.

Etowah

Cartersville, Georgia

On the north bank of the Etowah River, 4.8 kilometers south of Cartersville, lies the Etowah site
in a commanding position between a rich alluvial
valley and the Piedmont ecological zone to the
north. The site is bounded on the east, north,
and south by a dry moat and two quarries that
probably served to drain the site during heavy
floods at possibly five-year intervals. Lewis H.
Larson, Jr. (1972), found the moat to have a
7.6-meters-wide level bottom about 3 meters below adjacent grade with sides sloping upward at
an angle of 75 degrees above the horizon. Inside the moat, 4.6 meters, was a 3.6-meter-high
palisade consisting of upright wood posts, 30 to
35 centimeters in diameter, placed 30 centimeters apart, and set 1.2 meters into the earth.
The remains of an outward-projecting, 3-meter
square bastion were found, suggesting that additional bastions probably occurred at about 24-
meter intervals.

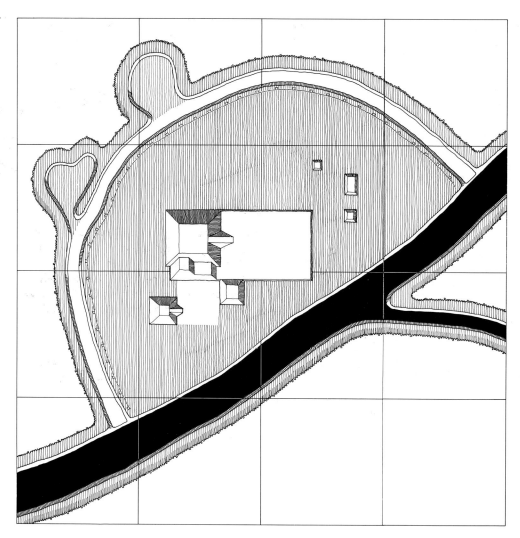

A.D. 800-1500

Within the palisade a town was arranged compactly around the mounds shown in this reconstruction, which is based primarily on Larson's schematic plan (1971, figure 1). The major structures were oriented very nearly to the cardinal points. Etowah's largest truncated pyramid rose 20.3 meters from an 85-by-110-meter base to a 51-meter square summit and had two terraces on its south side. Its sides sloped upward at 45-degree angles. This structure is estimated to have contained 121,813 cubic meters of material, about one-fifth the volume of Monks Mound at Cahokia. On the east side, a ramp led downward to an approximately 90-meter square plaza, constructed of clay and elevated 30 to 45 centimeters above adjacent grade.

Southwest of Etowah's main structure was a clay platform that rose about 6 meters from a 45-meter square base to an 18-meter square summit, with a ramp leading down to the east. Around the platform was a palisade with an opening at the base of the ramp. In each of five phases, a public building was erected on the platform. More than 350 burials with elaborate grave goods were removed from this temple platform. The temple or charnel house, platform mound, encircling palisade, and burials apparently constituted a mortuary complex.

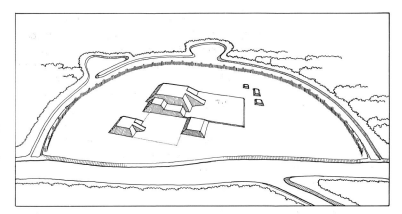

Southeast of the main structure, Etowah's third largest truncated pyramid rose 10.7 meters, from a 37-by-40-meter base to a 25-by-27-meter platform. Three platforms were located east of the plaza, one about 2.4 meters high with a 15-meter square base, and another about 3 meters high with an 18-by-24-meter base. The height of the third platform is not yet known.

The Etowah Valley was first occupied about 5000 B.C. Radiocarbon dating indicates that most of the mortuary complex burials occurred between A.D. 950 and 1450. Larson suggests that the earthworks and palisade probably were constructed between A.D. 1250 and 1550 (personal communication, 1979). For a modern-day view of Etowah, see Dache Reeves's aerial photograph on page 162.

Reference: Larson, 1971 and 1972.

Ocmulgee

Macon, Georgia

On the northeast bank of the Ocmulgee River near Macon are the remains of a large village and ceremonial center. The site was occupied intermittently after 2000 B.C. by small groups of shellfish-eating people who deposited shells in middens on which earth mounds later were built. About 100 B.C. early farmers began to settle at Ocmulgee, bringing increased stability and leisure. About A.D. 900, master farmers introduced corn agriculture and sophisticated economic and political systems. Until A.D. 1100 the population increased rapidly and religious ceremonialism flourished.

The site axis was established at a right angle to the centerline of the Ocmulgee River; today the river lies 200 meters further southwest than this reconstruction suggests. On the southwest side of the village three ramps apparently ascended the major temple mound, which rose to a height of more than 15 meters above its 91-meter broad base. A smaller temple mound lay a short distance to the north.

Five hundred meters to the north on the major temple mound's axis was a circular earth lodge, 12.8 meters in diameter with an extended passageway on the east. The earth lodge, or winter council house, was enclosed by a roof of heavy logs covered with sod. Forty-seven seats on a 15-centimeter-high clay bench were arranged around the interior wall. A central opening in the roof admitted light and emitted smoke from the council fire. A platform west of the central firepit contained three elevated seats and an altar forming an eagle effigy.

A short distance northwest of the winter council house was a platform mound, which was built in several successive stages. The wooden structure on this platform may have served as a summer council house.

On the west edge of the village was a burial mound, which was built in seven successive layers. The truncated pyramid shown here represents the third stage. Apparently on each succeeding level a charnel house was built, secondary interments occurred, and the charnel house was ceremonially burned before the next mantle of earth was placed. Another mound was erected to the east of the village 250 meters north of Walnut Creek, a tributary of the river.

To the north and east of the site were two linear excavations averaging about 2 meters deep and 5 meters wide. These excavations were generally parallel to the higher elevation of the village and may have formed a sunken passageway between the main elements of the site. They also may have been used as borrow pits or fortifications.

About A.D. 1350 a new village, Lamar, was constructed 4.8 kilometers south of Ocmulgee. Here a log palisade enclosed two major mounds, a central plaza, and residences on earth platforms. The larger mound was rectangular; the smaller mound (far right), was round. Whether its irregular sides once formed a spiral ramp or represented some other feature is not known. See Dache Reeves's aerial photograph of the remains of Ocmulgee.

Reference: Fairbanks, 1956.

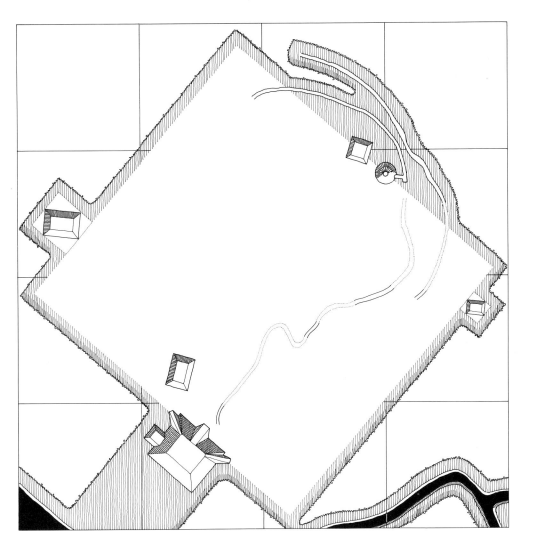

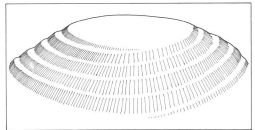

Kolomoki

Blakely, Georgia

Kolomoki is located 9 kilometers north of Blakely in southwest Georgia. Kolomoki Creek, a tributary of the Chattahoochee River, lies east of the site in a 26-meter-deep ravine. A swamp lies to the north. The largest of Kolomoki's eight structures rose from a 61-by-99-meter base to a two-level platform, 17.2 meters high to the south and 16.3 meters high to the north. William H. Sears (1956) found no evidence of a ramp here and suggested that probably log or clay steps once provided access to the summit.

Flanking the main structure were two 15-meter-diameter mounds, each 1.5 meters high. The southerly cone yielded evidence that 61- to 76-centimeter-diameter wood poles, possibly 3 meters high, had been inserted at various points about 1 meter into the earth, perhaps to serve as goal posts.

Toward the west across the plaza were two domical burial structures associated with ceremonial platform structures to the south, the latter rising 1.8 meters from 15-by-18-meter bases. The middle platform structure shown here contained a recent cemetery and was not excavated. The central domical burial structure contained the tomb of a single person and his retinue with elaborate grave artifacts. Built in a relatively brief period of time, it contained four successive earth structures: an 8-meter-diameter domical primary mound within a 9-by-15-meter truncated pyramid, 1.5 meters high, covered by a truncated cone, 25 meters in diameter, and topped by a domical mound, 30.5 meters in diameter and 6.1 meters in height. Kolomoki's second domical burial mound was an earlier and smaller-scale version of the central structure which was 366 meters to the east.

Village middens were grouped around the ceremonial plaza to the north, west, and south of the temple mound. Apparently the site's western area was used for mortuary purposes.

Kolomoki's structures were finished with red clay taken from the site, yellow clay taken from the creek, and occasionally thin layers of white sand. First occupied about A.D. 200 to 400, Kolomoki's plan apparently emerged about A.D. 500. The final 2-meter-thick cap of the multilayered main structure probably was placed about A.D. 700. Kolomoki's population may have been at most 2,000 with at least that number again in small villages along the watercourses within 8 kilometers.

Reference: Sears, 1956.

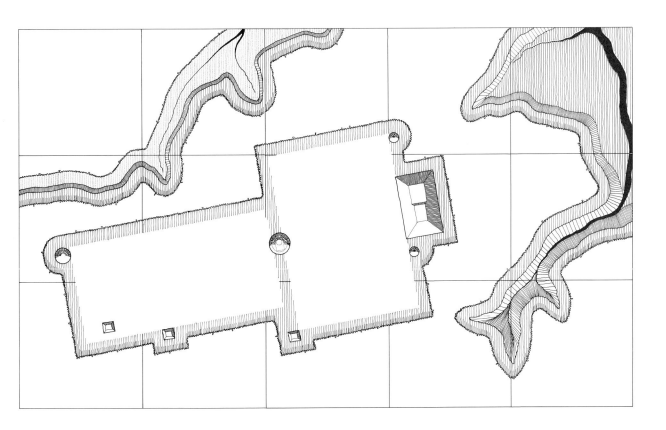

Irene

Savannah, Georgia

On the west bank of the Savannah River 8 kilometers north of Savannah is a 2.5-hectare peninsula that several centuries ago was bordered by
Pipemaker's Creek to the west and south. The
river extends northwesterly more than 300 kilometers from the Atlantic Ocean and is bordered
by swamps and islands except in the vicinity of
the Irene site, where a 3-to-4.5-meter-high embankment rises along the west bank. Intermittent
occupation of the site began some time after
2000 B.C. Intense occupation began about A.D.
1000 and continued up until the time of historic
contact. The reconstruction shown here suggests
its possible appearance during the fifteenth
century.

Irene's major architectural feature was a 49-
meter-diameter round-topped mound, 4.7 meters
high, the eighth and last of a succession of earth
structures built one atop another. The earliest
structure was a 38-centimeter-high enclosure
measuring 12 by 17 meters at its outer base and

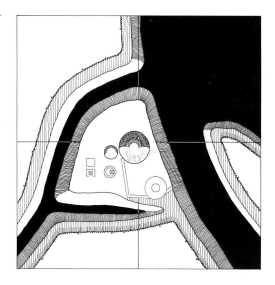

surrounding a 7.6-by-7.9-meter rectangular
wood building on original grade. This was buried beneath three successive enclosures of similar
configuration, each with a ramp leading toward
the southeast generally parallel to the riverbank.
The fifth, sixth, and seventh structures were truncated pyramids. Dashed lines in this site plan
and the perspective represent the seventh structure, which was three meters high and 26 meters
wide at its base. A palisade on its 20-meter-
wide platform surrounded a 4-meter square
wood structure near its center.

West of the main mound was a 76-centimeter-
high burial mound, 17 meters in diameter, possibly the site's oldest structure. A double palisade
encircled the mortuary 24 meters southwest of
the main mound. Across the ceremonial plaza to
the southeast was the rotunda, or winter council
house, connected by a double palisaded street to
the main mound.

Numerous houses, enclosures, walls, excavations, and other architectural features were found
at Irene, but their chronological relationships are
unclear.

Reference: Caldwell and McCann, 1941.

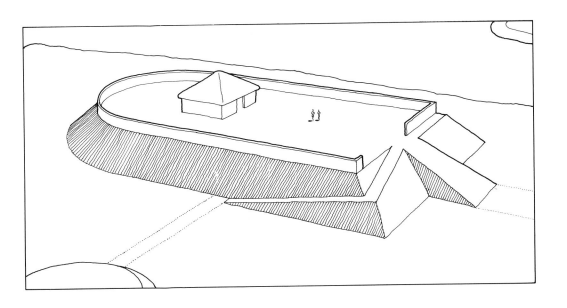

Florida Area

Shields

Jacksonville, Florida

The reconstruction of these unique earthworks on Mill Cove near Newcastle Island is based on the survey of F. W. Bruce and the detailed account of M. G. Miller accompanying Clarence B. Moore's report of 1895. The site is a high bluff on the south bank of the St. Johns River with a commanding view to the north. Inshore 137 meters the major sand mound rose about 5.5 meters, from a 65-meter-wide base to a platform 35 by 40 meters. In 1895 the mound's corners appeared rounded although originally they may have been square. A lower oval platform or apron engaged the major mound's north slope.

From the south face of the Shields mound a ramp 30 meters wide and 30 centimeters high proceeded southward 153 meters, diminishing in width to 6 meters and increasing in height to more than 4 meters. At this point the ramp turned sharply westerly and descended northward to grade. To the west of this ramp, 26

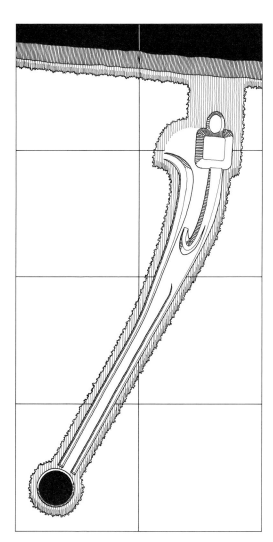

meters, a second embankment ran southward from the river, forming a basin below grade, where sand may have been quarried to construct the earthworks. The two slightly converging ridges "continued southward with [6 meter] widths elevated [15 to 25 centimeters] above grade to a point at which they became lost in the surrounding territory. . . . about [540 meters] southwest of the mound lies a small lake, to which the space between the low ridges . . . may have served as a covered way" (Moore, 1895, p. 11). Presumably the term "covered way" referred to an avenue flanked by low parallel ridge mounds, an element also found at nearby Mount Royal. Unfortunately both sites have lost their avenues due to erosion or cultivation.

The Shields mound site probably was occupied between A.D. 1 and 1500. The main structure appears to have served domiciliary purposes during its earlier occupation and subsequently to have become a repository for layered burials, mostly articulated.

Reference: Moore, 1895.

Mount Royal

Welaka, Florida

Near the east bank of the St. Johns River about 5 kilometers south of Welaka lie the remains of Mount Royal, its sunken avenue, and its artifical lake. The accounts of John Bartram (1769, of a 1766 visit), his son, William (1958, of a 1771 visit); Squier and Davis (1848), and Moore (1894 and 1896) provide conflicting dimensions for the earthworks. In the absence of thorough archeological examination to date, this reconstruction is based on a composite from these sources, which agree on the basic spatial arrangement. According to Moore, the conical mound was about 54 meters in base diameter and 6 meters high, although erosion may have reduced its original height. The approximately 800-meter-long avenue had a level floor, 46 meters wide, sunken below adjacent grade, and flanked by 60-centimeter-high embankments. The artificial lake measured at most 91 by 137 meters, with embankments 3.7 meters wide and 76 centimeters high.

Concerning Mount Royal, William Bartram wrote, ". . . what greatly contributed toward the magnificence of the scene, was a noble Indian

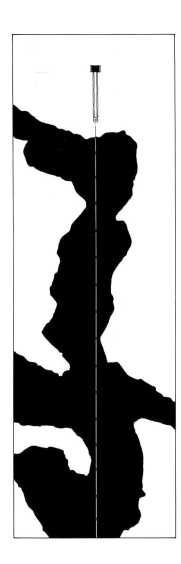

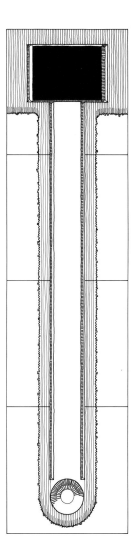

highway, which led from the great mount, on a straight line, . . . first through a point or wing of the Orange grove, and continuing thence through an awful forest, of Live Oaks, it was terminated by Palms and Laurel Magnolias, on the verge of an oblong artificial lake, which was on the edge of an extensive green level savanna . . . This grand highway was . . . sunk a little below the common level . . . Neither nature nor art, could any where present a more striking contrast as you approach this savanna. The glittering water pond plays on the sight, through the dark grove, like a brilliant diamond, on the bottom of the illumined savanna, bordered with a various flowery shrubs and plants; and as we advance into the plain, the sight is agreeably relieved by a distant view of the forests, which partly environ the green expanse on the left hand, whilst the imagination is still flattered and entertained by the far distant misty points of the surrounding forests."

Reference: Squier and Davis, 1848, figures 24 and 25.

Lake Jackson

Tallahassee, Florida

The Lake Jackson site consisted of six and possibly seven mounds on the southwest shore of McGinnis Arm about 7 kilometers north of Tallahassee. In recent decades the lake has been receding, and today it has become a marsh closer to the shore. High sloping bluffs rise to the south of the site and continue around the perimeter of a 16-kilometer-long valley. Oak and gum trees abound. There is a beautiful view of the lake and valley to the north from the major mound's platform. The soil is clay, more common to nearby Georgia than to most of Florida, where sand is more frequently found.

The largest truncated pyramid, located near the center of the group, rose to a height of about 8 meters from a 48-by-65-meter base. Originally a ramp may have led down from its northeast corner. The architectural relationship of the major mound to its surrounding mounds is suggested by three open spaces: two square spaces to the east and west and a rectilinear space to the north in the approximate proportion of 4 to 7.

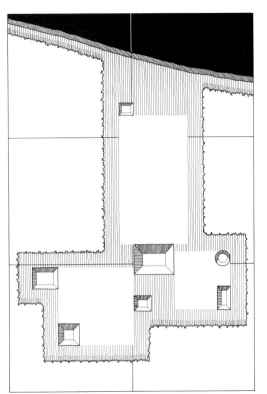

The west group consisted of a 3- to 4-meter-high mound with a 34-by-43-meter base at the northwest corner and two smaller mounds to the south. Between the two-meter-high northernmost mound and the main group, midden remains indicate an intensive village occupation. The southeasternmost mound was originally a clearly shaped truncated pyramid, 3 meters high, with steep sides. The 1-meter-high circular rise may have been a burial mound, but evidence of domiciliary structures also has been found.

Some of the Lake Jackson mounds appear to have been constructed by building up several successive layers of sand and middens, each capped by a red clay mantle. The site was occupied between 1300 A.D. and historic times and served as the political and religious center for small surrounding villages. In each village a small mound and nearby single-family farm plots have been found. Late period 3 burials with embossed copper breastplates have also been found recently at Lake Jackson.

Reference: Willey, 1949B.

Long Key

St. Petersburg Beach, Florida

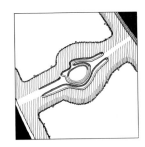

Long Key is an island, 8 kilometers long and about half a kilometer wide, located between the Gulf of Mexico and Boca Ciega Bay. Pass-a-Grille Channel lies to the south and Blind Pass lies to the north. Near the center of the island, a peninsula, about 600 meters long, projects southeasterly into the bay. The avenues suggested in this reconstruction lead to the bay on the northeast and southwest shores of the peninsula, but an accurate measure of their lengths has not been made.

When Clarence B. Moore located the earthworks, dense thickets surrounded the site. The oval mound was slightly more than a meter high and measured approximately 30 by 21 meters. The construction material was white sand. Midway to the summit, the oval appeared to be surrounded by a circumambulation that was connected, on the north, to a raised flat-topped embankment or causeway extending toward the northeast. To the south a second embankment flanked the oval to form an access at grade level, suggesting a processional way, about 3 meters wide to the northeast and 6 meters wide to the southwest.

The purpose of the earthworks is obscure. The only burial found apparently was a later intrusion. No artifacts were found. Moore mentioned no related earthworks or habitation sites in the area. Other Gulf Coast sites near Long Key included in this study are Crystal River and Terra Ceia.

Reference: Moore, 1903.

Philip

Marion Haven, Florida

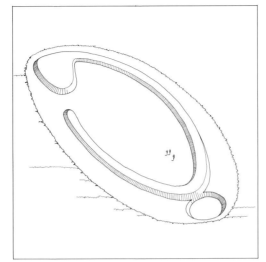

This 26-by-76-meter oval composition was located to the east of Lake Marion near Marion Creek. The oval-shaped mound to the east was 12.2 by 15.2 meters at its base and 1.2 meters in height. A ramp, which varied in height from 1.1 to 1.2 meters and in width from 3.7 to 4.6 meters, connected the mound to a 6.1-meter-diameter excavation to the west. At one time the excavation may have contained water. The ramp then continued back to the mound, stopping 1.5 meters short to form an entryway into the enclosure.

Earth for the structures was taken from the mound perimeter, the enclosure, and the excavation. Burial fragments, shell dippers, and ceramics were found at the site, which seems related to Shields and Mount Royal.

Reference: Benson, 1967.

Turtle

New Smyrna Beach, Florida

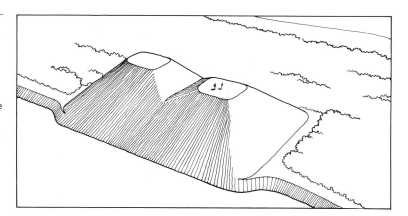

The Turtle Mound site lies on the east bank of the Intracoastal Waterway about 14.5 kilometers south of New Smyrna Beach. The Atlantic Ocean is a short distance to the east. Oaks, palmettos, hollies, and other coastal vegetation stabilize the surrounding dunes, which are subject to erosion. Yaupon plants grow on the mound's steep sides. It was from these or similar leaves that the Indians made the Black Drink, a ceremonial emetic.

Over a period of centuries the original inhabitants harvested oysters and discarded shells to form the structures at Turtle. Shells produce several times the volume of fill that a village midden would produce and, by firmly interlocking, maintain relatively steep sides. Whether the two summits were originally conical, rectangular, or amorphous middens is largely unknown due to lack of information and continuing erosion (Jerald T. Milanich, personal communication, 1978). Today the south summit stands approximately 13.5 meters high and the north summit

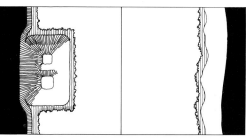

stands about 1.5 meters higher. Other shell structures in this study were found at Sapelo, Fig Island, Crystal River, Tick Island, and Terra Ceia.

Last used by the Timuquans, Turtle Mound may have served as a refuge from floods during hurricanes or coastal storms, an observation post, a signal platform, or a navigational reference.

Reference: Folsom, 1974.

Terra Ceia

Bradenton, Florida

The Terra Ceia site consists of an oblong ceremonial mound and two round burial mounds with
causeways connected to extensive village middens. The site is on low-lying terrain, at most 3
meters above the surrounding tidal areas of
lower Tampa Bay. Terra Ceia apparently was
first occupied some time after A.D. 1 and was
used by a comparatively small population until
about A.D. 1600. The hypothesis that this was
Uctica, the village occupied by De Soto after his
landing in 1539, appears unlikely. Mangrove
swamps lie along the shoreline to the south and
northeast of the site. Principal food sources were
fish, crabs, clams, conchs, and oysters taken
from the warm, shallow waters of Miguel Bay to
the west. The village middens also yielded bones
from deer, bear, alligators, turtles, birds, and
rabbits.

The northern habitation area, reported to have
been about 6 meters above the bay and a hectare in area, has been extensively quarried.

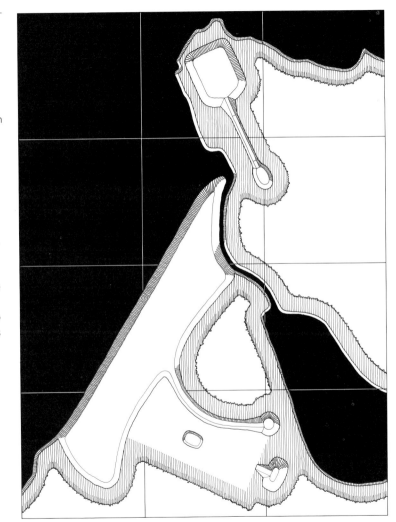

Here midden remains indicate occupation between A.D. 1450 and 1650. About 130 meters to the southeast is an oblong burial mound, approximately 1 meter high and 18 by 27 meters in plan. A causeway, elevated 46 centimeters above grade and more than 3 meters wide, connected the burial mound with the northern midden.

The southern village midden extended for 500 meters along Miguel Bay, exceeding 4 meters in height and varying from 68 to 136 meters in width. This midden was constructed by a small population over a period of possibly 800 years. A curving causeway was reported once to have connected the midden with the southern burial structure, the Prine mound, a 30-meter-wide conical knoll constructed by reshaping and augmenting a natural sand dune. Further to the south an

oblong ceremonial mound named Madira Bickel rose 6 meters from a 34-by-51-meter base. A ceremonial structure was built on its 8-by-21-meter platform. A ramp led down northwesterly to a hard-surfaced, level field that may have been a ball court or ceremonial plaza. Madira Bickel mound was built in several stages sometime after the burial mounds were constructed. In addition, the remains of a small shell midden were found midway between Madira Bickel mound and the southern habitation midden.

Reference: Bullen, 1951.

Big Mound City

Indiantown, Florida

Big Mound City was an intricate geometric arrangement of mounds and earthworks located 10 kilometers east of Lake Okeechobee in an area where the edge of the Everglades meets the higher ground of the pine woods. Eight mounds were connected to a semicircular embankment, 463 meters in diameter, by radiating causeways. All but one mound had a crescent-shaped embankment. An oval-shaped domiciliary mound, 91 meters long and 10 meters wide, defined the southwesterly edge of the composition. Within the central enclosure were five mounds, ranging in size up to 10.7 meters in diameter and 2.4 meters in height.

The largest mound outside of the main enclosure was 67 meters in diameter at its base and 7.6 meters high. It lay at the north end of a 39.6-by-186-meter court, which was elevated 1 meter above grade and flanked by 2.7-meter-high parallel causeways. A low semicircular embankment flanked the mound to the north. The second largest mound, 33.5 meters in diameter and 3.7 meters in height, was connected by two parallel causeways to the main enclosure. Between the largest and second largest mounds, a semicircular enclosure flanked a 76-centimeter-high oval mound that was connected to the main enclosure by three parallel causeways. The two westernmost mounds have parallel causeways in this reconstruction, but today extensive erosion has eliminated traces of these features. Additional mounds and earthworks lay to the south and west, but their relationship, if any, to the main composition is unclear.

The principal construction material was yellow and white sand except for the elongated domiciliary mound, which contained extensive midden remains. The earthworks may have served to elevate building foundations above the surrounding ground, which is flooded six months of the year.

The earliest time of activity at Big Mound City may have been about 500 B.C. Although the master plan appears to have been conceived all

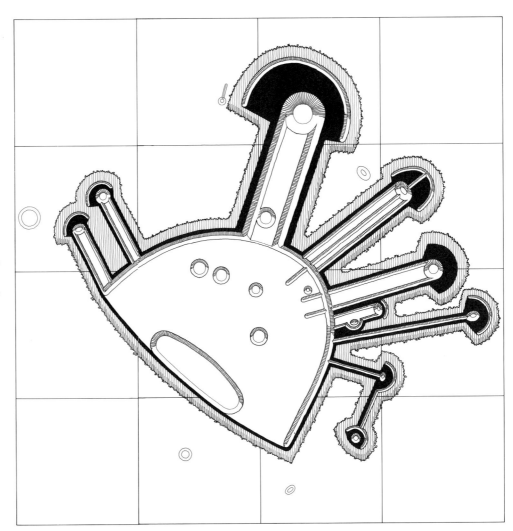

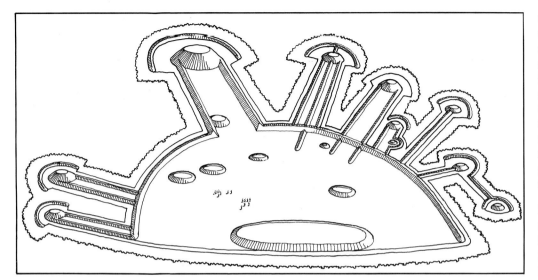

at one time, actual construction may have occurred over an extended period. Activity at the
site continued until the time of Spanish contact
about A.D. 1650, a chronology similar to that of
Fort Center on the opposite side of Lake Okeechobee. The last occupants of Big Mound City
were Calusas, who probably used the site primarily as a ceremonial center. Articulated burial
remains have been found in two mounds. Presumably temples or residences may have occupied some of the platforms, but evidence remains
to be found.

Due to its remoteness, Big Mound City has escaped major vandalism, cultivation, and quarrying, and recently has been added to the National
Registry of Historic Places. Continuing archaeological investigation may broaden our understanding of Big Mound City's original architectural characteristics.

Reference: Willey, 1949C.

Big Tonys

Clewiston, Florida

Big Tonys was located on a grassy prairie about 24 kilometers south-southwest of the Clewiston airport when Ross Allen visited it in early 1946. This reconstruction is based on his account including a sketch map and aerial photographs, published in 1948. While similarities exist between this site and two other South Florida sites in this study, Fort Center and Big Mound City, an accurate survey and more precise data on Big Tonys is needed.

The site lay between a deep sawgrass waterway to the northeast and a cypress swamp about 5 kilometers to the southwest. A 3- to 4.6-meter-wide embankment, 177 meters in diameter and 507 meters in perimeter, formed a semicircle around an area of low ground. Elevated embankments that were about 2 meters wide connected eight mounds with the semicircular enclosure. More than nineteen mounds and features were noted; some may have been natural formations. Tonys Mound measured 25 by 33.5 meters

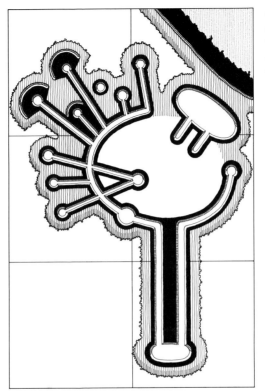

and lay 183 meters to the south of the semicircle. The two structures were linked by parallel 9-meter-wide linear earthworks set 21 meters apart. The excavation between the embankments formed a canal. In the semicircle's opening to the northeast was a 41-by-119-meter habitation site. Allen noted crescent-shaped earthworks beyond the outer mounds, three of which appeared in his aerial photographs and are shown in this reconstruction. Another large mound was noted about 400 meters to the northwest.

Allen observed that Big Tonys was located ideally near a waterway providing transportation and fishing, near attractive hammocks providing good hunting and palm materials for construction, and near cypress swamps abounding with deer and wild turkeys. Whether the site was used for habitation, ceremonialism, agricultural production, or other purposes is not known. Allen suggested that the excavations may have been interconnected to form a network of canals for water transportation linking habitation sites because the area was subject to flooding during wet seasons.

Reference: Allen, 1948.

Comparable Sites

Stonehenge
Trelleborg
Giza
Acropolis
Teotihuacán
Monte Albán
Angkor Wat
Piazza San Marco
Piazza San Pietro
Vieux Carré
Savannah
White House

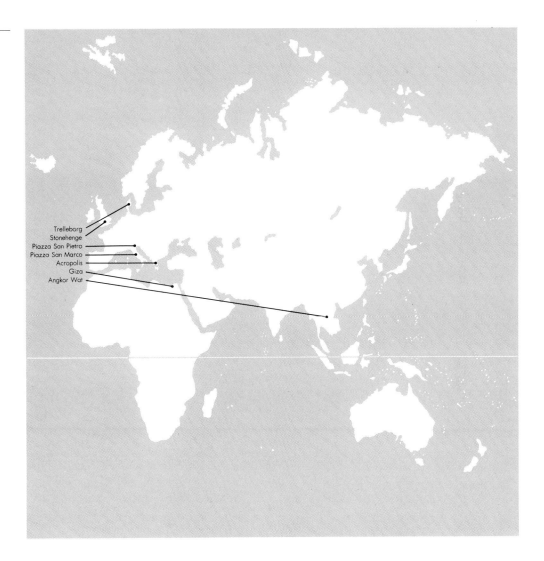

White House
Savannah
Vieux Carré
Teotihuacán
Monte Albán

On the following pages, twelve sites outside of the study area are presented for comparison with prehistoric American architecture. Each site is presented on a 200-meter square grid with north oriented toward the top of the page, and each description is followed by the name of a publication containing additional information. The sites are grouped generally according to geographical and chronological relationships.

The selection of these comparative examples was based on the reader's probable familiarity with the sites, availability of site plans and data, geographical and cultural diversity, and scale or conceptual similarities with sites in the prehistoric Eastern United States. Brief descriptions stress similarities rather than differences: Although widely separated by time, geography, and levels of cultural development, sites in this study share with the comparable sites certain conceptions that are easier to understand by comparing the two.

Except as noted, the comparable sites establish special senses of place, relate their physical elements to dominant topographical features, emphasize movement through space, and, perhaps most importantly, make architectural statements that subsume the ideas, concerns, and ambitions of their period and culture. At Stonehenge the aim was to capture the order of cosmic movement and ritually ensure the continuity of the seasonal life cycle. At Monte Albán, these aims were fused with the wish to reach heavenward in a claim for divine benevolence. At both Monte Albán and Teotihuacán artificial, stone-cased hills of pyramidal shape supported temples or observatories. At Giza the symbolic form of the pyramid was reserved for monumental royal burial mounds.

If one can sense something of the Egyptian search for immutable order and everlasting stability at Giza, a different, more dynamic kind of order comes across on the Acropolis of Athens. Here one becomes aware of measured perfection as part of the Greek ideal and, at the same time, the very direct manner in which the practical needs for protection were met by fortification. These needs are also met at the moated Khmer temple-citadel of divine kingship at Angkor and the fortified Viking camp at Trelleborg, whence the long boats set out on their ferocious raids.

Angkor Wat and Trelleborg rely as much on the accurate geometry of their layout as Bernini's piazza, built centuries later in front of St. Peters. The encompassing monumentality of St. Peter's piazza and the Piazza San Marco splendidly recall the unique contribution that Rome and Venice have made to European cultural tradition. In the same manner, the urbanity of Savannah's squares or the Vieux Carré in New Orleans recall traditions that, in their way, have become as essential to the built American environment as the traditions reflected in the monumental urbanism of Washington, D.C., where a traditional layout was made to serve revolutionary ideas and new purposes.

Stonehenge

Amesbury, England

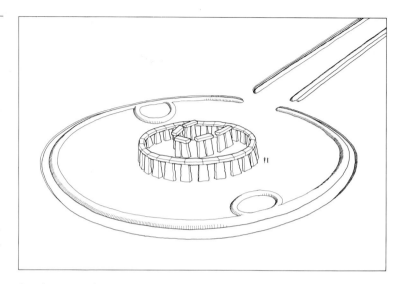

Four kilometers west of Amesbury is Stonehenge, a ceremonial site consisting of a moated embankment, 107 meters in diameter, enclosing a circular stone colonnade that surrounds a horseshoe of trilithons. According to radiocarbon dating, the sacred enclosure was erected primarily in three phases between about 1900 and 1550 B.C. and was used until about 1200 B.C. The earliest ceremonial structure was the circular embankment and moat. A single opening in the embankment led to a wooden structure in the center. Fifty-six holes containing human cremations were set at regular intervals just inside the embankment.

About 1800 B.C., a stone structure was erected in the central area and the entry was altered to align with the avenue, which was flanked by moated embankments leading to the river Avon 4 kilometers east of Stonehenge. This reconstruction suggests the appearance of the site about 1550 B.C.

Circular moated embankments associated with burials have been found at Marietta, Dublin, Bainbridge, South Charleston, New Castle, and other sites in the prehistoric Eastern United States. Avenues defined by embankments occurred at Newark, High Bank, Portsmouth "C," Shields, Mount Royal, and other sites. The monumental shell rings of Sapelo and Fig Island were constructed about the same time as Stonehenge.

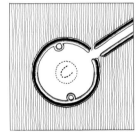

Reference: Hawkes, 1974.

Trelleborg

Slagelse, Denmark

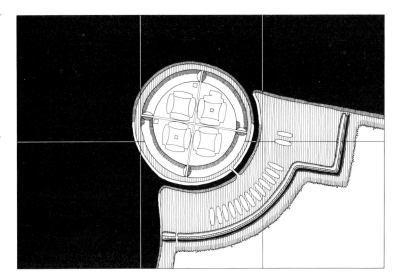

The fortified Viking encampment shown here was constructed in the latter half of the tenth century A.D. in Western Zealand, Denmark. Although the site today is surrounded by fields, it was originally a cape projecting into shallow water. Trelleborg's circular enclosure was a 4.9-meter-high embankment, 172 meters in diameter, with a moat around its inshore perimeter. A second moated embankment formed a concentric arc to the south and east, widening to enclose the site's cemetery. Two timber palisades originally lined the outer embankment, one on the inside and one on the outside. Fifteen wooden longhouses were arranged radially between the inner and outer embankments.

To enter the circular enclosure, the Vikings crossed the moat by way of a bridge from the southeast, then continued along a level passage between the moat and embankment to the east or south gates, which were roofed passageways. Within the enclosures, they continued along a boardwalk that interconnected the four entries and divided the interior space into quadrants.

Each quadrant contained four longhouses arranged around an open square. In the centers of the northeast and southwest squares were small wooden structures, similar structures were located inside the north and west entries. The steeply sloping rafters of the longhouses apparently were supported by vertical wood trench walls and were securely embedded in the earth at one end to eliminate interior posts.

Circular enclosures with moats have been found at Dublin, Bainbridge, New Castle, and other period 2 sites, but their moats lay within the embankments, suggesting ceremonial rather than military purposes. The shell ring enclosures of Sapelo and Fig Island, constructed about three millenia before Trelleborg, were smaller in size and apparently were used for ceremonial rather than domiciliary purposes.

Reference: Hawkes, 1974.

Giza

Cairo, Egypt

Several centuries before shell rings are known to have been under construction in Georgia, the pyramids of Giza were constructed on the west bank of the Nile River. During the second quarter of the third millenium B.C., three tombs were erected for fourth-dynasty pharaohs on a plateau at the edge of the limitless desert. Cheop's Pyramid, the northernmost and largest of the precise stone-faced monuments, rose 146.7 meters above its 230-meter square base. Mycerinus's Pyramid, the southernmost and smallest of the three, is not shown here.

Chephren's Pyramid, the second largest, is typical of the group. From the riverbank it was originally approached from the east along a processional way leading to the Valley Temple, which contained statues of the dead king and was probably used for purification and funerary rites. The eastward-staring Sphinx and its temple lay immediately to the north. From the Valley Temple a causeway led to the Mortuary Temple, where, from the courtyard, the top of Chephren's pyramid could be seen. Apparently the pyramid symbolized eternal life to the ancient Egyptians. Around the pyramid were tombs of Chephren's courtiers and officials.

At Sakkara, more than a century earlier, Zoser's Step Pyramid had been completed. The 60-meter-high, six-tiered structure suggested visual similarities with Monks Mound, Falling Garden, and other multiterraced truncated pyramids of the prehistoric Eastern United States. Like the ancient Egyptians, the prehistoric Americans apparently were more preoccupied with religious and funerary ceremonialism than with enclosing interior space. By comparison, Cheop's Pyramid was about two-thirds the area of Monks Mound and almost half again as high. Chephren's causeway was slightly shorter than the causeway at Shields. Poverty Point's earthworks originally contained about seventeen times the volume of Cheop's Pyramid. Both the ancient Egyptians and the prehistoric Americans sometimes embellished their important structures with carved wood portals and colorful murals on stucco, and both closely related their architectural compositions to dominant topographical features.

Reference: Edwards, 1975.

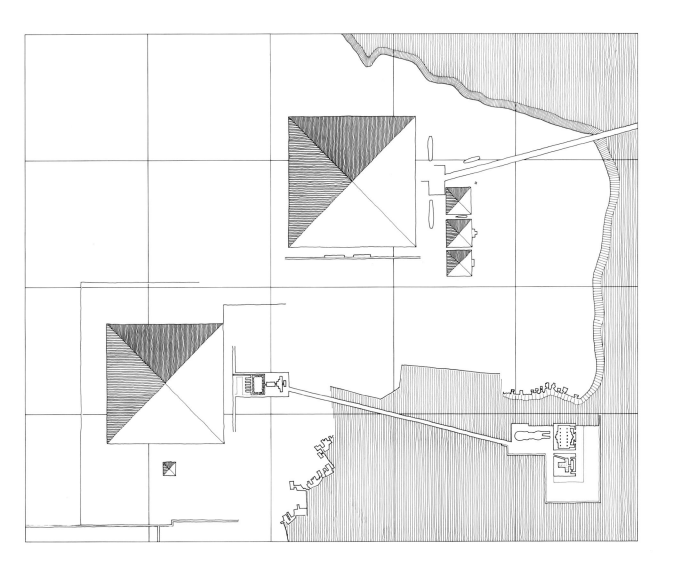

Acropolis

Athens, Greece

Between 600 and 479 B.C., Athens was contained within the perimeter enclosure shown in this reconstruction. Near the center was the Acropolis, a high plateau where, between 447 and 405 B.C., the Propylaea, the Erechtheum, and the Parthenon were built, forming a sacred precinct. About 200 meters northwest of the Acropolis was the Agora, Athens's marketplace, which evolved from an amorphous shape in 600 B.C. to a well-defined space by 400 B.C. Through the Agora, the Panathenaic Way led up the steep side of the Acropolis, through the Propylaea, past the Erechtheion, and around to the east end of the Parthenon, where processional groups assembled while their priests entered the sacred chamber containing the statue of Athena.

Greek and prehistoric American architecture share several similar conceptions: site organization with respect to dominant topographical features, movement through space in a sequence of experiences, and ceremonial areas often set apart from secular activities. Architectural elements were set in space like sculptures to be seen from many views but not to be entered by the populace. In land area early Athens was similar in size to the island on which Angel was built and to the area occupied by the central earthworks of Poverty Point. The Acropolis is slightly larger than the shaped, natural hill of Emerald and slightly smaller than the plateau of Anna. Spiro and Athens both are composed of two clearly separated zones. The linking together of separated areas, like the linking of the Agora and the Acropolis, was a characteristic of large period 2 enclosures in the Ohio Valley.

Like the early Greeks, the prehistoric Americans sometimes evolved their compositions over an extended period of time. Although their differences were many, both people exhibited the ability to conceive and execute large-scale projects in close harmony with their natural environments, an art lost in twentieth-century America.

Reference: Bacon, 1974.

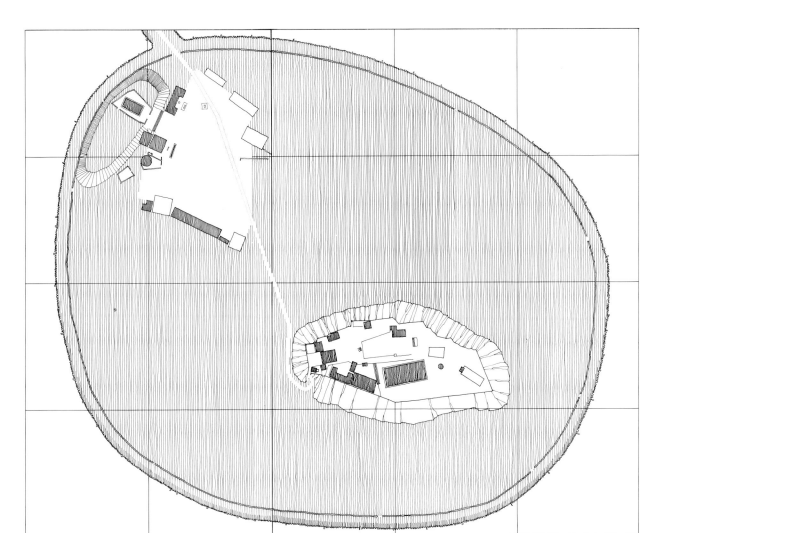

Teotihuacán

Mexico City, Mexico

Between 150 B.C. and A.D. 750, Teotihuacan became one of the largest centers in Mesoamerica, possibly exceeded in size only by Tenochtitlán. Although the extent of Teotihuacán's political control is not known, between A.D. 300 and 750 the city influenced the art and architecture of many Mesoamerican centers, including Kaminaljuyú in Guatemala. By A.D. 600, Teotihuacán had expanded to 20 square kilometers with possibly as many as 85,000 inhabitants. At the height of its development, the city apparently contained more than 500 craft workshops and 20,000 residences.

Early in its development, Teotihuacán was laid out in quadrants on a 57-meter square module. Through the center of the site was the Avenue of the Dead, oriented 15.5 degrees east of north and terminated in the north by the Plaza of the Moon, shown here. To the south were administrative and ceremonial compounds from which emanated west and east avenues, 90.0 and 91.5

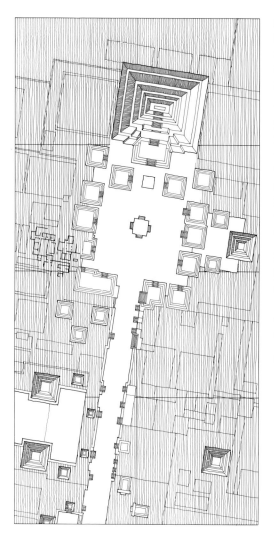

degrees to the Avenue of the Dead, respectively. From the city's center northward along the 45-meter-wide Avenue of the Dead were a series of extended terraces and, on the east, the Pyramid of the Sun, Teotihuacán's largest structure.

The symmetrical Plaza of the Moon was elevated 27 meters above the city's center. It was flanked by stone-faced pyramids, each composed of four-level platforms, which originally were topped by temples. The 46-meter-high Pyramid of the Moon consisted of four terraces and was 379,100 cubic meters in volume. A level platform projected from the pyramid into the plaza, emphasizing the broad entry stairs.

Harriet M. Smith (1973) and James A. Marshall (1969 and 1979) suggest that the 57-meter module, or a fraction or multiple of it, may have influenced the planning of some prehistoric earthworks in the Eastern United States, but a direct connection remains to be proved.

Reference: Millon, 1970.

Monte Albán

Oaxaca, Mexico

On a commanding plateau 360 meters above the valley of Oaxaca lie the remains of Monte Albán, a Zapotec urban center. The site was continuously occupied during the millenium preceding European contact, but major building activity occurred between A.D. 200 and 900, when the Zapotecs constructed platforms, tombs, palaces, courts, shrines, and related structures. Natural rock outcroppings and earlier structures sometimes were incorporated into the bases of the structures arranged around and within a 200-by-300-meter central plaza parallel to the ridge of an adjacent hill. Level terraces stepped down the eastern slope. For several kilometers along the ridge was an extensive complex of structures that, for the most part, have not been reconstructed.

Toward the south and near the middle of Monte Albán's plaza, the so-called observatory was placed in an orientation clearly different from that of the other structures. The central structure of Fatherland also obeyed a geometry of its own

for reasons that are not clear. In terms of size and complexity, Monte Albán is similar to Moundville, which consisted of twenty truncated pyramids arranged around a central plaza in several minor groups. Like Anna and Emerald, Monte Albán was placed on a natural eminence with a commanding view of a river valley. Cahokia's main plaza was subdivided into two smaller areas by minor structures, just as Monte Albán's plaza was divided by buildings.

No site in the prehistoric Eastern United States, however, possesses the magnificently carved stonework, architectural sophistication, and extraordinary setting of Monte Albán. Describing the site, Aldous Huxley (1934) wrote: "Few architects have had such a sense of austerely dramatic grandeur. Few have been given so free a hand. Religious considerations were never allowed to interfere with realization of a grand architectural scheme." Fortunately, Monte Albán escaped the attention of early Spaniards and has survived as an excellent example of Zapotec architecture.

Reference: Bernal, 1962.

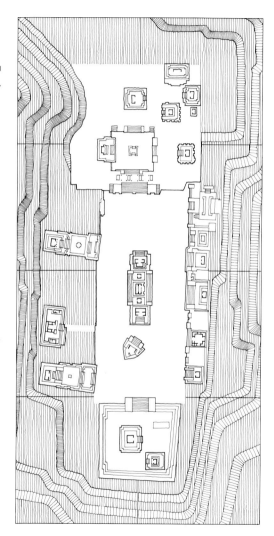

Angkor Wat

Siem Reap, Cambodia

At the time Cahokia was in the midst of its building activity and Gothic cathedrals were beginning to rise in France, the Khmers built one of the world's largest religious structures, Angkor Wat. Between A.D. 1112 and 1152, they created a moat around an 800-by-1,100-meter island with a causeway flanked by sculpted balustrades. Beyond the portalway and the raised ceremonial way flanked by two artificial lakes was the cruciform entry platform. Through the gallery enclosing the complex was an outer courtyard surrounding the central courtyard. From the central courtyard, steep stairs led to the inner terrace, containing the inner shrine with a 65-meter-high tower. The entire ensemble was conceived as a series of ascending terraces within a lake, symbolizing Mount Mehru, the home of Hindu gods worshipped by the Khmers. The extensive bas-reliefs embellishing the mausoleum/shrine portrayed Khmer epics appropriate to their grandest monument. Architectural influences from India were reinterpreted in Cambodia according to the local characteristics of the Khmers.

The causeway flanked by two lakes at Fitzhugh is similar to Angkor Wat's in conception and scale. The main shrine group of Angkor Wat is slightly smaller in area than Monks Mound, but its central tower probably rose higher than the ridge of Cahokia's main temple. Like the Khmers, the architects of Big Tonys and Big Mound City apparently employed watercourses and platforms elevated above low-lying terrain, utilizing a technology that apparently had been developed originally for agriculture. Angkor Wat's ceremonial island is about the size of the area within the main palisades of central Cahokia. Like the Khmers, the prehistoric Americans apparently reinterpreted influences from outside of their regions, emphasized movement through a sequence of spaces, reserved high places for important structures, and sometimes separated religious precincts from secular areas.

Reference: Groslier and Arthaud, 1957.

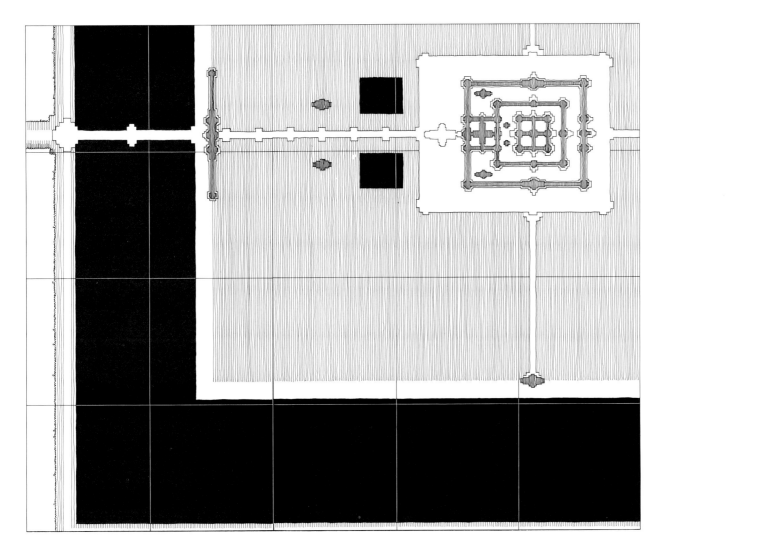

Piazza San Marco

Venice, Italy

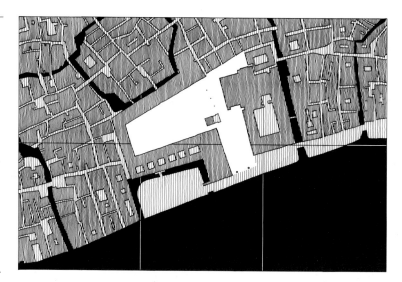

Venice was founded in the fifth century A.D. on the lagoon islands at the north end of the Adriatic Sea as a refuge from the barbarians. After five centuries of Byzantine rule, Venice attained its independence and developed its maritime interest to become a major European commercial center. The city's Piazza San Marco was constructed over a period of several centuries, symbolizing Venice's prosperity and orientation to the sea.

Toward the east end of the piazza lies the dominant structure, the Cathedral of San Marco. Arriving by gondola from the south, the cathedral is across the piazzetta, which is almost as large as the piazza itself. Moving around the pivotal bell tower, the entire space is visible.

Both the Piazza San Marco and the Piazza San Pietro illustrate European town planning ideas that are clearly different from those of the prehistoric Eastern United States. European cities were much more densely populated. Their plazas were defined by vertical planes of adjoining buildings in the case of the Piazza San Marco and flanking colonnades in the case of the Piazza San Pietro. These buildings, facades, and colonnades were constructed of masonry materials, utilizing a type of construction which is not found in the prehistoric Eastern United States.

Like the Venetians, the prehistoric Americans usually set their major structures to the side or at one end of their plazas and seldom in it. Monks Mound, for example, dominated the north end of Cahokia's main plaza. Most of the major spaces and structures of Venice and Cahokia were constructed during the same chronological period. Like Venice, many prehistoric American sites evolved over a period of centuries and were oriented toward waterways that apparently facilitated trade and communications.

Reference: Bacon, 1974.

Piazza San Pietro

Rome, Italy

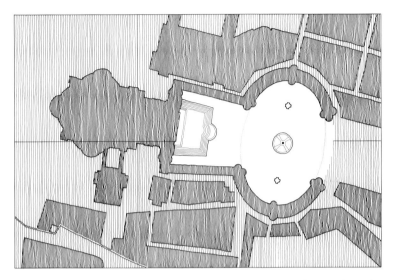

Between A.D. 1656 and 1667, the monumental baroque forecourt of St. Peter's Basilica in Rome was built according to Bernini's design. The piazza consists of a trapezoid opening into an oval, which is centered on an obelisk flanked by two symmetrically arranged fountains. A screen of columns defines the space to the north and south, emphasizing the Basilica to the west, which dominates the composition. Upon entering the slightly bowl-shaped piazza one can see not only the basilica and its colonnades but also as many as 300,000 spectators assembled on special occasions. To complete the composition, Bernini designed the opening to the east for an enclosing screen of columns, set out slightly from the oval's perimeter. In 1937, Mussolini ill-advisedly extended the Via della Conciliazione toward the center of Rome, creating a never intended axial movement through the piazza.

Symmetry, represented by the axial composition of the Piazza San Pietro, and asymmetry, represented by the plan of the Piazza San Marco,

appear in the designs of many sites and structures in the prehistoric Eastern United States, although never with the high level of sophistication found in European achievements of corresponding chronological periods. On both continents, plazas and other urban open spaces were principal elements of site designs and were used on special occasions for the assembly of large groups of people. According to early French observers, the south plaza at Fatherland served as

a kind of outdoor theater for the community to observe the ceremonial burial of a revered leader.

Like St. Peter's Basilica and Piazza, prehistoric American architecture often evolved over an extended period of time, involving changing functional requirements and design solutions. Civic spaces flanked by minor elements and dominated by a major structure appeared at Cahokia and many other prehistoric American sites.

Reference: Bacon, 1974.

Vieux Carré

New Orleans, Louisiana

The Vieux Carré is the historic old city in the center of New Orleans, which was founded by Bienville in 1718 and named for the Duke of Orleans, then regent of France. The city was created to serve as a trading post and administrative center for French commercial development in the New World. Following a period of unplanned and undisciplined growth, the military engineers De La Tour and De Pauger, in 1722, laid out the plan of the city on the northwest bank of the Mississippi River near a prehistoric portage route: a gridiron of 91.4-meter square blocks deriving its orientation from the axis of the river. The center block closest to the river was the public square with a church facing the river, as shown in this reconstruction. From the central plaza, the city was to extend four blocks in both directions and extend six blocks inshore, but this soon increased to a total of eleven blocks by six blocks, encompassing the entire 105 hectares of the Vieux Carré. In the symmetrical plan important public buildings were located on both sides

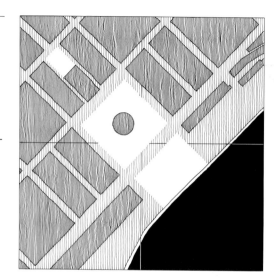

of the Church of St. Louis and on the flanks of the Place d'Armes, now called Jackson Square. Early residences were placed near the river, where the terrain was slightly higher, access to the water was convenient, and breezes were favorable. Typically residences were placed near streetfronts and had interior courts or gardens, some of which survive today.

Reference: Wilson, 1968.

Savannah

Savannah, Georgia

The classical rationalism of Vitruvius, a Roman architect of the first century B.C., and Renaissance architects such as Cattaneo and Scamozzi were well known to the designers of colonial towns in the New World. In 1733, James Oglethorpe laid out a beautiful and functional plan for a new town on the south bank of the Savannah River. The site's dominant topographical feature was the high bluff along the river. At a right angle to the bluff, a major street extended through the center of the plan and into the wilderness beyond, establishing the axis for continuing development for the next 120 years.

Oglethorpe's design was based on a basic cell approximately 200 meters square with a civic open space in its center. By 1856, the original four cells had grown to twenty-six and the expanded city was restructured along the riverbank by adding a city hall, Factor's Walk, and warehouses, most of which are preserved today. The

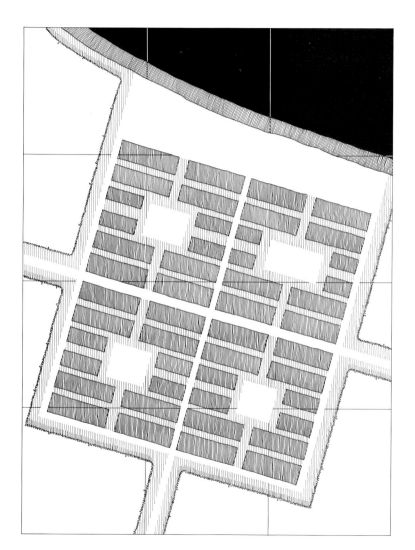

design meets the practical requirement of movement through the city with a gridiron of unobstructed streets between the cells. The consistent network of parks provides visual delight in two directions rather than in a single direction along a dominant axis, such as in Washington, D.C., and Paris.

In the prehistoric Eastern United States, the St. Louis site was composed of three open spaces in an orthogonal plan oriented with respect to the nearby Mississippi River. Parkin, Upper Nodena, and other settlements appear to have contained clearly defined open spaces in a fabric of structures. Like Savannah, many prehistoric settlements appear to have been oriented with respect to nearby watercourses or other dominant topographical features. No prehistoric settlements, however, are known to have equalled Savannah's clarity and order, and their plazas in most cases seem to have been much less clearly defined than Savannah's.

Reference: Bacon, 1974.

White House

Washington, D.C.

L'Enfant's plan of 1792 for Washington envisioned a new capital city closely related to its region, with sweeping vistas from the Capitol westward across the Potomac River to the Virginia hills and southward from the White House far down the river. To this end L'Enfant laid out orthogonal axes intersecting northeast of the river near the shoreline of the present-day Tidal Basin. From the axial intersection, the White House was placed 940 meters to the north and the Capitol was placed 2.4 kilometers to the east, with Pennsylvania Avenue interconnecting the two diagonally. L'Enfant's outward-reaching plan depended on exterior space planning and architectural design to achieve its purpose. The river was an integral part of the design conception.

The 1902 McMillan plan for Washington, however, called for a more self-contained design. The Lincoln Memorial obstructed the Capitol's westward view of the river, and the Jefferson

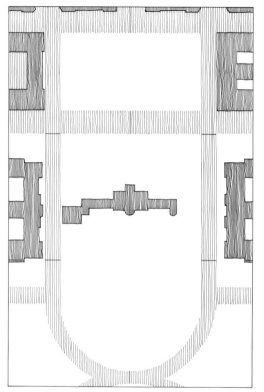

Memorial similarly blocked the southern vista from the White House. Potomac Park extended the land area of the Capitol to the southwest beyond the original shoreline.

The site plan presented here shows the Treasury Building and Old Executive Office Building, the two large structures flanking the White House to the east and west, respectively. Lafayette Park, to the north, is defined by buildings on three sides, forming an open space approximately 280 meters square. The South Lawn extends from the White House to the Ellipse and the Washington Monument.

Prehistoric American architects appear to have preferred a sequence of open spaces, sometimes impressive in size and related to each other hierarchally, such as those at Cahokia, to sweeping views, such as those of Washington. The distance from the White House to the Jefferson Memorial is about 1.8 kilometers and from the Capitol to the Lincoln Memorial is about 3.6 kilometers, compared to the 3.7-by-4.6-kilometer-long axes of Cahokia's diamond-shaped site.

Reference: Bacon, 1974.

Aerial Photographs

Newark
Serpent Mound
Ocmulgee
Marksville
Cahokia
Etowah
Miamisburg

Newark

Smithsonian Institution National Anthropological Archives,
Dache M. Reeves Collection, negative #196, 1934.

Serpent Mound

Marksville

Aerial Photographs

Smithsonian Institution National Anthropological Archives,
Dache M. Reeves Collection, negative #361 (left) and #354
(right), 1935.

Ocmulgee

Cahokia

Smithsonian Institution National Anthropological Archives,
Dache M. Reeves Collection, negative #422, 1936.

Etowah

Miamisburg

Smithsonian Institution National Anthropological Archives,
Dache M. Reeves Collection, negative #91, 1933.

Observations

On the foregoing pages, eighty-two sites constructed in the Eastern United States between about 2200 B.C. and A.D. 1500 have been presented in chronological and geographical groups. At this point it may be valuable to look at these achievements of prehistoric America in a more general way to emphasize certain ideas that may have been obscured by details and consider some questions that remain to be explored. The intent here is not to draw premature conclusions about prehistoric American architecture. This would clearly be a mistake in view of the relative dearth of information on this complex subject. To the student of architecture, the value of Squier and Davis's *Ancient Monuments of the Mississippi Valley* (1848) lies not in the authors' summary speculations but in the main body of the study, the factual presentation of many prehistoric American sites known in the early nineteenth century. This information is illustrated with often verifiable surveys, such as the survey of Newark, which Dache Reeves's aerial photograph clearly verifies. Similarly, Cyrus Thomas's *Twelfth Annual Report of the Bureau of Ethnology to the Secretary of the Smithsonian, 1890–91* contributed significantly to the study of prehistoric architecture in the Eastern United States with descriptions and illustrations of an extensive number of sites. In the light of these distinguished precedents, this study focuses its attention as clearly as possible on the knowledge presently at hand with the view of improving our understanding in the future as additional information becomes available.

Data

Of exceptional importance in the study of prehistoric American architecture is the need for basic data, verifiable facts to substantiate valid theories. The basic construction materials of the eastern North Americas, earth and wood, are subject to erosion and deterioration in a geographical area subject to comparatively high rainfall, floods, and the rapid growth of trees and underbrush. The architectural remains of the comparatively arid Southwestern United States have survived the forces of nature more successfully than those of the Eastern United States, rendering our understanding of the architecture of the former clearer than that of the latter. Our eastern sites require careful investigation, utilizing the most accurate methods available to modern archaeologists and other scholars. New data is now becoming available at a rapid rate, but its collection and analysis requires substantial time and effort. Even with improved support for data collection, these efforts will be of little avail without concomittant efforts to preserve our irreplaceable potential data sources.

Essential to broadening our comprehension of prehistoric architecture is the involvement of architects in the field, the type of involvement that has been successfully undertaken at early sites in Mesoamerica, the Mediterranean, and the Middle East, for example. Interestingly enough, one of the most valuable sources of documentation for preparing this study, *Archaeological Survey in the Lower Yazoo Basin, 1949–1955,* was prepared by Philip Phillips, who trained and practiced as an architect in Buffalo, New York, for some years before turning to archaeology. His insights and presentations make an invaluable contribution to architectural research as well as to archaeology. Another architect who made a significant contribution to the study of prehistoric New World architecture was Frederic Catherwood, who accurately recorded many Mayan sites during two visits to Yucatán with John L. Stevens late in the 1830s and early in the 1840s.

Catherwood's informative drawings illustrate *Incidents of Travel in Yucatán* (Stephens, 1963), an invaluable two-volume record of Mayan architecture.

Origin

Essential to an architectural prehistory of the Eastern United States are the questions of origins, such as when and where man first arrived in the New World and in the study area of this book. The beginning of agriculture often seems to be related to the beginning of formal architecture, but the important questions of when and where maize first was cultivated in the Eastern United States, and what, if any, influences did it have on the development of architecture are still unanswered. In some areas, such as the Southwest Gulf Coast of Florida, uncultivated food sources were readily available and agricultural production seems to have been unnecessary for architectural development. However, the converse seems to be true in most of the study area, such as in the Mississippi Valley, where architecture achieved a particularly high level of attainment during period 3. Agricultural production may also have played a role in the notable architectural achievements of period 2, such as that of Hopewellians in the Ohio Valley.

Another important question concerns the origin of ideas introduced in period 3. Truncated pyramids grouped around orthogonal plazas seems to suggest strongly a Mesoamerican origin, but exactly where and when did this conception appear in the Eastern United States? James A. Marshall (1969 and 1979) suggests that a 57-meter grid may have been the basic unit of planning period 2 earthworks in the Ohio Valley, such as Newark and High Bank. Harriet M. Smith (1973) suggests that fractions and multiples of a 57-meter unit may have influenced the design of Murdock Mound in period 3. René Millon (1967C) observed that, at Teotihuacán, the "basic modular unit of the plan is close to 57 meters. A number of residential structures are squares of this size. The plan of many of the streets seems to repeat various multiples of the 57-meter unit."

Architectural research in the future may shed important light on the question of a possible Mesoamerican connection with the prehistoric Eastern United States, which raises the issue of diffusion versus independent development, the subject of continuing debate among authorities. At the present time no hard data exists to prove direct Mesoamerican involvement in the study area, so I accept the idea of independent development until clear evidence of diffusion from abroad may appear in the future.

Chronology

This study establishes three chronological groups for the architectural ideas in the Eastern United States between about 2200 B.C. and A.D. 1500, based largely on current archaeological data. Because new data is becoming available rapidly, we may expect refinements in this grouping in the near future, quite likely pushing the periods of prehistory in the Eastern United States further back in time. Three decades ago the earliest verifiable evidence of man in North America was dated about 7000 B.C. Today this has been pushed back to 13,000 to 14,000 B.C., and recent discoveries may place man in the United States as early as 36,000 B.C. with even earlier dates possible in the future. Within three decades man's antiquity in the United States has been pushed two to five times further back in time.

Although clearly different in levels of achievement and influence, the architectural developments of the Mediterranean and Europe may be grouped into three chronological periods approximating those of the prehistoric Eastern United States. In 2200 B.C., the Pyramids of Giza had been completed for more than three centuries. Architectural development continued in Egypt and its influences spread northward to the islands and coast of the Mediterranean. Stonehenge and other structures had appeared in northern Europe by 1000 B.C., when Poverty Point was constructed in Louisiana.

Following a period of continuing development, a second period may be thought of as 500 B.C. to A.D. 200, which includes the classical architecture of Greece and the rise of Rome with distinctly new architectural ideas. This corresponds chronologically to the achievements of the Adena-Hopewell people in the Ohio Valley and related but different architectural developments in Tennessee, Lower Mississippi Valley, Florida, and other geographical areas of the Eastern United States.

The transition between period 2 and 3 in the Eastern United States corresponds roughly to the Dark Ages in Europe. By A.D. 800, the Romanesque was emerging in Europe, followed by the Gothic achievements in France and the Renaissance in Italy. During the same chronological period in the Eastern United States, architectural activity flourished in the five geographical areas presented in this study, with broad regional variations, until about A.D. 1500.

Although the chronological parallel between the New and Old Worlds is necessarily simplified, it may help us to understand the general sequence of architectural developments in the prehistoric Eastern United States.

In considering the chronological groupings of this study, it is important to bear in mind that significant architectural activity is known to have occurred at some sites in more than one period, such as in Marietta, Marksville, Pinson, Troyville, Fort Center, and Crystal River. In these cases, the distinguishing architectural characteristics of the site determined its grouping. A parallel here may be found in the architectural history of Rome: The architectural ideas of the Roman Empire and Republic (period 2) were clearly different from, although related to, those of the later Renaissance (period 3).

Hundreds of Archaic (7000– 2000 B.C.) sites are known to have been active in the Eastern United States prior to period 1. Architectural analysis of Archaic sites in the future may warrant their inclusion in a more comprehensive prehistory of architecture in the study area, although their architectural patterns presently are expected to be limited in scope, such as the plan of simple domiciliary structures.

Ceremonial architecture in Mesoamerica seems to have begun about 1000 B.C. in the "Middle Pre-Classic" or "Middle Formative" times, depending on the terminology. Jon Gibson (1974) suggests that the San Lorenzo site in the Veracruz province of central Mexico may date from about 750 B.C., which would have succeeded Poverty Point in Louisiana by about 250 years. Variations in radiocarbon dates, however, leave open the possibility that they may have been built about the same time. Even if these dates were proved, the question of diffusion of ideas versus independent development would remain open unless a direct connection between Mesoamerica and the Eastern United States could be established.

Terminology

The reader who may be somewhat familiar with the prehistory of the Eastern United States may wonder why the term "Adena-Hopewell" might not have been applied to period 2 or "Mississippian" to period 3, two terms frequently appearing in current anthropological literature. These terms are not used here because of the confusion that easily results from their use: They may refer to the cultural characteristics of a particular group of people or a given geographical area or a chronological period. The factors of culture, place, and time must be clearly differentiated in order to understand the development of architecture in the prehistoric Eastern United States.

Preservation

Today prehistoric American sites are disappearing so rapidly that within the foreseeable future almost all seem headed for extinction. The construction of roads, airports, dams with attendant upstream flooding, and similar projects are taking an accelerating toll. Suburban sprawl, industrial complexes, pothunters, and agricultural production contribute further to the eradication of more than three millenia of man's experience in the Eastern United States. Much remains to be learned in terms of architecture, planning, environmental adaptation, and other areas of concern for America today. Salvage archaeology, investigating sites one step ahead of the bulldozer under the pressure to time, diverts our limited scientific resources from an orderly investigation of prehistory. Below the present-day city of St. Louis lie the remains of a notable site. Tick Island, first occupied about 4100 B.C., recently was destroyed to provide oyster shells for a

road bed (Milanich, personal communication, 1979). The list of destruction is incredible and increasingly alarming, suggesting that our national priorities with respect to our irreplaceable prehistoric heritage are in need of immediate reevaluation.

Architectural Research

In the process of preparing this study, several areas for continuing architectural research have appeared. Because fully detailed information was not available on particular aspects of many sites, it would be advisable to verify the assumptions made here in the light of more current information. Substantial information on many sites not included in the study may expand our understanding further. These sites should be considered for inclusion in any future, and possibly enlarged, version of this study.

Structures of wood in the prehistoric Eastern United States deserve a full and systematic analysis. Structures of earth should be more fully explored with regard to internal reinforcement systems, steepness ratios, erosion control, methods of construction, and related factors. Measurement systems appear to have been required to design, lay out, and construct geometrically precise earthworks such as those in the Ohio Valley during period 2; yet the nature of these systems

remains to be explored architecturally. The possible use of sculptures, wall paintings, and other art related to architecture remains to be considered.

A study of overland transportation routes and an investigation of waterways for transportation would further broaden our understanding of how goods and ideas moved within the study area. The extent to which artificial moats, ponds, and natural watercourses were design determinants in prehistoric planning remains to be discerned. Studies of alluvium, silt deposited by running water, would indicate whether moats were water-filled or dry except during floods or heavy rain runoff. These and other questions remain to be explored.

Design Patterns

At the outset of this study we set forward as our objective to present an overview of prehistoric American architecture by synthesizing what is presently known, realizing that we do not know what the prehistoric architects actually intended or what, if anything, they understood their work to mean. The following is an overview of the design patterns that have appeared.

Period 1 The earliest clearly identifiable architectural designs were the circular shell rings found at coastal sites in South Carolina, Georgia, and northeastern Florida. At Sapelo and Fig Island, for example, the geometrically precise rings of various dimensions enclosed central areas apparently set aside for ceremonial purposes. About 1000 B.C., Poverty Point appeared in Louisiana, also arranged concentrically, but in a semicircle rather than a full circle. The large scale and geometric complexity of Poverty Point are its distinguishing characteristics. It is also the earliest example of axiality in the study area, apparently related to the natural bluffline overlooking Bayou Maçon to the east. Period 1 design patterns, including circles, semicircles, enclosures, large-scale plans, radials, and axiality, reappeared with broad variations in many later sites.

Period 2 The Adena earthworks of the Ohio Valley introduced to the study distinctly shaped conical and oval mounds related to burial ceremonialism and large-scale circular enclosures. Examples of these were found at Marietta, High Bank, Portsmouth Group "C," and Miamisburg. Effigy mounds, such as Serpent Mound in Ohio

and Lizard in Wisconsin, are also examples of Adena architecture, although effigies continued to be built by other groups over an extended period of time.

Closely following the Adena culture in the Ohio Valley was the widespread Hopewell culture, characterized by the placement of mounds opposite the breaks in square or octagonal earthworks, such as those at Newark, the central square at Marietta, Oldtown, High Bank, and Seal. Moats on the inner side of curvilinear enclosures were another period 2 characteristic that appeared at Dublin, Bainbridge, Kanawha, South Charleston, and New Castle. The large-scale geometric earthworks of period 2 in the Ohio Valley frequently did not conform to natural terrain.

In Florida during period 2, circular enclosures of increasing diameters appeared at Fort Center, but clear architectural design patterns were difficult to discern at Crystal River and Tick Island. During period 2 in the Lower Mississippi Valley, large-scale semicircular enclosures with outer moats and associated earthworks appeared at Marksville and Spanish Fort. Tchula Lake is a comparatively small-scale group of circular and oval platforms arranged around a circular open

space. Pinson, a very large-scale site in western Tennessee, represents a transition between the architecture of the Ohio Valley to the north and the Lower Mississippi Valley to the south. Pinson's circular mounds and large-scale enclosures are characteristic of period 2, although axial alignments do not appear with the geometric clarity found in other areas.

Period 3 The distinguishing architectural characteristic of almost all period 3 sites is an arrangement of truncated pyramids around a central rectangular plaza. Similar arrangements appeared early and widely in Mesoamerica, but a direct connection with North American developments has not been established.

Upper Mississippi and Ohio Area Except for the St. Louis site, the five important sites of this area continue to exist today. These comparatively large sites had palisaded enclosures and contained rectangular wood residences and truncated pyramids grouped around ceremonial plazas. Monks Mound at Cahokia contained four levels and a small conical platform. The main structures at Angel and Kincaid contained two levels, each with a small conical platform. Falling Garden at St. Louis is reported to have had three ascending platforms set at a right angle to the plaza rather than in a parallel arrangement more frequently found at period 3 sites. The palisades at Cahokia, Angel, Kincaid, and Aztalan contained outward-projecting bastions at intervals of 21, 36, 30, and 25 meters, respectively. Apparently this spacing was determined by the range of effective bow shots from two adjacent towers to provide an unbroken defense throughout the length of palisade (Larson, 1972). The number of truncated pyramids and other earth structures found at Cahokia, St. Louis, Kincaid, and Angel originally numbered about 120, 20, 19, and 11, respectively; Aztalan, which represents the northernmost spread of Mississippian influence in the study area, contained only two structures.

Lower Mississippi Area From this area, twenty-eight sites are reconstructed, beginning in southeastern Missouri and moving southward down the Mississippi River Valley. This is the largest single group of sites in the study, reflecting a greater wealth of information rather than greater architectural significance. The Lower Mississippi Area presents a broad spectrum of design ideas that lend themselves to subgrouping. Beckwith's Fort,

Lilbourn, Parkin, Upper Nodena, and Chucalissa were relatively compact sites enclosed by palisades and outer moats. Within the moats, rectangular houses were grouped around central plazas and truncated pyramids. These sites are located in southeastern Missouri, northeastern Arkansas, and eastern Tennessee, usually on higher ground near major watercourses.

Barney and Sherman were two multilevel curvilinear structures in eastern Arkansas. Very little data exists on Sherman, and nothing beyond Cyrus Thomas's 1894 account is known about Barney, suggesting caution in evaluating these sites. They contain features seldom found elsewhere in our study and do not appear to represent widespread influences.

Winterville and Toltec are large *D*-shaped sites originally oriented toward major watercourses to the northwest. They contain twenty-six and eighteen earthworks, respectively. Winterville has been partially restored, but relatively little has been published on Toltec, where archaeological investigations now in progress may reveal substantial new information on developments in the Lower Mississippi Valley during period 3 and possibly earlier.

Perkins was reported to consist of two truncated pyramids and two smaller circular mounds within a circular enclosure, an unusual composition. Conflicting early reports on its orientation should be verified if the site still exists and can be found again.

Alligator, Kinlock, Magee, Arcola, Haynes Bluff, and Mayersville illustrate typical smaller period 3 ceremonial centers of the Lower Mississippi Valley. All six of these sites contain truncated pyramids grouped around rectangular plazas, and all approach symmetry in their compositions. Perhaps the most nearly perfect example of this compositional theme is Alphenia, a relatively small-scale site closely approaching biaxial symmetry.

The major structure of Menard apparently was a truncated cone rather than a truncated pyramid, an infrequently found configuration, although not unprecedented. Jackson Place, now completely destroyed, is another example of a dominantly period 3 site with some features from period 2. Lake George is a large and significant site containing twenty-five earth structures, two principal plazas, and a moated enclosure built over a comparatively long time span. Winterville had a similar arrangement but apparently never had a moat.

Fitzhugh, now largely destroyed, was a large, well disciplined site with an unusual elevated causeway flanked by excavations. Jerden and Mott were similar D-shaped sites located near each other in northern Louisiana. Anna and its successor, Emerald, are comparable sites located on high natural bluffs near the Mississippi River north of Natchez.

Greenhouse is a small, well-composed site on a natural tear-drop–shaped island in the middle of an old river channel. Fatherland is a linear arrangement of three mounds and two plazas with a village nearby. Troyville's main structure apparently was originally a conical mound set on two truncated pyramids and linked by a causeway to a smaller platform. Linking of larger and smaller truncated structures also occurred at Winterville, Greenhouse, Fitzhugh, and Jackson Place.

Caddoan Area Represented by Mineral Springs and Spiro, the Caddoan Area of western Arkansas, southeastern Oklahoma, northeastern Texas, and northwestern Louisiana is more obscure than other areas of period 3. The Mineral Springs site plan has no clearly discernible pattern; the reconstruction presented is but one of several possibilities for this group, whose mound shapes remain to be verified.

Spiro's western group was arranged around an oval shaped rather than a rectangular shaped plaza. Its truncated pyramids are familiar period 3 features; however, the plaza's four smaller structures are buried houses, a characteristic of Caddoan architecture rarely found in other areas. Clearly separated from the ceremonial group to the west is the burial group to the east, which is dominated by the remarkable Craig Mound, unusually rich in mortuary artifacts.

Tennessee, Appalachian, and Piedmont Area Hiwassee, Obion, Lenoir, Shiloh, Mound Bottom, and Lindsley represent period 3 in Tennessee. Hiwassee seems somewhat less geometrical than many of its contemporary sites, but here the main structure is more complex than most truncated pyramids of comparable scale. The remarkable ramp providing access to the summit of Obion's principal truncated pyramid is almost as large as the main structure itself. Lenoir illustrates an unusual diamond-shaped apron or lower terrace engaging a higher truncated cove. Although a period 2 burial structure was found at Shiloh, the site's dominant characteristics clearly represent period 3. Mound Bottom is particularly well documented and is one of the most disciplined

arrangements in the study. Lindsley, a Cumberland Valley site, contained an unusual mortuary mound in which sixty burials were arranged like stacks of cord wood in a hollow square, almost suggesting that the remains presented a problem to be resolved with efficiency and dispatch. This is a remarkably different approach to the interment of the dead than that found in other sites and periods. In the Ohio Valley in period 2, reverence for the deceased apparently was a major preoccupation.

The Tennessee-Cumberland drainage basin presently is considered one of the likely areas for the rise of the Mississippian culture during period 3. One of the factors possibly contributing to development of that culture may have been a change in the significance of, or attitude toward, burial ceremonialism.

Town Creek in south-central North Carolina is a modest site representing the northeasternmost spread of Mississippian influence. Moundville in Alabama is one of the largest and best preserved sites in the Eastern United States. The largest of its twenty truncated structures is greater in volume than any structure in our study except for the principal structures at Cahokia and Etowah. Etowah contained only six structures, but like Moundville, its contemporary, it was large in scale. Enclosed by palisades with outward-projecting bastions, both Etowah and Moundville were major ceremonial sites located between diverse ecological zones and situated near major watercourses. Both contained numerous rectangular thatch-roofed houses typical of period 3 sites.

Ocmulgee is large in scale but does not reveal much information about site arrangement. Its reconstructed semisubterranean winter council house suggests the character of interior space typical in period 3.

Kolomoki's major truncated pyramid is architecturally well sited near a ravine, where a view of the structure is very impressive. The main mound at Irene was a domical rather than a truncated pyramid in its final form.

Florida Area Florida sites illustrate three distinctly different architectural design patterns. Lake Jackson in Northwest Florida is an example of the typical truncated pyramid and rectangular plaza arrangement found frequently in period 3 sites further to the north and west. Shields, Mount Royal, and Philip illustrate a second design pattern: a single truncated structure linked to a nearby excavation by an avenue flanked by earthen ridges. Long Key may have been a variation of this pattern; however, the structure is not located near an excavation but between two parallel ridges that curve outward to accommodate the mound. Turtle is massive, but its original shape and features remain to be ascertained.

The remains of the Terra Ceia group seems more randomly arranged in the pattern of Crystal River, a period 2 site further to the north. The linking causeways, elevated above low-lying terrain, are comparable to those of Tick Island to the northeast and Big Mound City and Big Tonys to the southeast. The latter two sites clearly illustrate Florida's third architectural design pattern, which is not found outside of the Everglades area: a radial composition made up of a circular or semicircular central space joined to outlying mounds by linear platforms elevated above low-lying terrain and flanked by moats.

Overview

The eighty-two prehistoric sites reconstructed in this study present an overview of architectural achievements in the Eastern United States during the 3,700-year period preceding the arrival of Europeans in the New World. Altogether, they express a simple dignity in architecture.

In terms of planning, no sites of the scale and density of the principal prehistoric centers in Mesoamerica and South America have been found in our study area, where the environment is favorable for the concurrent development of relatively decentralized, self-sufficient communities. The prehistoric North Americans exploited their environment with ingenuity, skill, and increasing success before the arrival of Europeans. Their major monuments were constructed of earth, utilizing a relatively low level of technology. Where they have been left undisturbed in recent centuries, these impressive works of architecture have stood the test of time and record for us today the attainments of their builders.

In terms of design, the prehistoric architects created a broad variety of geometrically disciplined structures, often large in scale and sometimes complex in detail.

In view of the distinguished achievements of prehistoric architecture in the Eastern United States and our present-day concerns for the built environment of man in America, we may be well advised to consider more thoroughly the implications of our authentic past in relation to our future.

Bibliography

Adair, James. *The History of the American Indians.* New York: Johnson Reprint Corp., 1968. First published in 1775.

Allen, Ross. "The Big Circle Mounds." *The Florida Anthropologist,* nos. 1–2, May 1948.

Anderson, James A. *A Cahokia Palisade Sequence.* Illinois Archaeological Survey, Inc., Bulletin No. 7, pp. 89–99. Urbana, Ill.: University of Illinois, 1973.

Appleton, Leroy H. *American Indian Design and Decoration.* New York: Dover Publications, Inc., 1971.

Atwater, Caleb, "Description of the Antiquities Discovered in the State of Ohio and Other Western States." *Archaeologia Americana, Transactions and Collections,* vol. 1. Washington, D.C.: American Antiquarian Society. Reprint of an 1820 edition.

Bacon, Edmund N. *Design of Cities,* rev. ed. New York: The Viking Press, Inc., 1974.

Bartram, John. *A Journal of a journey from St. Augustine up the river St. John's as far as the Lakes,* 3rd ed., much enlarged and improved. Sold by W. Nicoll, London, 1769.

Bartram, William. *The Travels of William Bartram,* edited by Francis Harper. New Haven: Yale University Press, 1958.

Belmont, John S. "Revisions of Architectural Drawing and Description of the Greenhouse Site." Personal communication, Peabody Museum, Harvard University, Cambridge, 28 February 1979.

Benson, Carl A. "The Philip Mound: A Historic Site." *The Florida Anthropologist,* vol. 20, nos. 3–4, 1967.

Bernal, Ignacio. *Official Guide of Monte Alban* [and] *Mitla.* Mexico, D.F.: Instituto Nacional de Antropologia e Historia, 1962.

Bernal, Ignacio. *Mexico Before Cortez: Art, History, Legend.* Translated by Willis Barnstone. Garden City, N.Y.: Dolphin Books, Doubleday and Company, Inc., 1963.

Bernal, Ignacio. *Los pueblos y senorios teocraticos.* Mexico, D.F.: Instituto Nacional de Antropologia e Historia, 1975.

Black, Glenn A. *Angel Site: An Archaeological, Historical, and Ethnological Study,* 2 vols. Indianapolis: Indiana Historical Society, 1967.

Bohannon, Charles F. *Excavations at the Mineral Springs Site, Howard County, Arkansas.* Arkansas Archaeological Survey, Research Series No. 5. Fayetteville, 1973.

Brain, Jeffrey P. *Mississippian Settlement Patterns.* Studies in Archaeology Series, edited by Bruce D. Smith. New York: Academic Press, 1978.

Brain, Jeffrey P.; Copeland, Peter; De La Haba, Louis; Harrell, Mary Ann; Loftin, Tee; Luvaas, Jay; and Schwartz, Douglas W. *Clues to America's Past.* Washington, D.C.: National Geographic Society, 1976.

Broster, John B., and Schneider, Lee, eds. *The Pinson Mounds Archaeological Project: Excavations of 1974 and 1975.* Research Series, No. 1, Division of Archaeology, Tennessee Department of Conservation, Nashville, 1975.

Broster, John, and Schneider, Lee. "Pinson Mounds: A Middle Woodland Mortuary Center in West Tennessee." *Newsletter,* Tennessee Archaeological Society, vol. 21, no. 4, April 1976.

Brown, James A. *Spiro Studies,* Description of the Mound Group, vol. 1. First part of the Second Annual Report of Caddoan Archaeology, Spiro Focus Research, University of Oklahoma Research Institute, Norman, 1966.

Bullen, Ripley P. *The Terra Ceia Site, Manatee County, Florida.* Florida Anthropological Society Publications, no. 3. Gainesville: University of Florida, 1951.

Bullen, Ripley P. "Stelae at the Crystal River Site, Florida." *American Antiquity,* vol. 31, no. 6, 1966.

Bullen, Ripley P. "Regionalism in Florida during the Christian Era." *The Florida Anthropologist*, vol. 23, no. 2, 1970.

Burland, Cottie; Nicholson, Irene; and Osborne, Harold. *Mythology of the Americas*. London: Hamlyn Publishing Group, 1970.

Caldwell, Joseph, and McCann, Catherine. *Irene Mound Site, Chatham County, Georgia*. Works Project Administration, Archaeological Project. Athens: University of Georgia Press, 1941.

Caldwell, Joseph R. "The Archaeology of Eastern Georgia and South Carolina." *Archaeology of Eastern United States*. Edited by James B. Griffin. Chicago: University of Chicago Press, 1952.

Chapman, Carl H. "Internal Settlement Designs of Two Mississippian Tradition Ceremonial Centers in Southeastern Missouri." *Culture Change and Continuity: Essays in Honor of James B. Griffin*. Edited by Charles E. Cleland. New York: Academic Press, 1976.

Cisco, J. G. "Madison County." *American Historical Magazine* 3(1902): 329.

Coe, Joffre L. *Town Creek Indian Mound*. Research Laboratories of Anthropology, University of North Carolina, 1976.

Cole, Fay-Cooper, et al. *Kincaid, A Prehistoric Illinois Metropolis*. Chicago: University of Chicago Press, 1951.

Cotter, John L. "Stratigraphic and Area Tests at the Emerald and Anna Mound Sites." *American Antiquity*, 1951.

Cottier, John M. *Towosahgy State Archaeological Site*. Missouri Department of Natural Resources, 1974.

Culin, Stewart. *Games of the North American Indians*. Bureau of American Ethnology, 24th Annual Report, pp. 1–811. Washington, D.C., 1907.

Cushing, Frank Hamilton. *Exploration of Ancient Key Dwellers' Remains on the Gulf Coast of Florida*. Introduction by Philip Phillips. Published by AMS Press, Inc., New York, for Peabody Museum, Harvard University, Cambridge, Mass., 1973.

Davidson, Marshall B. *Lost Worlds*. New York: American Heritage Publishing Company, 1962.

Davis, Hester A., "An Introduction to Parkin Prehistory." Reprinted from the *Arkansas Archaeologist*, vol. VII, no. 1–2, Spring–Summer 1966.

Edwards, I. E. S. *The Pyramids of Egypt*. London: Penguin Books, Ltd., 1975.

Erasmus, Charles J. "Monument Building: Some Field Experiments." *Southwestern Journal of Anthropology*, vol. 21, no. 4, Winter 1965.

Fairbanks, C. H. *Archaeology of the Funeral Mound, Ocmulgee National Monument, Georgia*. National Park Service, Archaeological Research Series, no. 3. Washington, D.C. 1956.

Fischer, F. W., and McNutt, C. H. "Test Excavations at Pinson Mounds, 1961." *Tennessee Archaeologist*, vol. 18, no. 1 (1962): 1–13.

Fitting, James E. *The Development of North American Archaeology*. Garden City, N.Y.: Anchor Press/Doubleday, 1973.

Folsom, Franklin. *America's Ancient Treasures*. New York: Rand McNally and Company, 1974.

Ford, James A. "Greenhouse: A Troyville—Coles Creek Period Site in Avoyelles Parish, Louisiana." *Anthropological Papers*, American Museum of Natural History, vol. 44, part 1, 1951.

Ford, James A., and Webb, Clarence H. "Poverty Point, A Late Archaic Site in Louisiana." *Anthropological Papers*, American Museum of Natural History, vol. 46, part 1, 1956.

Forshey, C. G. "Description of some Artificial Mounds on Prairie Jefferson, Louisiana." *American Journal of Science and Arts* XLIX (1845): 38–42.

Fowler, Melvin L., *Explorations into Cahokia Archaeology*. Illinois Archaeological Survey, Inc., Bulletin No. 7. Urbana: University of Illinois, 1973.

Fowler, Melvin L. *Cahokia: Ancient Capital of the Midwest*. An Addison-Wesley Module in Anthropology, no. 48. Milwaukee: University of Wisconsin, 1974.

Frankfort, Henri; Frankfort, H. A.; Wilson, John A.; and Jacobsen, Thorkild. *Before Philosophy*. Chicago: University of Chicago Press, 1946.

Gibson Jon L. "Poverty Point, The First North American Chiefdom." *Archaeology*, vol. 27, no. 2, 1974.

Giedion, Sigfried. *Space, Time and Architecture*, 4th ed., enlarged. Cambridge, Mass.: Harvard University Press, 1965.

Goggin, John M. *Space and Time Perspective in Northern St. Johns Archaeology, Florida*. Yale University Publications in Anthropology, no. 47. New Haven: Yale University Press, 1952.

Griffin, James B., editor. *Archaeology of Eastern United States*. Chicago: University of Chicago Press, 1952.

Groslier, Bernard Phillippe, and Arthaud, Jacque. *Angkor: Art and Civilization*. London: Thomas and Hudson, 1957.

Hardman, Clark, Jr. "The Primitive Solar Observatory at Crystal River and its Implications." *The Florida Anthropologist*, vol. XXIV, no. 4, 1971.

Hawkes, Jacquetta. *Atlas of Ancient Archaeology*, New York: McGraw-Hill Book Company, 1974.

Hemmings, E. Thomas, "Preliminary Report of Excavations at Fig Island, South Carolina." *The Institute of Archaeology and Anthropology Notebook*, vol. II, nos. 9– 12, Sept.– Dec. 1970.

Herold, Elaine Bluhm. *The Indian Mounds at Albany, Illinois*. Davenport Museum Anthropological Papers, no. 1. Davenport, Iowa, 1971.

Holmes, William H. "Certain Notched or Scalloped Stone Tablets of the Mound-Builders." *American Anthropologist*, vol. 8, no. 1 (1906): 101– 108.

Hudson, Charles L. *The Southeastern Indians*. Knoxville: University of Tennessee Press, 1974.

Hurley, William M. *An Analysis of Effigy Mound Complexes in Wisconsin*. Anthropological Papers, No. 59, Museum of Anthropology, Ann Arbor: University of Michigan, 1955.

Huxley, Aldous. *Beyond the Mexique Bay*, 1934. Reprint. Westport, Ct.: Greenwood Press, 1975.

Jennings, Jesse D. "Prehistory of the Lower Mississippi Valley." In Griffin, James B., editor. *Archaeology of Eastern United States*, pp. 256– 271. Chicago: University of Chicago Press, 1952.

Jennings, Jesse D. *Prehistory of North America*. New York: McGraw-Hill Book Company, 1974.

Jennings, Jesse D. *Ancient Native Americans*. San Francisco: Freeman Press, 1978.

Kaplan, David. "Men, Monuments, and Political Systems." *Southwestern Journal of Anthropology* 19(1963): 397– 410.

Kneberg, Madeline. "The Tennessee Area." *Archaeology of Eastern United States*. Edited by James B. Griffin, pp. 190– 206. Chicago: University of Chicago Press, 1952.

Kuttruff, L. Carl (Director), and O'Brien, Michael J. (Co-Director). Report of the Mound Bottom Archaeological Project, Department of Archaeology, State of Tennessee, May 1974. Includes a survey entitled "Mound Bottom Archeological Complex."

Larson, Lewis H., Jr. "Archaeological Implications of Social Stratification at the Etowah Site, Georgia." *American Antiquity*, Memoir 25, vol. 36, no. 3, part 2, 1971.

Larson, Lewis H., Jr. "Functional Considerations of Warfare in the Southeast during the Mississippi Period." *American Antiquity*, vol. 37, no. 3, 1972.

LeMoyne de Morgues, Jacques. "Settlement of Florida." *Breris Narratio*. Frankfort, Germany: Theodor de Bry, 1591. English translation by Fred B. Perkins. *Narrative of LeMoyne*. Boston, Mass., 1875.

Lewis, T. M. N., and Kneberg, Madeline. *Hiwassee Island*. Knoxville: University of Tennessee Press, 1946. Third printing, 1976.

Lewis, T. M. N., and Kneberg, Madeline. *Tribes that Slumber*. Knoxville: University of Tennessee Press, 1958.

Marrinan, Rochelle A. "Ceramics, Molluscs, and Sedentism: The Late Archaic Period on the Georgia Coast." Ph.D. dissertation, University of Florida, 1975.

Marshall, James A. "Engineering Principles and the Study of Prehistoric Structures: A Substantive Example." *American Antiquity*, vol. 34, no. 2, April 1969.

Marshall, James A. "Geometry of the Hopewell Earthworks." *Northwestern Archaeology*. Northwestern University, Evanston, Spring 1979.

Mason, Carol L. "The Archaeology of Ocmulgee Old Fields, Macon, Georgia." Ph.D. dissertation, University of Michigan, 1963.

McGimsey, Charles R., III. *Indians of Arkansas*. Arkansas Archaeological Survey Publication on Archaeology, Popular Series No. 1. Fayetteville, 1968.

McKinley, William. *Mounds in Georgia*. Smithsonian Institution, Annual Report, 1872, vol. 27 (1873): 422–428.

McMichael, Edward V., and Mairs, Oscar L. *Excavations of the Murad Mound, Kanawha County, West Virginia, and an Analysis of Kanawha Valley Mounds*. Report of Archaeological Investigation no. 1. Morgantown: West Virginia Geological and Economic Survey, 1969.

Milanich, Jerald T. *The Southeastern Deptford Culture: A Preliminary Definition*. Bureau of Historic Sites and Properties, Bulletin no. 3. Tallahassee: Division of Archives, History and Records Management, State of Florida, 1973.

Millon, René. *El problema de la integracion en la sociedad Teotichuacana*. Mexico, D. F.: Instituto Nacional de Anthropologia e Historia, 1967A.

Millon, René. *Extension y poblacion de la ciudad de Teotihuacan en sus differentes periodos: un calculo provisional*. Mexico, D.F.: Instituto Nacional de Anthropologia e Historia, 1967B.

Millon, René. "Teotihuacán." *Scientific American*, vol. 216, no. 6 (June 1967C): 38–48.

Millon, René. "Teotihuacan: Completion of Map of Giant Ancient City in the Valley of Mexico." *Science* (1970): 1077–1082.

Millon, René. *Teotihuacan Map*. Austin, Texas: University of Texas Press, 1971.

Millon, René. *El valle de Teotihuacan y su contorno*. Mexico, D.F.: Instituto Nacional de Anthropologiae Historia, 1972.

Mooney, James. *The Sacred Formulas of the Cherokees*. Bureau of American Ethnology, 7th Annual Report. Washington, D.C., 1886.

Moore, Clarence B. "Certain Sand Mounds of the St. Johns River, Florida," parts I and II. *Journal of the Academy of Natural Sciences of Philadelphia*, second series, vol. 10, 1896.

Moore, Clarence B. "Certain Sand Mounds of Duval County, Florida. Two Sand Mounds of Murphy Island, Florida. Certain Sand Mounds of the Ocklawaha River, Florida." Advance sheets of the *Journal of the Academy of Natural Sciences, Philadelphia*, vol. X, part 4, 1895.

Moore, Clarence B. "Certain Aboriginal Remains of the Northwest Florida Coast." *Journal of the Academy of Natural Sciences of Philadelphia* vol. 12, part 2, (1902): 126–355.

Moore, Clarence B. "Certain Aboriginal Mounds of the Florida Central West-Coast." Reprint from the *Journal of the Academy of Natural Sciences of Philadelphia*, vol. XII, part 3, 1903.

Moore, Clarence B. "Certain Aboriginal Remains of the Black Warrier River. Certain Aboriginal Remains of the Lower Tombigbee River. Certain Aboriginal Remains of Mobile Bay and Mississippi Sound. Miscellaneous Investigations in Florida." Reprint from the *Journal of the Academy of Natural Sciences of Philadelphia*, vol. III, 1905.

Moore, Clarence B. "Moundville Revisited. Crystal River Revisited. Mounds of the Lower Chattahoochie and Lower Flint Rivers. Notes on the Ten Thousand Islands, Florida." Reprint from the *Journal of the Academy of Natural Sciences of Philadelphia*, vol. XIII, 1907.

Moore, Clarence B. "Certain Mounds of Arkansas and of Mississippi: Mounds & Cemeteries of the Lower Arkansas River, part I. Mounds of the Lower Yazoo and Lower Sunflower Rivers, Mississippi, part II. The Blum Mounds, Mississippi part III." Reprint from the *Journal of the Academy of Natural Sciences of Philadelphia*, vol. XIII, 1908.

Moore, Clarence B. "Some Aboriginal Sites in Louisiana and in Arkansas." Reprint from the *Journal of the Academy of Natural Sciences of Philadelphia*, vol. XVI, 1913.

Moore, Clarence B. "Aboriginal Sites on Tennessee River." *Journal of the Academy of Natural Sciences of Philadelphia*, vol. XVI, 1915.

Moorehead, Warren K. *Fort Ancient: The Great Prehistoric Earthwork of Warren County, Ohio.* Cincinnati: Robert Clarke & Company, 1890.

Moorehead, Warren K. *The Cahokia Mounds.* Bulletin, vol. 26 no. 4. Urbana: University of Illinois, 1928.

Morse, Dan F. *Nodena, An Account of 75 Years of Archaeological Investigation in Southeast Mississippi County, Arkansas.* Arkansas Archaeological Survey, Publications in Archaeology, Research Series no. 4. Fayetteville: Arkansas State University, 1973.

Muller, Jon David. *Mississippian Settlement Patterns.* edited by Bruce Smith. New York: Academic Press, 1978.

Myer, William Edward. "Recent Archaeological Discoveries in Tennessee." *Art and Archaeology*, vol. 14, no. 3 (Sept. 1922): 140–150.

Nash, Charles H. "Chucalissa: Excavations and Burials through 1963." Occasional Papers, no. 6. Memphis: Memphis State University Anthropological Research Center, 1972.

Neitzel, Robert S. *Archaeology of the Fatherland Site: The Grand Village of the Natchez.* Anthropological Papers of the American Museum of Natural History, New York, vol. 51, part 1, 1965.

Norwich, John Julius, general ed., *Great Architecture of the World.* New York: Random House, Inc., 1975.

Nuckolls, John B. "The Pinson Mounds." *Tennessee Archaeologist*, vol. 14, no. 1, 1958.

Nuttal, Codex (also called Codex Zouche). *Codex Nuttal: Facsimile of an Ancient Mexican Codex Belonging to Lord Zouche of Harynworth, England.* Introduction by Zelia Nuttal. Cambridge, Mass., 1902.

O'Brien, Michael J. *Intrasite Variability in a Middle Mississippian Community.* Ph.D. dissertation, Dept. of Anthropology, University of Texas, 1977.

Orr, Kenneth G. "Survey of Caddoan Area Archaeology." In *Archaeology of Eastern United States.* James B. Griffin, editor. University of Chicago Press, 1952.

Panofsky, Erwin. *Meaning in the Visual Arts.* Garden City, N.Y.: Doubleday Anchor Books, 1957.

Peale, Titian Ramsey. *Ancient Mounds at St. Louis, Missouri, in 1819.* Smithsonian Institution Report, pp. 386–391. Washington, D.C., 1861.

Peebles, Christopher S., and M. Kus, Susan. "Some Archaeological Correlates of Ranked Societies." *American Antiquity* vol. 42, no. 3, 1977.

Pfeiffer, John. "America's First City." *Horizon*, vol. XVI, no. 2 (1974): 58–63.

Phillips, Philip. "Introduction to the Archaeology of the Mississippi Valley." Doctoral dissertation, Peabody Museum, Harvard University, 1939.

Phillips, Philip. *Archaeological Survey in the Lower Yazoo Basin, Mississippi, 1949–1955,* parts 1 and 2. Papers of the Peabody Museum of Archaeology and Ethnology, vol. 60. Cambridge, Mass.: Harvard University, 1970.

Phillips, Philip, and Brown, James A. *Pre-Columbian Shell Engravings from the Craig Mound at Spiro, Oklahoma,* vols. 1–3. Cambridge: Peabody Museum Press, 1975.

Phillips, Philip; Ford, James A.; and Griffin, James B. *Archaeological Survey in the Lower Mississippi Alluvial Valley, 1940–1947.* Papers of the Peabody Museum of American Archaeology and Ethnology, vol. 60. Cambridge, Mass.: Harvard University, 1951.

Pope, G. D., Jr. *Ocmulgee National Monument—Georgia.* National Park Service Historical Handbook Series No. 24. Washington, D.C., 1956.

Potter, W. B. "Archaeological Remains in Southeastern Missouri." *Contributions to the Archaeology of Missouri.* St. Louis Academy of Science, pp. 5–19. Salem: Mass., Naturalists Bureau, 1880.

Price, James E., and Griffin, James B. "The Snodgrass Site of the Powers Phase of Southeast Missouri." *Anthropological Papers,* no. 66, Museum of Anthropology. Ann Arbor: University of Michigan, 1979.

Putnam, F. W. *Archaeological Explorations in Tennessee.* Eleventh Annual Report of the Peabody Museum of American Archaeology and Ethnology. Salem, Mass.: The Salem Press, 1878.

Reed, Nelson A. *Monks and other Mississippian Mounds.* Illinois Archaeological Survey Bulletin No. 7, pp. 31–42. Urbana: University of Illinois, 1973.

Ritzenthaler, Robert E. *Prehistoric Indians of Wisconsin.* Milwaukee Public Museum, Popular Series, No. 4, Handbook Series, No. 4. Milwaukee, 1970.

Robertson, D. S. *A Handbook of Greek and Roman Architecture.* London: Cambridge University Press, 1954.

Robertson, Donald. *Pre-Columbian Architecture.* New York: George Braziller, Inc., 1963.

Rolingson, Martha Ann. *Prehistoric Arkansans at Toltec Indian Mounds State Park.* Arkansas Archaeological Society Field Notes No. 145. Fayetteville; Arkansas Archaeological Society, 1977.

Scott, Geoffrey. *The Architecture of Humanism.* Garden City, New York: Doubleday and Company, Inc., 1956.

Sears, William H. *Excavations at Kolomoki, Final Report.* University of Georgia Series in Anthropology. Athens, Ga., 1956.

Sears, William H. "Food Production and Village Life in Prehistoric Southeastern United States." *Archaeology,* vol. 24, no. 4, 1971.

Silverberg, Robert. *Mound Builders of Ancient America.* Greenwich: New York Graphic Society, Ltd., 1968.

Smith, Bruce D., editor. *Mississippian Settlement Patterns.* Forward by James B. Griffin. New York: Academic Press, 1978.

Smith, Gerald P. *Ceramic Handle Styles and Cultural Variations in the Northern Sector of the Mississippi Alluvial Valley.* Memphis State University Anthropological Research Center, Occasional Papers No. 3, 1969.

Smith, Harriet M. *The Murdock Mound: Cahokia Site.* Illinois Archaeological Survey Bulletin No. 7, pp. 49–88. Urbana: University of Illinois, 1973.

Squier, Ephraim G., and Davis, Edwin H. *Ancient Monuments of the Mississippi Valley.* Smithsonian Contributions No. 1. Washington, D.C., 1848.

Stephens, John L. *Incidents of Travel in Yucatan,* vols. 1 and 2. New York: Dover Publications, Inc., 1963.

Stirling, Matthew W. *Indians of the Americas.* Washington, D.C.: National Geographic Society, 1955.

Stuart, George E., and Stuart, Gene S. *Discovering Man's Past in the Americas.* Washington, D.C.: National Geographic Society, 1969.

Stuart, George E. "Who Were the 'Mound Builders'?" *National Geographic,* vol. 142, no. 6, 1972.

Swanton, John R. *Indian Tribes of the Lower Mississippi Valley and Adjacent Coast of the Gulf of Mexico.* Bureau of American Ethnology, Bulletin No. 43, 1911.

Swartz, B. K., Jr. *The New Castle Site: A Hopewell Ceremonial Complex in East Central Indiana.* Contributions to Anthropological History No. 2. Muncie: Ball State University, 1976.

Thomas, Cyrus. *Twelfth Annual Report of The Bureau of Ethnology to the Secretary of the Smithsonian Institution, 1890–91.* Washington, D.C.: Government Printing Office, 1894.

Thurston, Gates P. *The Antiquities of Tennessee and the Adjacent States.* Cincinnati: Robert Clarke & Co., 1898.

Toth, Alan. *Archaeology and Ceremics at the Marksville Site.* Anthropological Papers No. 56. Ann Arbor: University of Michigan, 1974.

Valadés, Adrian Garcia. *The City and Its Monuments.* Mexico, D.F.: Instituto Nacional de Antropologia e Historia, 1976.

Walker, Winslow M. *The Troyville Mounds, Catahoula Parish, La.* Smithsonian Institution Bureau of Ethnology, Bulletin No. 113. Washington, D.C., 1936.

Walthall, John A. *Moundville: An Introduction to the Archaeology of a Mississippian Chiefdom.* Alabama Museum of Natural History, University of Alabama, 1977.

Waring, Antonio J., Jr., and Holder, Preston. "A Prehistoric Ceremonial Complex in the Southeastern United States." *American Anthropologist,* vol. 47, no. 1, 1945. Reprinted in *The Waring Papers.* Edited by Stephen Williams. Papers of the Peabody Museum, Harvard University, vol. 58.

Wauchope, Robert. "Archaeological Survey of Northern Georgia." *American Antiquity,* vol. 31, no. 5, part 2, 1966.

Weaver, Muriel Porter. *The Aztecs, Mayas and Their Predecessors.* New York: Seminar Press, 1972.

Webb, Clarence H. "The Poverty Point Culture." *Geoscience and Man,* vol. XVII. Baton Rouge: Louisiana State University, School of Geoscience, 1977.

Webb, William S., and DeJarnette, David L. *An Archaeological Survey of Pickwick Basin in the Adjacent Portions of the States of Alabama, Mississippi and Tennessee.* Smithsonian Institution, Bureau of American Ethnology, Bulletin No. 129. Washington, D.C., 1942.

Willey, Gordon R. "Crystal River, Florida: A 1949 Visit." *The Florida Anthropologist* vol. II, nos. 3–4, November, 1949A.

Willey, Gordon R. *Archaeology of the Florida Gulf Coast.* Smithsonian Miscellaneous Collections, vol. 113 publication 3988. Washington, D.C.: The Smithsonian Institution, 1949B.

Willey, Gordon R. *Excavations in Southeast Florida.* Yale University Publications in Anthropology, no. 42. 1949C.

Williams, Stephen. "Settlement Patterns in the Lower Mississippi Valley." *Settlement Patterns in the New World.* Edited by G. R. Willey. Viking Fund Publications in Anthropology, no. 23, 1956.

Williams, Stephen. "The Eastern United States." In W. G. Haag, editor. *Early Indian Farmers and Villages and Communities.* Washington, D.C.: National Park Service, Dept. of Interior, 1963.

Williams, Stephen, editor. *The Waring Papers: The Collected Works of Antonio J. Waring, Jr.* Papers of the Peabody Museum, Harvard University, vol. 58, 1968.

Williams, Stephen, and Brain, Jeffrey P. *Excavations at Lake George, Yazoo County, Mississippi, 1958–1960.* Papers of the Peabody Museum. Cambridge, Mass.: Harvard University, in preparation, n.d.

Wilson, Rex L. *Excavations at the Mayport Mound, Florida.* Contributions of the Florida State Museum, Social Sciences, no. 13. Gainesville: University of Florida, 1965.

Wilson, Samuel, Jr. *The Vieux Carre, New Orleans. Its Plan, Its Growth, Its Architecture.* New Orleans, La.: Bureau of Governmental Research, December 1968.

Wittry, Warren L. *The American Woodhenge.* Illinois Archaeological Survey, Bulletin No. 7, pp. 43–48. Urbana: University of Illinois, 1973.

Wu, Nelson I. *Chinese and Indian Architecture.* New York: George Brazillier, Inc., 1963.

Index